HISPANIC

HISPANIC

WHY AMERICANS
FEAR HISPANICS
IN THE U.S.

GERALDO RIVERA

A CELEBRA BOOK

Celebra
Published by New American Library, a division of Penguin Group (USA) Inc., 375 Hudson Street,
New York, New York 10014, USA • Penguin Group (Canada), 90 Eglinton Avenue East, Suite 700,
Toronto, Ontario M4P 2Y3, Canada (a division of Pearson Penguin Canada Inc.) • Penguin Books
Ltd., 80 Strand, London WC2R 0RL, England • Penguin Ireland, 25 St. Stephen's Green, Dublin 2,
Ireland (a division of Penguin Books Ltd.) • Penguin Group (Australia), 250 Camberwell Road,
Camberwell, Victoria 3124, Australia (a division of Pearson Australia Group Pty. Ltd.) • Penguin
Books India Pvt. Ltd., 11 Community Centre, Panchsheel Park, New Delhi - 110 017, India • Penguin
Group (NZ), 67 Apollo Drive, Rosedale, North Shore 0632, New Zealand (a division of Pearson
New Zealand Ltd.) • Penguin Books (South Africa) (Pty.) Ltd., 24 Sturdee Avenue, Rosebank,
Johannesburg 2196, South Africa

Penguin Books Ltd., Registered Offices:
80 Strand, London WC2R 0RL, England

First published by Celebra, a division of Penguin Group (USA) Inc.

First Printing, March 2008
10 9 8 7 6 5 4 3 2 1

Copyright © Maravilla Production Company, Inc., 2008
All rights reserved

Grateful acknowledgment is made for permission to reprint an excerpt from the following
copyrighted material: "With God on Our Side" by Bob Dylan. Copyright © 1963; renewed 1991
Special Rider Music. All rights reserved. International copyright secured. Reprinted by permission.

CELEBRA and logo are trademarks of Penguin Group (USA) Inc.

LIBRARY OF CONGRESS CATALOGING–IN–PUBLICATION DATA:

Rivera, Geraldo.
   His panic: why Americans fear Hispanics in the U.S./Geraldo Rivera.
      p. cm.
   ISBN 978-0-451-22414-9
   1. United States—Emigration and immigration—Social aspects.   2. Illegal aliens—United
States.   3. Latin Americans—United States.   I. Title.
JV6475.R58 2008
305.868'073—dc22   2007044524

Designed by Elke Sigal • Set in Bembo

Printed in the United States of America

For Howard A. Levy, lionhearted attorney, beloved husband, adored father, adoring grandfather, unabashed Cleveland civic cheerleader, mentor to many, and friend to me. Go, Tribe.

And also to my bold and courageous grandparents, whose faith, vision, and passion continue to inspire our family today.

Geraldo Rivera with his grandparents, aunt, and cousin in San Juan, Puerto Rico, 1959

ACKNOWLEDGMENTS

To anthropologist Oscar Lewis, the pessimistic pioneer and rabbi's son who first explored modern life in El Barrio, authored *La Vida* and *The Children of Sanchez*, and who I hope is wrong about the "culture of poverty"; Cheech Marin, Renaissance brown brother; Herman Badillo and Cesar Chávez, the pathfinders; Chicano historian Nicholas Kanellos, who rediscovered the "Black Legend"; the Anti-Defamation League and the Southern Poverty Law Center, who use truth to shame the anti-immigration bullies, and Roger Ailes, visionary boss, loyal friend.

CONTENTS

Contents

HISPANIC

Preface

Welcome to America

My televised confrontation with Bill O'Reilly was as close as I've ever come to a fistfight without actually punching someone. The explosion—unscripted and unexpected as it was—came on *The O'Reilly Factor*, Fox News Channel's number-one-rated show, on a Thursday night in April 2007. The prominent media critic Howard Kurtz, writing in the *Washington Post*, called it, "A trash-talking, vein-popping, finger-thrusting shoutfest," and the subject was illegal immigration.

In the immediate aftermath of the clash, I hoped that the episode, which was viewed by millions on cable and by millions more on YouTube, would become a landmark in the contentious debate over pending reform legislation, if not a turning point. Instead, in a stunning setback for President Bush, most of his fellow Republicans in the Senate, aided by a handful of knee-jerk, protectionist Democrats, torpedoed the legislation. The June 2007 vote left our divided nation's immigration policy in tatters.

An irresistible uprising of the conservative grass roots, enraged by a savage talk-radio campaign more potent than any before, including the one that warped Bill Clinton's blow-job lies into impeachment, overwhelmed legislators favoring reform, frightening enough of them away from the bill to ensure its resounding defeat.

"You wake up the next day and your country has got a mess on its hands," said Senator Lindsey Graham, one of the architects of the defeated legislation. "Not only does it have a broken immigration system, it's got a broken Congress."

At the time of my altercation with O'Reilly, though, reform was still possible. That's why the stakes were so high. O'Reilly styles himself as the American mainstream's "Culture Warrior" and views the issue of immigration as crucial to U.S. national security, the economy, and identity. Like other commentators, including Fox's Sean Hannity and the more reckless Lou Dobbs of CNN, O'Reilly has taken to highlighting the negative acts of individuals living in this country illegally, a number generally thought to have reached at least 12 million at the time of our televised collision.

"An illegal alien robbed a bank today." "An illegal alien raped a teenager." "An illegal alien pushed an old lady." "An illegal alien ate my baby." The atmosphere got so poisonous that in August 2007 the dogmatically conservative Web site WorldNetDaily theorized that the tragic I-35 W Minnesota bridge collapse was caused by an increase in truck traffic from Mexico brought about by the NAFTA treaty. As far as I can determine, NAFTA has yet to have any effect on road traffic in Minnesota.

O'Reilly and I had tangled before when he played the blame game, insinuating that the deaths of nine West African immigrants, eight of them little children, in a terrible house fire in the Bronx, New York, in March 2007 was the direct result of their being here illegally. "Your so-called compassion helped kill those kids," he chastised pro-immigration reformers on the March 9 edition of his program. "These kids are dead because of the pro–open border people. They're dead because of them. . . . My opinion is this is another example of people dying because of a chaotic immigration system." His point was that New York City's lax immigration enforcement had created a climate wherein officials like fire inspectors were reluctant to do their jobs. There is an unspoken rule in the Big Apple, his theory goes, that stops officials from doing anything that might expose the status of someone who is in this country illegally to federal authorities. New York City's role as a so-called sanctuary city was therefore thought by O'Reilly to be the main reason those kids were dead. Coming on later in the program, I told him the notion was preposterous, that the children died because an adult had been negligent with a space heater. This time we agreed to disagree, but the scene was set for the showdown, which came the following month.

It started as a debate about a drunk driver in Virginia Beach who killed two teenage girls in a terrible accident. The loser, who had previous misdemeanor convictions for public drunkenness and drunk driving, happened to be an illegal alien from Mexico, and O'Reilly excoriated the mayor of Virginia Beach for allegedly being soft on immigration policy, running another sanctuary city and essentially allowing this wretched man to murder two Virginia girls who had their whole lives ahead of them and everything to live for.

When it was my turn to speak, I forcefully challenged O'Reilly's focus on the immigration status of the driver and asked why he hadn't reported on any of the other drunk-driving fatalities in Virginia, 347 of them in 2005, the last full year for which statistics were available at the time of the debate. I asked angrily what difference the driver's national origin made. "He could have been a Jewish drunk, an Italian drunk, or an Irish drunk, would you still care?"

O'Reilly thundered, "It makes plenty of difference! He doesn't have the right to be in this country! He should have been deported!"

I roared back that it was a "cheap political point!" O'Reilly accused me of wanting anarchy on the nation's borders. I said that what I wanted was fairness and he sneered, "Fairness? Bull! You want to let them all in!"

Actually, I don't want to "let them all in," as O'Reilly put it. But I do oppose the maddening tendency in this country to want to burn the immigrant bridge as soon as your particular crew has come in over it.

"Positively No Irish Need Apply"

—Popular U.S. nineteenth-century public notice

My Irish-American media colleague and fellow Fox News commentator is relatively more moderate on this issue than many flame-throwing conservatives, whom I will address later. And as I pointed out to him, the more things change with immigration, the more they stay the same. In the nineteenth century, native-born Americans, themselves sons and daughters of immigrants, fearful of being overrun by newcomers from overseas, posted the above kind of unwelcome-to-America notice for newly arrived Irish.

In the same way, fear of being overrun infects many native-born Americans these days, but now it is not just the general fear of immigrants from across the seas, but more specifically of Latinos, who look and sound different than we do, coming across our southern border. It is fear of America's changing face, masquerading as the immigration debate that has become our most divisive passion in the twenty-first century, surpassing even debates on the war in Iraq in vitriol. How will the nation cope with the dynamic growth of the Hispanic population? What are the consequences? Aside from what the country will look like in the next few decades, will we be better off or worse?

In *His Panic*, I try to address fairly the public's fears about immigration good, bad, and ugly, and also the broader issue of the changing face of America. I believe most of the fears are groundless and are based on myth and propaganda, which are driving us to reject and persecute newcomers we should be embracing. They are a dynamic force that will assimilate and strengthen our country as immigrant groups before them, like the Irish, have done.

1

Proud to Be an American

First, let me tell you my family's story, just one Hispanic family among millions. Like the overwhelming majority of immigrants, Hispanic or otherwise, the Riveras of Puerto Rico worked hard, served our country in many different ways, and made enormous efforts to assimilate, despite the obstacle of prejudice.

My dad always wanted to fit into America, his "new" country. Well, technically the country wasn't new, because U.S. citizenship had been bestowed on him and all current and future Puerto Ricans by legislation called the Jones Act in 1917. The United States had been in possession of the lovely tropical island it had conquered and won from Spain for only twenty years, and Cruz Rivera was just two years old, the sixth of seventeen children born to Juan and Tomása Rivera of Bayamon, Puerto Rico.

"How could you have so many children?" I remember asking my grandmother, a woman of enormous patience and good humor who wore her snow-white hair pulled back, contrasting dramatically with her angular, chocolate-colored face made leathery by the sun. "Times were different then," she replied in fabulous understatement, referring to their modest agrarian lifestyle in the sugarcane and coffee economy that dominated the island in the days before the commonwealth. My grandfather helped manage one small operation, and each child became another income earner, cutting and stacking cane, watched over by a slightly older sibling.

With citizenship bestowed, the new Americans were free to roam and the Puerto Rican diaspora began, with island residents leaving their then largely rural society for the far-flung corners of the industrialized mainland United States. Most, like my dad, came to New York City.

When the now twenty-one-year-old Cruz arrived on board one of the New York and Porto Rico Steamship Company's "banana boats" in 1937, more than fifty thousand of his fellow islanders lived here. The number had been higher, nearly double earlier in the decade, but the Great Depression had unleashed a torrent of bitter racism toward the newcomers, who, like the immigrants of today, were thought to be stealing jobs from "real" Americans. So thousands had gone home to the island. My dad and several of his siblings were determined to stay.

He met my mom, Lilly Friedman, at Stewart's Cafeteria on Sixth Avenue and 42nd Street. He was a counterman there; she was a pretty brunette from Jersey City who cleared dishes and waited tables. She is Jewish, he was Catholic, but he spoke English fluently, having learned as the valedictorian of his Bayamon high school. He proposed marriage, promised to convert to Judaism (which as a lay deacon of the church he never got around to doing). He had been on the mainland for only three years and was keen on assimilating, becoming even more American.

To that end, and to ease the angst of my mom's parents over their daughter marrying a man whose name, Cruz, translates as "Cross," he adopted the name Allen, becoming Allen C. Rivera when he married. "Why Allen?" I asked my mother. "When he came here he was ridiculed and put down. He was called Chico or Pancho and it really upset him. He just wanted to be an American.

And he spoke English perfectly, with no accent at all, except when he was on the phone. So he never wanted to speak on the phone." My parents went so far as to give my older sister, Irene, and me the last name Riviera, as in the French or Buick Riviera, to further disguise our roots. It was the only thing they ever did that I'm still mad at. No one was fooled. All it did was confuse our school records, and by the time my brother Wilfredo arrived from Puerto Rico and my sister Sharon and brother Craig were born, the artifice was dropped.

Dad and Mom worked hard and we moved from Orchard Street near the main thoroughfare of Houston Street on the Lower East Side of Manhattan to a small apartment in the Williamsburg section of Brooklyn. It was a perfect neighborhood for our blended family. It was divided by Broadway, the teeming boulevard under the elevated subway that sliced through two radically different neighborhoods. One side of the street was nearly all Puerto Rican, the other almost all Orthodox Jewish. The family joke was that we were the only ones who could cross the street with impunity. Then in 1944, Pop got drafted.

Like many Puerto Ricans during World War II, he served honorably in the army, restricted as many Hispanics were in those days of military segregation to kitchen duties. "He was stationed out in Sacramento," Mom told me. "When his unit was being shipped out to Okinawa, the people running the Officers Club where he worked wouldn't let him go. They loved his spicy cooking. Otherwise, the army food was so bland."

After the war, Dad drove a New York City taxi until, with the benefits of the G.I. Bill, my parents were able to buy a modest home for $8,000 in a blue-collar neighborhood in West Babylon, Long Island. With his own extended family, Wilfredo still lives in the old house our family bought in 1950.

On Long Island, Dad got the job that helped him ease us into the upper working or lower middle class, supervising the largely Puerto

Rican kitchen staff of the cafeteria concession of the Republic Aviation Corporation in the town of Farmingdale. Now defunct, it was where they built the F-84 Thunderjets used in the Korean War and later the F-105 Thunderchiefs that saw service in Vietnam.

During the booming postwar economy of the 1940s and early 1950s, the Puerto Rican population in the States recovered dramatically, skyrocketing to well over a half million, still mostly living in New York. Puerto Ricans were on the traditional immigrant track to assimilation. But as the community grew, because of factors largely out of its control, so did economic and social tensions. While many people had been gainfully employed in the expanding postwar economy—women mainly in the garment industry, men like my father in hotel and restaurant kitchens—the accelerating shift of manufacturing jobs out of the inner cities displaced and impoverished many Puerto Rican and other immigrant families.

Ironically, an equal but opposite phenomenon was unfolding back on the island. There a government program called Operation Bootstrap was moving agrarian families off farms and sugar plantations and into cities, where they were lured by jobs in newly subsidized industries. While there are obviously widespread and sometimes spectacular exceptions, in some ways the inner-city segment of both communities never recovered, many falling into a trap of welfare dependency, broken families, and drug and alcohol abuse.

Still, despite income levels lower than those in the States (median family income for 2006 was measured at $20,045 in Puerto Rico while the lowest state was Mississippi at $42,805), and an economy far too dependent on public jobs, there is enormous pride of place. We call our band of brothers and sisters *Boricua*, which derives from Boriken, the pre-Columbian, Taino Indian name for the island. Visited by Christopher Columbus during his second New World voyage in 1493, the lush, mountainous, and now crowded little island's heart is her capital, major port, and the oldest city under the U.S. flag, San Juan. On its modern outskirts, there is the usual collection of tourist hotels lining the beautiful Atlantic beaches, although curiously lacking are the kind of supercasinos that are remaking cities like Las Vegas and Atlantic City. The heart of the old city, though, is unmatched by those synthetic meccas. It is a charming, 465-year-old neighborhood within the old walled section built to withstand invasion. There, with cobblestone streets, elegant government buildings, and hundreds of carefully restored sixteenth- and seventeenth-century Spanish colonial structures surrounded by La Fortaleza and other massive fortifications, the best of life under Old Spain is easily conjured.

Too much of the rest of the island has fallen under the plows of random development, urban poverty, and grinding, often chaotic traffic, although lovely pockets remain. As an expression of solidarity with the land of my father and his father for generations out of memory, several years ago I bought an undeveloped mangrove island off the south coast we use for vacations and enormous family reunions. A mile-square jewel located three miles off the modest coastal village of Salinas, I intend gifting it to the people of the commonwealth as a park, and to be buried there.

What is fascinating, given the island's profound social problems, is how satisfied Puerto Ricans seem with their lot in life. We invented irrational exuberance. To prove that thesis, just watch one Puerto Rican Day Parade in New York City. It is billed as the world's largest, with as many as half a million marchers watched by 2 million of their closest friends. The colorful pageant is a giant demonstration of pride in community. I've marched in at least two dozen going back to 1971, and was once honored as Gran Mariscal, the grand marshal. It was one of my dad's proudest days, even though a torrential downpour that drenched Fifth Avenue interrupted the procession midway.

While we certainly have our share of strivers and success stories, curiously we are among the least envious, most inherently happy people on the planet, content to make a living, make love, and debate politics. Without bragging or being condescending, there is an openness and innocence about Puerto Ricans that in all my world travels I have found unmatched. Strangely, in my experience it is Afghans who come closest to our extraordinary willingness to welcome strangers and our perhaps disproportionate hometown pride of place. Italians and Lebanese also come close. One Puerto Rican's success is every Puerto Rican's success. Again, if you don't believe me, watch the parade just one time and see how it seems to be a gigantic family gathering. When the young and old, men and women cheer Jennifer Lopez or Ricky Martin, they do it without an ounce of insincerity or envy, only pride.

If only our ambition for education and achievement matched our compassion or ability to love. In his book, *The Governor's Suits*, my longtime friend and confidant Dr. Guillermo Gonzalez, an island-born and -trained psychiatrist, believes that part of the reason for our community's tranquility is that as the world's oldest continuous colony, claimed for Spain by Christopher Columbus on November 19, 1493, and invaded by the United States on July 25, 1898, someone else has always been in charge of us. As a child prospers emotionally in the absence of anxiety and responsibility, our centuries-long colonial status has meant less stress for us. The big bad world wolf is not our problem. But we have sacrificed self-determination and drive for tranquility, the assurance that Uncle Sam will always take care of us.

My first professional hero, role model, and mentor, Herman Badillo, the first Puerto Rican congressman, is even more pessimistic about our community's current plight. Badillo blames our persistent social problems and relative lack of success on an addiction to entitlements and preferential public programs, like bilingual education and open admission to public colleges, programs he not only benefited from, but, until leaving the Democratic Party and becoming a late-in-life Republican, also championed. "We act as if our New York neighborhoods were part of Puerto Rico," Herman told me in an interview. "We haven't taken advantage of the assets we have available to us here, like the City University. We're becoming part of a permanent underclass."

Widely criticized by current community leaders like the fiery congressman Jose Serrano and former Bronx borough president and losing mayoral candidate Fernando Ferrer, Badillo has written a scathing but not entirely mistaken commentary on our current situation titled *One Nation, One Standard: An Ex-Liberal on How Hispanics Can Succeed Just Like Other Immigrant Groups*. In the book, Badillo points to the relative success of our cousins from the nearby Dominican Republic (DR). They didn't have the same advantages we did when they got here. The DR was suppressed for years by a series of brutal dictators, principally Rafael Trujillo, who ruled with an iron hand from 1930 until he was assassinated in 1961. The island nation, which is next door to Puerto Rico and separated only by the sixty-mile-wide Mona Passage, is now free and unfettered. Unlike Puerto Ricans, who are U.S. citizens all, many Dominicans came to America as visitors or trespassers with no advantages, but with immigrant vigor. They are now turning vast swaths of New York City into upwardly mobile enclaves. Once a ghetto, Washington Heights is a thriving Manhattan neighborhood heading straight into the middle class thanks to its hardworking residents, largely from the DR and Mexico. Unmistakably Latino, the Heights are a vastly more stable, safe, and prosperous neighborhood than they were just twenty years ago.

I respect both Herman and Guillermo tremendously, but I see the root of our problem in our ambiguous status. Puerto Rico is neither an independent country nor a state of the union. We get many of the benefits nationhood or statehood would bring, but not the responsibility or respect. Our island is a stepchild in the family of nations, charming, ebullient, and attractive, but a stepchild nevertheless. And until that status is resolved with either independence or, my preference, statehood, the stubborn social problems will persist as they have for more than a half century. The stepchild needs to grow up and become an equal member of the American family. To mix metaphors, Puerto Rico has to pick a lane.

When the Ozzie and Harriet ideal was sweeping the nation in the Eisenhower days, hard times in the inner city intensified residential and racial segregation, crime and unemployment increased, public schools spiraled downward. I have an image of my dad coming home from work in the afternoon and scouring the crime stories in our hometown newspapers, *Newsday* and the *Long Island Press*, hoping that the perpetrator of some particularly vicious act was not a Puerto Rican or other Latino for fear that the dirty deed would only make our efforts at assimilation more difficult.

My father's response to the growing discrimination and backlash against the community was to align our family with the Anglo mainstream, becoming suburban "us" to the inner-city barrio's "them." His fear of being racially stereotyped and his malignant communal shame at any dreadful or embarrassing act committed by any Hispanic is something I can never forget. As a young adult, it was what caused me to reject his cautious assimilation and adopt a flamboyant ethnic identity, growing a mustache I haven't shaved in forty years, habitually wearing a Che Guevara–like purple beret, permanently becoming Geraldo (don't call me Gerry unless you want a fight), and throwing my lot in with a grassroots East Harlem radical group called the Young Lords.

Actually, I forced myself on them. I graduated from Brooklyn Law School, interned at a community legal services office in the heart of Harlem at 116th Street and Eighth Avenue, and then became the cochairman of an activist group of minority lawyers we called the Black and Brown Lawyers Caucus. In August 1969, I gained radical credibility when our group literally seized Donald Rumsfeld. The future two-time secretary of defense was then head of the Office of Economic Opportunity (OEO). We all worked for Federal Legal Services, which was part of OEO, so Rumsfeld was our ultimate boss. As part of a larger movement to protest Nixon administration policies toward the poor (which included us), we invaded and occupied Rumsfeld's Washington office, holding him captive until we were all arrested. Hosting an inaugural gala for the wounded veterans at Walter Reed Army Medical Center in D.C. in January 2004, I recounted the story for the secretary and a group of generals. I got big laughs.

But in the day, there was nothing funny about our commitment to radical social change. By 1968–69, the Young Lords were advocating community services, like free breakfast programs and testing for lead-paint poisoning for neighborhood children, campaigning for the independence of Puerto Rico, occupying a local hospital that was notorious for substandard care, confronting local police and other authority on behalf of barrio residents, seeking common cause with similar civil rights and antiwar activists around the country in a grand, multiracial Rainbow Coalition, and idealizing a semi-socialist society. The Lords were led by a unique combination of college-educated activists and several street-smart, old-school leftist organizers. Some of the former are still active in public life, like the poet and commentator Felipe Luciano, the *New York Daily News* columnist and former head of the National Association of Hispanic Journalists Juan Gonzalez, and the WCBS correspondent Pablo Guzman. The Lords were the first homegrown—that is stateside— Puerto Rican activist group concerned with social issues like poverty and police brutality rather than focusing, as most PR groups did at the time, on the island's independence.

The Lords were getting press and not all of it was bad, staging protests, organizing confrontations with the local precincts, and dealing aggressively with the somewhat sympathetic administration of Mayor John V. Lindsay. At the time the group was being represented by several traditional young white lefties from the Lawyers Guild. That's when I forced myself on them, rushing into their office, typical of the radical 1960s—a smoky, crowded, and poster-filled room in the shadows under the Park Avenue elevated train—and demanding that since I was the only Puerto Rican radical lawyer around who was their age, they were mine to represent. They were bemused—some still tell that story—but my offer/demand was accepted.

In May 1970, the Lords seized possession of the block-square building owned by the Spanish Methodist Church on 111th Street and Lexington Avenue in the impoverished, almost exclusively Puerto Rican "El Barrio" neighborhood. I was often their spokesman, and in that role was interviewed then on the *Today* show. The church is still there, and though the neighborhood has somewhat gentrified, and like many in New York and elsewhere is much more Mexican than in the old days, it retains its rough ghetto edge. Well-maintained public housing faces rehabilitated tenements; larger markets sit side by side with the traditional bodegas, and there are combination grocery-department stores where you can still cash a check, buy a whole pig for roasting, and overpay for almost everything.

In nice weather there are scores of mostly poor people on the street; the cops watch the action up and down Lexington Avenue with an eye-in-the-sky crane on which an officer sits in a glass-enclosed perch thirty or so feet up. On the streets below, the legend of the Young Lords is passed down from generation to generation. The seizure of the church almost forty years ago has become the stuff of local lore, one of those seminal events that everybody remembers and many claim to have participated in. Over the years, many strangers have come up to me to say that they were there, although like a Puerto Rican *Mayflower*, they couldn't possibly have all fit in.

On the air giving interviews during that crisis, my job was to explain the benevolent nature of the group's seemingly hostile act: that the Lords wanted to put the church complex to work for the community. The congregation, many of whom had prospered and moved out of the city, kept the buildings shuttered during the week, only using the sanctuary for Sunday services. The building takeover was not unusual for those turbulent times. The Kent State National Guard shootings had just taken place and the nation was being frequently disrupted by antiwar demonstrations and plagued by urban unrest.

I was spotted on television by Al Primo, the founder of WABC's *Eyewitness News*, who was forging a news team that reflected the diverse community it served. The only other Puerto Rican on television at the time was a local CBS reporter named Gloria Rojas, and she recruited me into the business. Primo hooked me up with the legendary newsman Fred Friendly for a crash course at the Columbia University Graduate School of Journalism.

As my urgent ethnicity and radicalism simmered down during a four-decade-long public career, what remained was a reflex opposition to racial and ethnic stereotyping. That stance has frequently brought me into highly publicized, sometimes violent confrontation with hatemongers from the KKK to neo-Nazis and skinheads advocating white power and terrorizing minorities. There aren't many people in this country who have been called both a Spic and a dirty Jew in the same street brawl with neo-Nazis, as I had the pleasure of being in Janesville, Wisconsin, in 1992.

Right now in America, the group being singled out for the most destructive negative emotion is Hispanic immigrants, both legal—families who have been in the country for generations—and illegal—people who may have crossed over the border yesterday. All this destructive hostility is the manifestation of what is now a national panic. Despite this hate, I can say that as a proud Puerto Rican, I am proud to be an American.

2

Probing the Panic

T o appreciate the visceral nature of the fear and loathing of Hispanic immigrants, we need to look at the parallels between the great immigration of the nineteenth and early twentieth centuries and today. In the years we Americans were going west, taking the Southwest from Mexico to fulfill our "Manifest Destiny," hundreds of thousands of illegal—that is, undocumented—unsanctioned, and uninvited immigrants, mostly Catholic, many from Germany, but many more from Ireland, were pouring into American cities. In the case of the Irish, they were driven from home by the disastrous potato famine of 1847–48 and by oppression by the English rulers and ruling class. This giant surge of men, women, and children abandoned their stricken homeland. Entire cities, villages, and towns were deserted in the Old Country and a questing, undaunted, and desperate community of immigrants came ashore en masse in New World cities like New York, Boston, Charleston, Savannah, and New Orleans.

In those two years alone a staggering 650,000 Irish men, women, and children arrived in New York, in a historic instant becoming almost a third of the city's population. By 1850, the Irish made up 43 percent of New York's foreign-born population. Militant anti-Catholics like William "Bill the Butcher" Poole (whose story is fictionalized in Martin Scorsese's film *Gangs of New York*, based on Herbert Asbury's classic book) became alarmed that the newcomers would overwhelm them and give control of the country's political processes to the pope. Anti-Irish gangs were formed; rioting and violence became commonplace, and, routinely, signs reading "Positively No Irish Need Apply" appeared on businesses and residential buildings. Anglo-Protestant nativists formed their own political party, the Know-Nothings, which fought to suppress Irish immigration and keep the newcomers from becoming naturalized citizens.

What is striking in recalling the Know-Nothing movement of the mid-nineteenth century is how closely it reflects the sentiments of contemporary citizen organizations like the Minutemen. The Minutemen have been very effective in bringing out the worst in today's Americans on the issue of immigration and, by extension, the role of the country's growing Hispanic population. On his deathbed "Bill the Butcher" Poole was still so fixated on the influx of Irishmen that he said, "Good-bye, boys: I die a true American," by which he meant he was blessedly born in the USA. Poole's militant successors are again raising the ugly head of nativism, which I define as about equal parts nationalism and racism, working to do all they can to make the latest wave of Hispanic immigration as unpleasant as possible.

Their stated goal is to prevent potential illegal aliens from crossing our southern border by direct action. But it doesn't take a gumshoe or forensics expert to suspect their real fight is against the demographic surge of Latinos that is changing the face of America. As you will see, the racial nature of their opposition is written bold in their manifestos, and the debate is getting dangerous. In early May 2007, a federal grand jury indicted six Alabama men described as members of an antigovernment, anti-immigrant paramilitary group. Federal agents seized scores of hand grenades and other weapons the group allegedly intended to use to attack Mexicans who had been moving into their small town in surprisingly large numbers.

The influx of Latinos and the explosive growth of the number of American-born Hispanics are causing tension and reaction everywhere along the political spectrum, but most frighteningly at the fringes, where panic reins. According to the Anti-Defamation League's civil rights director, Deborah M. Lauter:

> The Ku Klux Klan, which just a few years ago seemed static or even moribund compared to other white supremacist movements such as neo-Nazis, experienced a surprising and troubling resurgence during the past year [2006]. The KKK believes that the U.S. is drowning in a tide of non-white immigration, controlled and orchestrated by Jews, and is vigorously trying to bring this message to Americans concerned or fearful of immigration.
>
> If any one single issue or trend can be credited with re-energizing the Klan, it is the debate over immigration in America. Klan groups have witnessed a surprising and troubling resurgence by exploiting fears of an immigration explosion, and the debate over immigration has, in turn, helped fuel an increase in Klan activity, with new groups sprouting in parts of the country that have not seen much activity.

Since the year 2000 alone, the number of anti-immigrant racist hate groups, covering the spectrum from the KKK to the neo-Nazis, has risen by 40 percent, according to the Southern Poverty Law Center (SPLC), a watchdog agency based in Montgomery, Alabama. According to Mark Potok, of the SPLC, "The immigration furor has been critical to the growth we've seen." And the growth of the hate groups is being fueled by a wildfire of aggressive anti-immigration rhetoric by relentlessly nativist crusaders, like CNN's Lou Dobbs. "I think that AM talk radio and cable news has played an extremely

vile role in the immigration debate, popularizing conspiracy theories, promulgating false statistics and conjuring up fake public health
dangers," Potok told me in an interview. "This demonizing of an
entire class of people by a mainstream player like Dobbs is brand-
new. I know Fox has higher ratings, but Dobbs commands the most
important news hour on the most important news channel. Every
newsroom in America has CNN on someplace. It helps direct other
people's coverage. And it is just amazing that CNN doesn't try to
control or at least check the accuracy of Dobbs's reporting."

"This kind of really vile propaganda begins in hate groups,"
Potok wrote in the SPLC's "The Year in Hate" report, "makes its
way out into the larger anti-immigration movement, and, before you
know it, winds up in places like *Lou Dobbs Tonight* on CNN. This
country needs a robust debate on immigration, but it does not need
a debate based on racist allegations and bogus conspiracy theories."

While Democrats like Senator John Edwards frequently criti-
cize the objectivity of Fox News and refuse to appear on it because
it is "slanted" against liberal politicians like him, he is robust in his
support of CNN, the network that is home to the most virulently
anti-Hispanic immigrant show on television. In fairness, my on-air
colleague, the Fox News commentator Sean Hannity, has also done
his share of damage to the cause of immigration reform. Hannity is
the stubborn defender of all things right wing, a consistent and
unembarrassed conservative rabble-rouser and a charming, slightly
more predictable, more sincere, male version of Ann Coulter. Like
Dobbs, Hannity has frequently given chunks of airtime to spokes-
men for radical groups like the Minutemen or to bogus social scientists from the Heritage Foundation. Sean even rode horseback with
the citizen vigilantes along the southern border, a dumb, destructive
stunt I ridiculed to his face on television. But aside from his being a
personable guy and a friend of mine, there are important substantive
differences between his program and Dobbs's propaganda. First,
people like Alan Colmes and me temper Hannity's position.

Regularly we get roughly equal time to point out how closed-minded and dogmatic Sean is on the issue. Furthermore, until recently, Dobbs's show broadcast at six p.m. ET. Now moved to seven p.m., it is still dressed as a news program, unlike Hannity's, which is a classic late-evening cable news commentary and debate show.

Neither Brit Hume, the Washington managing editor for Fox News and anchor of our six p.m. ET news, nor Shep Smith, the anchor of our *Fox Report* at seven p.m., would engage in the sort of populist hatemongering, like the Dobbs crusade to free two border patrol agents, Jose Compean and Ignacio Ramos. Compean and Ramos were convicted of shooting a drug-dealing illegal immigrant (he was shot in the ass) as he fled across the border, then covering up the incident. Dobbs made the men martyrs of a runaway, pro–illegal immigrant federal government and has championed their cause on 131 broadcasts as of this writing. According to an investigation in *Texas Monthly* magazine called "Badges of Dishonor," CNN's *Lou Dobbs Tonight* "glossed over nearly all of the damning facts at trial," including the failure of the agents to report the shooting or to claim self-defense until a month after the incident. "Set against the backdrop of the national debate over immigration, a new narrative emerged, one in which Ramos and Compean were recast as 'American heroes,' unjustly persecuted by a government that cared more about amnesty for illegal immigrants than about border security."

O'Reilly did get this one right on his show when he admonished the Colorado congressman Tom Tancredo, who had jumped on the agents' bandwagon after they were convicted of the shooting and cover-up. "They shot the man in the back, Congressman," O'Reilly said.

Dobbs plods doggedly on with his anti-immigrant crusade, assisted by an on-air supporting cast disguised as reporters, who, when called upon, assume the role of fellow immigrant bashers whose job seems to be digging up "facts," like a fake leprosy epidemic they recently conjured up and blamed on immigrants. The "anchorman" was once a respected business journalist and still pretends to be one. But after his ratings plummeted in the face of the Fox News ascendancy, as I said several times on the air, he has resurrected a failed career on the backs of these poor immigrants.

Lou Dobbs came up to me and my wife, Erica, when we were speaking with my longtime agent, Jim Griffin, at the William Morris Agency annual TV cocktail party reception at the Four Seasons restaurant in New York in May 2007. I swear that at the moment Dobbs approached the three of us, I was telling Jimmy, my dear and trusted comrade, that I was embarrassed for the agency that they represented this demagogue. The instant that sentence was finished, here was Dobbs saying, "Hello, Geraldo." Recovering from the shock and guided by forty years' experience in random public encounters like this, I said flatly, "Hello, Lou." I couldn't even bring myself to shake his hand, so destructive have his editorial choices and solemnly delivered bullshit been to the cause of sensible dialogue and what the SPLC called the "robust debate on the issue of immigration." I immediately turned to Jimmy and said, "I've got to get a drink," grabbed Erica's lovely arm and steered her toward the bar.

Dobbs has been given unprecedented freedom to voice his vitriolic opinions about immigration because his now relatively higher ratings help lift CNN's otherwise flagging prime-time fortunes. But Dobbs publicly stubbed his editorial toe when he was chastised for advertising a fund-raiser for his favorite town, Hazelton, Pennsylvania. Various immigrant groups had sued the town's mayor, Lou Barletta, who had essentially declared his community an illegal alien–free zone. Barletta vowed to arrest any illegal immigrant, and severely fine anyone offering them food, shelter, or employment, and in doing so he became Dobbs's darling. The newsman even had the gall to ask for cash to support the city's legal fight on the cable news channel's official Web site.

After initially arguing that the posting was only on Lou Dobbs's Web page, CNN president James Walton agreed to take down the link to CNN's site after being harshly criticized by the National Institute of Latino Policy, and blasted by an editorial in *El Diario/ La Presna*, the principal New York Latino newspaper, which complained that the network was actively rallying support for anti-immigrant measures.

Among Barletta's other supporters is the New Jersey–based Confederate Knights of the Knights of the Ku Klux Klan, which offered to hold a rally in Hazelton, saying it supported the city's efforts "100%." Happily, the mayor declined their assistance. In June 2007, just hours before Barletta's ordinances targeting the immigrants were set to go into effect, a federal judge blocked the city of Hazelton from enforcing them. U.S. District Judge James Munley ruled that landlords, tenants, and businesses that cater to Hispanics faced "irreparable harm" from the proposed laws and issued a temporary restraining order blocking their enforcement. The judge added that there was "a reasonable probability" the laws would be declared unconstitutional, which they were in August. In fact, many of the communities that tried to follow Hazelton's lead in passing restrictive anti-immigrant ordinances have since pulled back in the face of mounting legal costs and a series of adverse court rulings.

One of the things I can't figure out in this roiling immigration controversy is how the children of such recent arrivals can be so resolutely anti-immigrant. Mayor Lou Barletta, like the aggressively radical congressman Tom Tancredo, is the descendant of Italian immigrants. The parents of the anti-immigrant hawk Michelle Malkin hail from the Philippines. According to the *Filipino Reporter*, the authoritative media outlet for that community in the United States, there are 1 million Filipino illegal aliens in this country, third only to Mexicans and Chinese among undocumented immigrant groups. Malkin and I have had several bitter exchanges over her proposition that it is every citizen's duty to report suspected illegal aliens to federal authorities. Would she turn in a Filipino maid cleaning the Georgetown condo next door to hers? What if she was a distant relative?

The New Haven, Connecticut, mayor John DeStefano is another child of Italian immigration but he's my new hero. DeStefano has embraced the illegal aliens who make up perhaps 10 percent of the population of his city of 120,000. Recognizing the integral part they play in the daily life of his city, he rationalized that the city could regularize their existence. He initiated a municipal identification card that would enable the immigrants to open bank accounts, learn English, and be legitimate participants in city life.

The same day the mayor's visionary IDs became available, federal immigration officials raided households of suspected immigrants, roughly separating men from women and children. Thirty-two immigrants were arrested and put in jails throughout New England. Two days later the spunky mayor appeared on *At Large*, my Fox News weekend show, and angrily accused the federal government of retaliating against the city for its ID initiative. Following the mayor's lead, the Yale law professor Michael Wishnie specifically alleged that the motive for the operation was unconstitutional retaliation against New Haven for the ID program. Homeland Security chief Michael Chertoff defended Operation Return to Sender and claimed improbably that the timing was just coincidental.

By early fall 2007, the legal blowback from the misguided raids came in full force. A massive federal lawsuit alleged that agents from Immigration and Customs Enforcement (ICE) had unlawfully forced their way into the homes of Hispanic families without court warrants or other legal justification, sometimes pushing down doors in the middle of the night in search of alleged illegal aliens. Many of the Hispanic plaintiffs were American citizens; others were legal residents. They told harrowing stories of predawn raids by heavily armed ICE agents crashing into their homes in search of the undocumented.

Their suit also alleged that under pressure from the Department of Homeland Security, the agents had been given a quota of one thousand immigrants captured and deported per team per year, and that they were using unconstitutional means to bag their catches.

In the case of Adriana Aguilar and her mother, Elena Leon, both legal residents awaiting naturalization, agents burst into their home in East Hampton, New York, on the hunt for Ms. Aguilar's ex-husband, an illegal immigrant ordered deported because he had a criminal record. The problem, according to the Puerto Rican Legal Defense and Education fund (of which I was a longtime member of the board), is that Ms. Aguilar has not seen her ex-husband since they separated four years ago.

The East Hampton and New Haven raids are emblematic of a federal policy in disarray in the wake of the failed immigration legislation. The government drifts and improvises between enforcement and benign neglect while immigrants live in terror and businesses are confused about hiring conditions. Activists like Dobbs, Barletta, the militant Minutemen, the KKK, and the (so-far few) nut jobs like the crew in Alabama are demonstrating how malignant the fear and loathing of Latino immigrants is becoming in America. This hatred has become the new wedge issue in America's culture war. It is driven by public officials like the Iowa Republican congressman Steve King, whose frequently uttered but provably false statistics claim among other sins that illegal aliens are killing twenty-five native-born people a day (a figure that King says he "extrapolated" from national statistics to include twelve murdered and thirteen killed by drunk drivers).

The Rise of the Neo–Know-Nothings

Because they offer a glimpse into the sour heart of anti-immigrant, anti-Hispanic sentiment, I would like you to see some of the thoughtful e-mails I have received lately from viewers. All are presented exactly as they were sent, except some of the names have been changed. Here is one I received in April 2007.

> Dear Gerarldo,
>
> I thought you came to your senses after 9/11. You support of the invasion of our country by illegals is disgraceful. What part of illegal don't you get? I resent my tax dollars being used to provide health care, education, housing, food stamps etc. to people who are in this country illegally. They say Social Security will be bankrupt by 2021, it will for sure if all the people here illegally are allowed to become citizens. Common sense tells me they will be eligilble for for all the public and social services that I have paid into my entire life.
> Jane
> Missouri

In a raging debate that recalls the fury of the Know-Nothings, a swelling, vocal, and by now almost organic anti-immigration movement has taken its cause to the forefront of domestic issues, surpassing even abortion or gay marriage to rank as the nation's most divisive. Check out this e-mail sent on June 9, 2007, by a guy calling himself "FreedomBob."

> Geraldo,
>
> You must be the only dumb ass at Fox about this obvious issue! I always thought Puerto Ricans of all people would not have such ignorance about Mexicans! Why don't you use your influence about how unjust the Mexican Government is—The light skinned ones who treat the dark skinned indigents like 3rd class citizens, they even give them maps, then send them here! HAVE SOME BALLS AND BRING THAT UP, OR TAKE ME ON!—BECAUSE BILL [O'Reilly] DOES NOT HAVE THE BALLS!!
> One of over 200 Million,
> Bob

Whether he is one of over 200 million, "FreedomSteve" has obvious anger issues and apparently wants to kick my ass, but one blogger on MCDC Forums, the "Official Forums for Minuteman Civil Defense Corps," who calls himself "usa today," went further in his posting:

> *From usa today; Location: Nevada; Posted: Sun May 13, 2007 5:23 pm; Post subject: This one will get me kicked of;*
> *A call to lynch Geraldo Reveria*

Lynch me? Not just kill me, but a lynching, just like the good old days. "FreedomBob" and "usa today" are obviously over the top, but most opponents of immigration are not so easily dismissed. Many of their professed concerns, like Jane's above, are based on the uninformed fear of negative change, like increased crime, taxes, and unemployment, the threat of terrorist infiltration, dilution of English-language supremacy, and the overwhelming of public schools, social security, welfare, and other social services.

It is certain, however, that a deep, dark passion drives the anti-immigrant movement. Another e-mail, one of scores I continue to receive:

❝ YOUR MEXICANESS,
DOES THIS BOTHER YOU AT ALL? SEEMS LIKE ANYTHING SOME ILLEGAL MEX DOES YOU HAVE SOME RIDICULOUS EXCUSE FOR THEM.
IF THIS STUNT DOESN'T PENTRATE THAT TINY MIND OF YOURS, YOUR IN THE WRONG COUNTRY [sic].
DB
California ❞

(e-mail received May 2007)

Another message:

> To: Geraldo Rivera
> From: John
> Go home!!
> Take your illegal loving friends with you!!

Go home? I am home—I was born on 17th Street in Manhattan!

Seldom in my long career have so many people been so disdainful, physically hostile almost, to my stance on a volatile issue. Aside from a fear of change, what many of the messages have in common is raw anger. People who in their regular lives are probably as peaceful and open-minded as any one of us have been driven to fury and distraction bordering on apoplexy by any suggestion of immigration reform as opposed to a single-minded enforcement of border controls. Moreover, their emotional investment in the issue is causing spillover resentment toward those Hispanics who have long been citizens of the United States. A hardened or at least hardening eye is being directed at the greater Latino community. To many, there is a gnawing feeling that we are all "foreign," that we don't belong here whether we were born in this country or not.

Give those anti-immigration vigilantes credit. Aided and abetted by an eager corps of histrionic shock jocks, commentators, and opportunistic politicians, these noisy neo–Know-Nothings have been the obnoxious catalyst for the scary embrace by millions of a political position that can be summarized as "close the border, find, report, imprison, then kick out all illegal aliens with prejudice and without pity or doubt." It is a position held not just by the political extreme right but also by many people we used to call Reagan Democrats—mostly white blue-collar or middle-class folk, many at or near retirement age who have never met or even seen an illegal immigrant, except in their nightmares. One of their new heroes is a controversial player with a somewhat shady background named Chris Simcox.

> *The Minutemen are now a force to be reckoned with, and I will continue to lead these proud and patriotic Americans until we achieve total victory. We're not leaving the border until we're relieved from duty by the U.S. military or National Guard. There will be no compromise.*
>
> *(Chris Simcox, Minutemen founder at America First rally, Chicago, 2006)*

Having discovered the mother lode of nativist reaction, Simcox and his comrades are propagating that classic fear of "outsiders" coming to steal our stuff, assault our women, and pollute our race, which societies crueler than ours have used in the past to justify terrible acts. In this agitated climate they work hard to create and maintain, a majority in Congress and sadly among the American people now deeply resent any attempt to normalize the status of the "illegals" among us, insisting that they be rounded up and thrown out and that we physically wall ourselves off from Mexico and the rest of Latin America. Even former mayor Rudy Giuliani, who helped insulate New York's immigrants from federal enforcement during his tenure as mayor, is now talking about building a real and a "virtual" fence.

The Wall

> "We build too many walls and not enough bridges."
> —SIR ISAAC NEWTON

If that longed-for border wall is ever completed, the long-term consequences will be deeply harmful to the nation and to the cause of assimilation and integration. President Bush's trip to South America in February 2007, in which he encountered anti-U.S. demonstrations at the same time that Venezuela's Hugo Chávez was being widely lauded in his travels around the continent, should have been an eye-opener to those advocating the construction of a mighty wall to keep Latinos out. We build that wall and we fuel the radical movement led by Chávez and his left-wing comrades who say, "See—the gringos hate us."

"It will give voice to the very anti-U.S., very anti-democracy, very anti-globalization interests. It will give them something to point to," said the former Mexican foreign minister Jorge Castaneda in a May 2007 speech at the University of Texas, San Antonio. "It's become a symbol of American unfriendliness to Latin America, and to Mexico in particular."

Wall building exacerbates, radicalizes rather than regulates, the flow of illegal immigrants. Remember Berlin? Is there a person reading this who believes that a man with a hungry family who has marched across the length and breadth of Mexico and miles of parched desert because his family back home is hungry will be seriously impeded by a wall? Don't Mexicans have ladders? Or are we going to shoot them like the Stasi and the border guards did in East Germany? And once they get over or under the wall are they still going to go and come as they do now with the ebb and flow of seasonal jobs, risking running afoul of stricter border enforcement? Or will they just stay in the United States, worried they won't be able to make it back over that terrifying fence?

I remember doing a *20/20* report in 1982 in which my camera team and I hooked up with a group of several dozen Mexican farmworkers about to cross the Sonora-Arizona desert border. This particular group consisted of men, women, and young teenagers headed up to the Phoenix area to pick the ripening fruit crops, as most of them had been doing for years. The forty-mile trek was across a bleak, parched landscape. By the time we got to Arizona proper, the Border Patrol was waiting, alerted by the footprints our group had made crossing a patch of raked sand that serves as a distant early-warning system near the no-man's-land along the border.

When the patrol's assault began, the group scattered, hiding from the Jeep patrols on the ground and the helicopters overhead. I lost track of them and was worried that they had turned back, and, now waterless, were attempting to recross into Mexico. Instead, in a few days most had made it to the orchards around Phoenix and were quietly picking fruit as they had always done. A wall would not have stopped that hardy crew. And what are we going to do now if their descendents do manage to climb over or tunnel under the multibillion-dollar boondoggle?

George from New Jersey has an idea. Here is the e-mail he sent me on June 14, 2007:

> " The first order of business is to secure our southern border by installing two parallel fences, 12 feet high and about 25 feet of separation with land mines in between. Signs on the fences should indicate that mines are present. The border patrol should have high-powered rifles, with a warning shot fired first and if the intruder doesn't stop, aim straight.
> George
> New Jersey "

"It should be legal to kill illegals," a sixty-nine-year-old retired Special Forces veteran who claims he fought in Vietnam told a young law student monitoring the Minutemen anti-immigration vigilantes along the Arizona border for the Southern Poverty Law Center. "Just shoot 'em on sight. That's my immigration policy recommendation. You break into my country, you die."

"I agree completely," a man named Michael is quoted as saying by the SPLC. "You get up there with a rifle and start shooting four or five of them a week, the other four or five thousand behind them are going to think twice about crossing that line."

"I don't really like violence, but if we did start doing what you're talking about, it would show we mean business for a change," the group's only woman is quoted as saying. "It would say, 'This is the USA, don't fuck with us!'"

Senator Richard Burr of North Carolina, a moderate Republican who contemplated supporting the reform bill, told the *New York Times* that his office received a telephone call during the debate that "made a threat about knowing where I lived. There were enough specifics to raise some alarm bells."

"There is racism in this debate," Senator Lindsey Graham told the *Times* on the eve of the failed crucial vote on the proposed 2007 immigration bill. "Nobody likes to talk about it, but a very small percentage of people involved in this debate really have racial and bigoted remarks. The tone that we create around these debates, whether it be rhetoric in a union hall, or rhetoric on talk radio, it can take people who are on the fence and push them over emotionally."

Aside from the insanity of vigilantes threatening members of Congress and the only half-joking proposals to impose the death penalty on otherwise innocent people sneaking across the border seeking economic opportunity, the unmistakably racist tinge to the screechiest opposition to immigration reform is complicating the effort to confront legitimate areas of concern squarely, like national security. "We've seen people from Missouri and Kentucky militias involved in border-vigilante activity, especially with the gung-ho Arizona group Ranch Rescue that used face paint, military uniforms and weapons," Mark Pitcavage, the fact-finding director of the Anti-Defamation League, told *Time* magazine in May 2006. "It's a natural shift. Militias fell on hard times, and this anti-immigration movement is new and fresh."

And the xenophobic fear of a "brown tide" washing over America's white shores is being exacerbated by mob-inciting commentators like Lou Dobbs, and overtly racialist books like Pat Buchanan's *State of Emergency: The Third World Invasion and Conquest of America*; Michelle Malkin's *Invasion: How America Still Welcomes Terrorists, Criminals, and Other Foreign Menaces to Our Shores* (Malkin wrote an earlier book praising the forced internment of Japanese civilians during World War II, *In Defense of Internment: The Case for Racial Profiling in World War II and the War on Terror*); and Congressman Tom Tancredo's *In Mortal Danger: The Battle for America's Border and Security.*

In our panic, aren't we missing some very practical considerations amidst all the rhetoric? Aren't we turning our backs on Latin America, a huge and strategically important region that since the Monroe Doctrine we have sought to hold close? With a U.S. unemployment rate of less than 4.5 percent, where would we find the workers to replace the 12 million undocumented workers who are here? There are areas of the country where scarcely a child is cared for, a lawn mowed, a restaurant dish washed, a part assembled in a small factory, or a roof shingle nailed other than by an illegal alien. In other areas of the country scarcely a head of beef or a pig or chicken is processed but by an undocumented worker. Unless the current economic downturn becomes a full-fledged depression, there are not enough citizen hands to do the work of the nation.

Right now the nation is frightened by the enormous demographic changes that loom. "There is an ugly backlash that is taking place," former congressman Badillo told me, putting some of the blame on the president. "He meant well with his so-called comprehensive immigration reform. But he had no idea how to get it passed. And in the debate the American public suddenly realized that we Hispanics are the biggest minority group and we're getting bigger. And they feel that we're not qualified to be citizens, to be real Americans. We have to follow the Italians, Greeks, Germans, Jews, and everyone else that came before us. We've got to learn the language and get an education and everything else that defines citizenship. People are scared that we keep coming. That's why they're talking about building that wall and the higher the better. And the backlash is going to get worse. Wait another five or ten years."

3

The Threat to America's
Traditional Identity

"The single most immediate and most serious challenge to
America's traditional identity comes from the immense and
continuing immigration from Latin America, especially from
Mexico."

—SAMUEL HUNTINGTON,
Who Are We? The Challenges to America's National Identity

It is inconceivable that Huntington's fear for the fate of our "traditional identity" would be a major issue were it not for the role of race. The "we" in his "Who Are We?" question refers to white people, particularly Anglo-Protestants. He argues for a reaffirmation of the nation's Anglo-Protestant heritage, and views its resurgence as essential to avoiding a bifurcated, disunited America. Although joined in the New World over the centuries by other immigrants—Catholics, Jews, African- and Hispanic Americans, Asians, and so forth—Anglos are still the nation's dominant culture. This is a racial, religious, and ethnic equilibrium Huntington clearly believes passionately it is critically important to maintain, since he made its perseverance the central theme of his work.

If you have any doubts concerning the racial reality underlying the current immigration debate, picture it revolving around an influx of Northern European illegal aliens sneaking over the border from Canada. Now imagine the thousands of volunteer, vigilante Minutemen mustering the energy to get up off their couches, taking out the old shotgun, and making their way to our long and until recently unprotected northern frontier with the Great White North. "I've got a job to do, Mabel. Those pesky Swedes are infiltrating over the Minnesota line again! Alert the FBI, the CIA, the NHL!"

The dynamic demographic shift happening in the United States is fueling a wildfire of immigration resentment more raw and widespread than any the nation has experienced since the mid-nineteenth century. Firsthand reporting, combined with instinct and experience, convince me that the contemporary debate over immigration is a surrogate for the deeper, more fundamental concern: the mostly unspoken but widely acknowledged fear that America's essential racial and ethnic character, indeed our national identity, is being altered.

Consider this sad e-mail:

❝ Geraldo, while my urge is to resort to the invective, when it comes to you, as I find you a truly despicable person, I shall try to remain civil.

Your comments that the failure of the Immigration bill was due to poor leadership and even racism are patently nonsense. Why is it that Hispanics always attribute their own failure to measure up as racism?

The last thing we need in this country is another class of well-coached moochers. Hispanics have made it into a profession. They bring nothing to the American party, but their pregnant bellies and low IQs.

Why would we embrace these moochers? I count myself among those who would round them up and deport them. The country would be the better for it.

If the US becomes a Hispanic country . . . we are doomed. Within a generation, two at the most, the U.S. will look just like Mexico does now . . . a 3rd World Country.

I suggest that it is you who are the racist . . . promoting people of your race, regardless of the damage they do. It's singularly their race that you find compelling . . . that's racism.

Please take your genes back to Puerto Rico, or whatever God-Forsaken place it hails from.

Hispanics are the proverbial turd in the American punch bowl. When you throw a turd into a punch bowl, you don't elevate the stature of the turd . . . you poison the punch bowl. That is what is happening with all the hispanic invasion into this country.

Regards

Nick M. "

(received July 2, 2007)

However gross and obnoxious his sentiments, Mr. M. is at least honestly expressing the widely held resentment and unease directed at Hispanics living or working in the United States right now. While the nation's expanding African-American and Asian populations are part of America's undeniably and rapidly changing face, it is Hispanics who demographically are taking the country to a place she has never been. If current trends continue, the Anglo, white American majority will in less than a century swap places with Hispanics, now the nation's largest minority.

Since people like Nick M. are so agitated by that prospect, let me borrow Huntington's question and ask of my fellow Hispanics, "Who Are We?" The question is more complicated than it sounds because race and ethnicity are separate and distinct concepts, not only to the federal government but to us as well. Certainly, there are *caudillos* and *caballeros* from Cuba or Argentina or Spain who think of themselves as ethnically Hispanic and/or Latino, but consider themselves racially as white men. They would be horrified to be described as "brown" (a term I have enthusiastically embraced to describe our disparate community; my California-based friend Cheech Marin and I call each other "my brown brother").

A new study on Hispanic immigrants, "Are Latinos Becoming White?" presented at the American Sociological Association conference in August 2007, confirmed this deep and dramatic difference within the Latino community on racial self-identification. The researchers from the University of Cincinnati reported that 91 percent of Cubans surveyed self-identified as white, as compared to just 56 percent of Puerto Ricans and 49 percent of Mexicans, who preferred "other" when asked whether they were white, black, or something else.

Just as interestingly, the researchers found that the longer people remained in the United States, the less likely they were to identify as white, gravitating instead toward a Spanish racial self-identification. What makes this so intriguing is that it is in sharp contrast to the experiences of previous immigrants from Italy and Ireland, and the European Jews, all of whom campaigned aggressively against being classified as "other" and insisted on being incorporated into the "white" category.

To me, brown, like black or white, is an all-encompassing cultural, ethnic, even geographical and historic reference rather than a strict description of someone's skin tones. And it works for the Riveras. In my own huge family, my army of first cousins on my father's side ranges from fair-skinned, with orange-red hair, through subtle tan brown skin, with eyes and hair to match, to dark chocolate skin and black hair that is virtually indistinguishable from that of many Afro-Caribbeans. The potpourri is a function of Puerto Rico's colonial past, during which time native Arawak and Taino Indians, European conquistadors, Spanish expatriates, African slaves, American servicemen, traders, pirates, and adventurers all added to the hybrid broth. And while you would think that my mixed-race family of Puerto Rican islanders would have very little genetically in common with, say, an Aztec-Mayan-European Mexican like Cheech Marin, there is an unmistakable bond, which is made more powerful by the all-encompassing term "Hispanic."

Later in life, when he came to be reconciled with our culture for all its strengths and weaknesses, my father and I used to joke, *"La unica diferencia entre nosotros, Los Hispanos, es el color de nuestros frijoles."* (The only difference between us Hispanics is the color of our beans.) Yes, Mexicans prefer brown beans, Cubans black, and Puerto Ricans red, but our point was that we Hispanics are all in the pot together, sharing something both tangible and spiritual that is in varying degrees race, color, creed, language, geography, history, gene pool, social and economic challenges, and religion.

"What's in a name?"

—William Shakespeare

So where did the word "Hispanic" come from? Some quick history is required. "Hispania" was the collective name for the four principal Christian kingdoms on the northern half of the Iberian Peninsula where Spanish was spoken. That was in the days before Queen Isabela and King Ferdinand threw the Muslims out of Western Europe at the end of the fifteenth century after an eight-hundred-year occupation.

In the years following the Christian triumph over the Moors and the later separation of Portugal into an independent country with its own language, an expanded, modern Spain, still known also as Hispania, was created. And the principal ruler of those lands became known as the King of all the Hispanics (*Rex Omniae Hispaniae*).

The term "Hispanic," then, has for at least 425 years referred to people from the original mother country of Spain, its far-flung subjects around its once mighty, world-girdling empire, as well as to its Spanish culture and language. So Hispanics can be black, brown, red, or white; Catholic, Protestant, Jewish, Muslim, or Buddhist; and residents of Spain, Puerto Rico, Cuba, the Dominican Republic, or other Caribbean, Mexican, Central or South American nations. The exceptions in South America are Brazil, where Portuguese is spoken, and the trio of former European colonies perched on the continent's right shoulder: Surinam (formerly Dutch Guiana), Guyana (formerly British Guiana and still best remembered as the site in 1978 of the infamous Jonestown murder–mass suicide, which followed the murders of California congressman Leo Ryan and four others, including my friend, NBC cameraman Bob Brown), and French Guiana (home of the European spaceport and Devil's Island, the infamous prison from which Papillon escaped).

The combined Hispanic groups that will represent about 25 percent of the entire U.S. population by 2040 are therefore persons of any Spanish culture or origin, regardless of race and whether they even speak the language. I often refer to the entire crew simply as "Spanish people."

What then is a Latino? In modern usage, it is not a word that relates either to Latin, the language of ancient Rome, or to other Romance languages (like French or Italian). Rather, it is a political-geographic description of people who either live in Latin America or their descendents in the United States.

The confusion is all Napoleon III's fault. In the early 1860s, with America distracted by our epic civil war, the French ruler (and nephew of Napoleon I) hatched a plot to invade and colonize Mexico and expand his New World holdings. Having fought their own protracted and bloody war of independence against Spain (1810–21), and having later lost Texas (in 1835) and what is now the entire southwestern United States (1846–47) to us, the war-ravaged Mexicans still resisted the French, most famously at the Battle of Puebla. There, on May 5, 1862 (the event celebrated as Cinco de Mayo), a force of four thousand locals, under leaders like Porfirio Diaz (later the dictator of Mexico) defeated the foreign legions of France.

But the reinforced French recovered the military and political initiative, occupied Mexico City, and installed their ill-fated puppet regime. To lessen popular resistance, Napoleon III sought to emphasize the common heritage, however remote, between this New World country and France. He therefore popularized the term "Latino." He could pretend that since French and Mexican people both spoke a Romance or Latin-derived language, they were all related. It was along the lines of, "I'm a Latino, you're a Latino. Can't we all just get along?"

The too-clever ruse didn't work. The monarchs he installed, the hapless Austrian Archduke Maximilian, who became Emperador Maximiliano I de Mexico, and his crazy wife, the Belgian princess who was his Emperatriz Carlota, were undone when the United States invoked the Monroe Doctrine, which prohibited further European colonization of the Americas and refused to recognize their government.

Facing continued stubborn military resistance from Mexican insurgents who were being supplied by the United States, and threatened in Europe by Iron Chancellor Bismarck's restless Prussian army, which would soon defeat and depose him, Napoleon III decided the ambitious New World scheme wasn't worth the price in men and money and withdrew his army.

With the French force gone, after just three years, 1864–67, Max was overthrown by Mexicans under the command of Benito Juarez and executed. This original Latino had never gotten around to learning Spanish. His last words were "Poor Carlota" (*Pauvre Carlotta*). By that time, she had already fled for Europe. The empress was in the Old Country trying to drum up support for her doomed husband when she got the news of his execution. She was later declared insane.

The fake imperial family's grim fate aside, and despite complaints that it ignored the heritage of the indigenous people who were here before any Europeans arrived, Napoleon III's term "Latino" has stuck around much longer than his empire did. So now, if you live in or are descended from Spain or Latin (Spanish) America, you are a Latino.

To curtail what later became a largely semantic debate that festered in the 1960s through the 1980s and to end tiresome bureaucratic confusion, in 1997 the federal government officially adopted both "Latino" and "Hispanic" terms, declaring them essentially synonymous. At the risk of becoming tiresome myself, I must add that neither "Latino" nor "Hispanic" has the same meaning as the more recently evolved term "Chicano."

Anglo farmers in the Southwest once used "Chicano" to signify a lowly regarded Mexican or Tex-Mex peasant laborer. Then, in the way some African-Americans of the same period were claiming and repositioning the vile and pejorative "nigger," in the 1960s, Mexican-American social and political activists adopted "Chicano" as their own proud, preferred self-description. But "Chicano" refers only to someone of Mexican-American origin, not to the Latino/Hispanic community at large. As a Puerto Rican, I am Latino and Hispanic, but not a Chicano.

Whatever you call us, the community is growing explosively. Alarmists and demagogues inflame public passions proclaiming the peril of a de facto state within a state created by America's expanding Latino population. As you will see, the claim is hogwash, but while the sea of Irish fleeing oppression and famine in 1840–65 comes close, there is no denying the current surge of Mexican-Hispanic-Latino-Chicano population growth is historically exceptional.

"Before the storm, only 2 percent were Hispanic; now about 96 percent are Hispanic."

—Beth Perrilloux, head nurse, Metairie health unit
of Louisiana Department of Health and Hospitals

A Hispanic baby boom has hit hospitals in the New Orleans area in the wake of Hurricane Katrina, as immigrant families flood into the Crescent City looking for work amidst the monumental rebuilding effort. It is one tiny example of a tsunami sweeping the nation. In 1950 there were fewer than 4 million Hispanics living in the United States. By 2007, according to U.S. Census Bureau estimates, there were over 45 million, at least 12 million of whom were here illegally, most of these of Mexican origin. Forty-five million! Only the nation of Mexico and the South American country of Colombia have larger Hispanic populations than the United States. Arizona, California, Colorado, Florida, Georgia, Illinois, Massachusetts, Nevada, New Jersey, New Mexico, New York, North Carolina, Pennsylvania, Texas, and Washington State each has at least half a million Hispanic residents.

While the name Smith still ranks as the most common surname in the United States, for the first time, according to a survey released by the Census Bureau, two Hispanic surnames—Garcia and Rodriguez—are among the top ten. Another, Martinez, was narrowly edged out for tenth place by Wilson.

The number is huge and expanding hourly. "To me Hispanic immigration is like a lava flow," says Cheech Marin. "You can stand in front of it and try to block it with walls and Minutemen or you can try to channel it in positive directions. I want my kids to be both proud Hispanics and proud Americans. One big problem is that we have been excluded from the fabric of America when in fact we're one of the main threads. If you took out the Hispanic influence from American society none of the West would have names and there'd be nothing good to eat in restaurants. Immigration is saving small towns from extinction. It's the single most powerful new voice in American culture. Salsa is already more popular than ketchup. It may not be unfolding exactly how we would like it, but I think it's all going to work out. We have to keep a positive attitude."

But the issues raised by the burgeoning population of Latinos are manifest. Alone, Hispanics here illegally are already roughly equal to the entire populations of the nation's two largest cities, New York and Los Angeles. The sheer magnitude of that population should rationally dictate future policy decisions and their accommodation inside the country. Clearly, any suggestion of forced mass deportation is not only frightening, it is absurd. Yet, as one hateful wag among many put it in a mass e-mail message sent to the Senate and copied to multiple offices during the immigration debate, "They need to be taken out by ANY MEANS."

"Taken out," as in eradicated, or merely removed? If removed, by what means—livestock trains? I saw that movie already and it was called World War II. The extent of the extreme horror wrought by the Nazis was unprecedented. The world has never seen anything like their fascist racial purification, so any comparison with it is doomed. Yet can individuals like the Fox News contributor Michelle Malkin, who proposes mass deportation, deny its similarity to, say, the universally condemned actions of Serbia in the 1990s in attempting to evict all ethnic Albanians (Muslims) from areas of the Balkans controlled by them? Or the expulsion of the Armenians (Christians) by the Turks in the early twentieth century or the Jews from Spain, France, and England during the Middle Ages?

> **"The Mexicans are physically, mentally and morally an inferior and 'low flung' race."**
>
> —Brigadier General Stephen Watts Kearny,
> *Letter Book 1846–1847*

J. D. Hayworth, the hapless hard-liner and former Arizona Republican congressman, is now a radio shock jock advocating among other final solutions to the problem of illegal immigration that all undocumented immigrants be given 120 days to leave the country or face a massive, forceful roundup and deportation. The Atlanta-based syndicated radio host Neal Boortz put it even more colorfully in a June 2007 broadcast. After assuring his audience that he did not sanction mass roundups ("We're not gonna throw these people out of airplanes with taco-shaped parachutes)," he urged the government to "build a double fence along the Mexican border, and stop the damn invasion. I don't care if Mexicans pile up against that fence like tumbleweeds in the Santa Ana winds in Southern California. Let 'em."

Doesn't the suggestion of forced mass deportation of those in America illegally meet the internationally recognized definition of "population transfer," which is "the forced movement of a large group of people from one region to another by state policy or international authority, most frequently on the basis of ethnicity or religion"?

Putting aside the ugly mask worn by many of those most vocally opposed to immigration reform, whose illogic I will address, the fact remains that the current 45 million Hispanic-American population is expected to double again in the next twenty years. That rate of growth will far outpace all other groups, including African-Americans and Asians, strengthening and enhancing the Latino position as the nation's largest minority. Some demographers suggest that if unchanged (with or without illegal immigration), the current trend will make the United States a majority Hispanic nation by the end of the twenty-first century, no doubt much to the dismay of Nick M. and my other e-mail friends.

The reasons are clear and unavoidable. As America's predominantly white baby boomers move out of their childbearing years and their children opt for smaller families, the growth in the number of Hispanics accounts for almost half of the country's total population growth. And while one in seven individuals already claims Hispanic ethnicity, given their relative youth and accelerated birth rate, plus the current cascade of immigrants, an unprecedented 40 percent of the most recent coming from Mexico alone, the face of America is becoming more Latino at a geometrically increasing rate.

In Los Angeles, whites are already the minority, representing just 30 percent of the population, compared to 48 percent Hispanic. The "Browning of America" process is now inevitable, absent either another white baby boom, a gigantic influx of whites from abroad, or a run on Scandinavian sperm banks, each of which is historically unlikely.

Despite so much attention being paid to the role of immigration, most of the population increase will be homegrown. In cities like Houston, Dallas, and, especially, San Antonio, the relative growth in the Latino population is being fueled mostly by natural increase, not by immigration. These are births here in the United States, not of so-called anchor babies, whom I will also address later, but of kids born of Hispanic-American citizens.

In the golden summer of 2000, in that last full year of innocence before the Twin Towers went down, along with actor Eddie Olmos, funnyman Paul Rodriquez, actor Esai Morales, and my soul brother actor-comedian Cheech Marin, I participated in the Latino Laugh Festival, now an annual event, which uses comedic themes to celebrate Hispanic culture in exaggerated and often side-splitting parody. The burlesque and over-the-top humor is not unlike TV's Comedy Central using a "Senior National Public Restroom Correspondent" to tell the story of Republican senator Larry Craig's Minneapolis Airport misfortune in 2007.

Between tequila shots in our San Antonio, Texas, hotel suite following the performance, I joked that since we were all U.S.-born Latinos of varied backgrounds who had "made it" in America, that maybe the five of us should pose for a Hispanic mini–Mt. Rushmore. Maybe it could be carved in a cliff in East L.A. or into the Palisades over the Hudson River facing Manhattan's Washington Heights from New Jersey. Olmos especially, I kidded my longtime friend, has the craggy face for monumental sculpture. Coincidentally, Eddie went to Montebello High School, in a then relatively middle-class neighborhood east of L.A., with my Jewish-Sicilian ex-wife, Sheri, the mother of my firstborn child, Gabriel Miguel. Gabriel's grandfather still lives there, in a neighborhood that has become almost totally Hispanic and politically engaged in the intervening years.

The Emmy Award–winning star of everything from *Zoot Suit* to *Kojak, Miami Vice* to *Battlestar Galactica*, Eddie exudes a calm that is the counterpoint to every cliché about overexcited Latinos. His

1988 film *Stand and Deliver,* based on the life of the educator Jaime Escalante and how he managed to turn around a group of kids in East L.A.'s Garfield High School and help them succeed in Advanced Placement Calculus, was not only inspirational but showed that given the chance, poor Hispanic youth could compete with students from across town in Beverly Hills.

Esai Morales was not yet the heartthrob he would soon become with *NYPD Blue,* but this Nuyo-Rican (New York–born-and-bred Puerto Rican) son of a garment worker was already well known. The wry (for a Latino), Mexican-born, East L.A.–bred Paul Rodriquez scored a hit with ABC television's *AKA Pablo,* and as such is a crossover star, since statistically you can't have a hit show on network television unless it appeals to a broad demographic. His son Junior, known as "P-Rod," is a famous, goofy-footed professional skateboarder. I'll tell you about Cheech in a minute. The point is that the five of us that night in San Antonio were known by almost everybody with a television in the United States. To the extent that anyone thought of us at all, they wouldn't have thought of us as anything but fellow Americans.

In 2000, San Antonio was already the Tex-Mex capital of the country. As such, it is a good indicator of the likely evolution of Hispanic America. If you want to know what the United States will be like when and if Latinos are ever the demographic top dogs, just visit the "Alamo City." It's the de facto capital of south Texas, a gigantic area that stretches from El Paso in far west Texas to Laredo on the Mexican border, to Brownsville and Corpus Christi on the Gulf of Mexico in the southeast. San Antonio is the second largest city in Texas, with a population of about 1.3 million, more than double since 1970, and nearly 70 percent of its residents are Hispanic.

San Antonio de Bexar, the old missionary town laid out by the Spanish in 1731, is now strongly middle class. The city has a diversified economy; it is surrounded by big military installations like Fort Sam Houston and the Lackland Air Force Base. It boasts a first-class basketball team, the Spurs, which trounced my beloved Cleveland Cavaliers and LeBron James in four games in 2007 for their fourth NBA title. There is a vibrant tourist trade that centers on the legendary heart of Texas pride, the Alamo, where 189 brave souls perished holding off the entire Mexican army for almost two weeks.

Given the role the Battle of the Alamo played as one of American history's pivotal moments, it is perhaps ironic that most of the residents of the city more closely resemble the attacking army than the mission's heroic defenders. Walking through downtown, I've often marveled at the public buildings gaily colored pink, green, and red, the resurrected and very Latino Market Square, and the grace of the River Walk, where folkloric displays and civic celebrations make it a kind of year-round Latino Colonial Williamsburg. The city offers everything from ranchero music and mariachis to flamenco dancers, traditional street vendors, winter night light shows, and some of the best restaurants, hotels, shops, and museums in Texas, including the recently opened Museo Alameda, which is affiliated with the Smithsonian, but unlike its stodgy uncle is dressed in flamboyant pink and green and holds, among its treasures, Emperor Maximilian's emerald ring.

"If you draw a line from El Paso across the state through the Rio Grande Valley to San Antonio and Corpus Christi, every member of Congress, all six of them, are and have been Hispanic for many years," the longtime social and civil rights activist and Texas lawyer Tony Bonilla told me in an interview. "And that power of seniority translates in chairmanships. So from the political standpoint, Mexican Americans dominate the scene in south Texas, just as we dominate the economic and cultural scene." It is an impressive and unprecedented lineup of Latino congressmen, stretching from Silvestre Reyes in the west to Ruben Hinojosa, Henry Cuellar, Ciro Rodriquez, Charlie Gonzalez, and Solomon Ortiz in Corpus Christi to the east. Other than the usual cohorts of old white guys, there is no similar grouping of a single ethnic group. Rodriquez was actually born in Coahuila, Mexico, the border province known as Mexico's Front Door, through which most of the commerce with the United States passes. Tony's folks were also born south of the border.

"My parents were born in Monterrey, Mexico, my dad emigrated here at the age of fifteen, in 1905," my dear old friend Tony told me in an interview. "My mom came two years later." Tony and his lovely wife, Olga, have been my hosts and guides to all things Texan since we were both honored in 1980 at a meeting of LULAC, the awkwardly named League of United Latin American Citizens, which was founded in Corpus Christi in 1929, making it the oldest political advocacy group for Latinos in the United States. Tony's family's story is instructive and comforting to anyone who fears the rise of Hispanics in America. His father, Ruben, worked as an immigrant laborer, "digging ditches in the oil fields," as Tony told me.

Settling in central Texas, Ruben Bonilla worked his way up from gas station attendant to owner of his own full-service Texaco in the old cotton plantation town of Calvert—population 1,400—where blacks still outnumber browns by a wide margin, the "colored" folk living on one side of the railroad tracks, whites on the other. Like my own father, Tony's emphasized the importance of education for his children, and as a result all eight of them went to college. Calvert is strategically located on State Route 6, and became the rest stop for politicians traveling between Houston and Dallas. Even though he was self-taught in English, Ruben became involved in local politics, meeting and greeting passing senators and congressmen, including a lanky, young, and dynamic man by the name of Lyndon B. Johnson.

Of Ruben and wife Maria's eight children, two became educators, four became lawyers, and two became successful businessmen. All were initiated by Dad into politics. When most of the family relocated to Corpus Christi in 1960, Mexicans working in the post office were still not allowed to serve the public, nor answer the telephone. "The thing that drew us all into local politics and activism was the fact there was still so much discrimination in the 1950s and 1960s. It was the natural progression of our education," Tony said. Three of the Bonillas would serve as national presidents of LULAC, becoming allies of and visiting their old friend, the then president Lyndon Johnson, in the White House; bringing lawsuits to end school segregation; and working to get local officials elected. "Hispanics played a significant role in getting John F. Kennedy and our friend Lyndon Johnson elected. Now the hands that picked cotton helped pick the president of the United States."

Root for Immigrant Success

I hope that the immigrant success story represented by the Mexican-American Bonilla family is comforting, because there is no force on earth that can stop the nation from becoming more Latino, not the Minutemen, not the militias, and neither walls nor the National Guard can reverse this trend. Since there is no way to turn back the demographic clock, what are the consequences, fearful, fanciful, and factual?

Harshly stated, the neo-nativist fantasy sweeping the nation in 2007 wonders whether America's essential character as an English-speaking, democracy-loving, law-abiding, hardworking, Anglo-Protestant–dominated society will be lost in a flood of welfare-grubbing, Social Security–sucking Hispanics, many of them Catholic strangers, who trace their roots to that mysterious, probably decadent, criminal and immoral culture south of the border. If you think I am exaggerating, check out this e-mail:

> I am furious and horrified!!!!!this is insane!!!!
> These illegal lawless Mexicans (and other illegals) are never going to
> abide by any laws. They are lawless.

Illegal aliens are invading our country and are a huge burden on our country and they pay no taxes and they will never pay taxes regardless of how you try to tell us they will. They won't.
THIS IS HORRIFYING! THIS IS TEARING APART THE VERY FABRIC OF OUR ONCE VALIANT NATION!!!
FENCE FIRST AND FOREMOST AND SEND THESE LAWLESS CRIMINAL ILLEGALS BACK TO MEXICO ONCE AND FOREVER!!! WE ALL SEE THROUGH WHAT YOU LEADERS ARE DOING AND LYING TO US WHILE YOU SELL OUT OUR NATION AND MAKE US PAY PAY PAY FOR ALL THESE ILLEGALS AND ALL THEIR RELATIVES WHO GET A FULL FREE Ride ON OUR BACKS!!!!!!!!!!!!!!!!!!!!!!!!!!!!!!!!!!! !!!!!!!!!!!!!!!!!!!

R. **77**

(May 18, 2007)

While we pause to allow R. to catch his or her breath, we must recognize there is the legitimate question of whether the impact of demographic change on mainstream culture, on the American identity, will be destabilizing. Will the newcomers distort the uniqueness of our nationhood? Will they wreck the American dream?

There is a legitimate conclusion based on the last half century of objective, measurable social and economic data and observable anecdotal evidence like the Bonilla, Rivera, and Marin family sagas. It is that our extraordinary national culture will do as it has always done: change immigrants more than immigrants change America. To the extent that the fabric of our society is changed by the latest wave of immigrants, it will be woven richer, stronger, and more colorfully.

I don't want to sound too much like an ethnic cheerleader, but sometimes it seems the achievements of the Latino "Our Crowd" are overlooked, while our sins become grist for the Minutemen and Malkin mill.

In August 2007, for example, a particularly outrageous, cold-blooded, execution-style triple slaying of three African-American college kids in Newark, New Jersey, garnered almost no national attention for several days. I went on television expressing my frustration with the lack of coverage and opined that it would have been different if the victims had been white kids from Orange County, California. With sixty murders already that year in Newark, the media had simply ignored the slaughter as more of the same black-on-black crime.

Then, two days later it was revealed that the alleged ringleader of the gang of thugs who killed the black teenagers was a Latino illegal immigrant from Peru. Suddenly, the story was everywhere, receiving tabloid headlines and widespread attention from cable news networks like my own. There was a barrage of interviews with former House Speaker Newt Gingrich, who angrily demanded a new federal law requiring state and local cops to check the immigration status of all prisoners and parolees. He even insisted that "the war here at home" against illegal immigrants is "even more deadly than the war in Iraq and Afghanistan." Because the statement was so breathtakingly naive, uninformed, or just intentionally inflammatory, I guessed immediately that Newt Gingrich has never been either to Iraq or Afghanistan. In November 2007, when the ex-Speaker appeared on Fox News, in the green room of John Gibson's show I asked him directly. "No, I've never been to either," he told me. "Only vicariously, through your reporting."

Bill O'Reilly used the occasion of the Newark homicides to once more protest the existence of "sanctuary cities," which he said allowed these predators to prowl our streets. Viewer David S. agreed with him, sending me this rotten e-mail shortly after the segment aired:

“ From: David S.
To: Rivera, Geraldo
Sent: Mon Aug 13 22:41:54 2007
Subject: heres to you . . .

geraldope, i can only hope that your daughters have a
runin with the likes of the illegal gamboa brothers
and suffer the fate you invite on so many who BELONG
HERE. go fuck yourself.
David S.
Louisiana 🙶🙶

One of my most unimpeachable findings is that the debate over
illegal immigration is exposing something deep and dark in the
American psyche. Nobody can contradict me because no one has
been better placed to feel the ugly venom of that rage in the months
following the O'Reilly confrontation. It is one thing even to call
for my "lynching." It is much more wicked to hope for the victim-
ization of my children. In Mr. W's case, I did something I rarely do:
I wrote back, and after calling him sick, told him to go fuck himself.

On Bill O'Reilly's show that night, the host did concede, albeit
reluctantly, after I forcefully made the point about the lack of media
attention initially paid the dreadful crime, that the mainstream
media's habitual inattention to inner-city crime was an "interesting
point." But when I added that in substantive terms, what the Newark story was really about was the fact the alleged perpetrator was an
accused child rapist out on ridiculously low bail, that his bail was
the issue and not his immigration status, O'Reilly claimed the right
to have the last word and reverted to another rant against "sanctuary
cities" like Newark.

The most tragic aspect of the demonizing of illegal immigrants
like the Newark assassin or the Virginia drunk driver is the spillover
effect that negatively impacts the legion of Latino innocents, immigrant and otherwise. Statistically, we are neither drunker nor more
murderous than any other group in this country. It is one of those
cosmic misfortunes that, in the current climate of acrimony over
immigration, when Latinos could certainly use some good public
relations, the goodwill generated by Hispanic Americans who are

successful is not as effectively attaching to the community as are the misdeeds of the minority of misfits.

The pity is that the criminals among us are easy to spot, and if you miss them, one of the rabble-rousing, right-wing, throwback protectionists will point them out to you.

While individual transgressions like these, allegedly committed by a Peruvian or a Mexican, tend to hoist blame and shame on the broader Hispanic community, our success stories generally get folded into the broader American national community's successes.

There are exceptions. Some of our crossover Hispanic-American heroes have gone out of their way to emphasize their Latino heritage, usually either for comic result or to play the "Latin lover" roles that became so popular when I was a kid. In 1952 the Cuban-born bandleader, actor, producer, and performer Desi Arnaz made history by adorably loving Lucille Ball with an exaggerated accent the gifted comedienne mimicked in her own endearing way. As a couple, Ricky and Lucy Ricardo were so haplessly charming and approachable that despite initial race-based resistance by network producers fearful of a negative response, a generation of television viewers ended up falling in love with both of them.

The Mexican-born actor Ricardo Montalban has had an enduring sixty-year career in theater, film, and television, but he only soared to fame in the United States when he used his elegantly Spanish-accented English to extol the virtues of rich Corinthian leather in Chrysler automobile commercials.

The Spanish-born, Cuban-bred mambo king Xavier Cugat was mostly famous to a particular generation for marrying the ever-effervescent entertainer Charo, who personified sexy, comic Las Vegas excess even though her real skill is the Spanish guitar. The Argentine-born Fernando Lamas was a suave partner to mermaid and actress Esther Williams in film and in life, as well as to the incomparable Arlene Dahl, but he really only made his mark through the comedy of Billy Crystal. After watching an appearance of Lamas on the *Tonight Show*, Crystal created the character "Fernando" on *Saturday Night Live*. Borrowing something the real Fernando said to Johnny Carson, Crystal regaled late-night America with his faux Spanish accent, advising us that "it is better to look good than to feel good," and that, darling, "you look marvelous."

The widely adored, incomparably romantic Julio Iglesias crossed over into female America's heart only when he teamed with Willy Nelson in their ode to "All the Girls We Loved Before." Antonio Banderas became the heir to the older generation of on-screen Latin lovers and even surpassed their passion. He received great plaudits when he played, ironically enough, a gay guy in an incredible performance opposite Tom Hanks in *Philadelphia*, and also with the visionary director Robert Rodriquez's mystical "Mariachi" trilogy, culminating in *Once Upon a Time in Mexico*. Penelope Cruz crossed over only after her well-publicized liaison with Tom Cruise (no relation).

The road for today's Hispanic comics was long ago paved by some of the greatest of the craft. Even in television's early days, there was Spain's Wenceslao Moreno, better known as Señor Wences to Ed Sullivan's television audience, and another on-screen regular, the brilliant deadpan funnyman known as "Mexico's Charlie Chaplin," Mario Moreno Reyes, aka Cantinflas. Following in the professional footsteps of my friend, the late Freddy Prinze, who rocked in the pioneering 1970s sitcom *Chico and the Man*, in the modern era successful and talented comedians like George Lopez, also known as "America's Mexican"; his Taco Bell rival Carlos Mencia; together with the aforementioned Paul Rodriquez and Cheech Marin, have made millions laugh with routines that lovingly but sometimes bitingly reference Hispanic lifestyles of the not so rich or famous. Cheech's once and future partner Tommy Chong disparagingly called it being "a professional Mexican."

Incidentally, how many times has any of that crew been on the *Tonight Show* or *Saturday Night Live*? Not many. And Garrett Morris's wonderful Latino ballplayer character, Chico Escuela, doesn't count, although he did utter the unforgettable line "Baseball's been berry, berry good to me," which Sammy Sosa later adopted during his historic home-run derby with Mark McGwire. "They don't have a thing against Hispanics, they always book Tony Orlando," Cheech cracked, breaking into a spontaneous rendition of "Tie a Yellow Ribbon Round the Ole Oak Tree." You ever notice how *SNL* has always had a black guy, but never a Spanish guy, at least until they got [Chilean] Horatio Sanz? "I guess they didn't deem us worthy," Cheech deadpanned.

When it comes to the larger community's exemplars and role models, people often don't notice the individual's ethnic background. In the way consumers don't automatically equate Toyota to Japan, Bic pens to France, or LEGO to Denmark, crossover actors like Cameron Diaz, Eva Longoria, Salma Hayek, Edward James Olmos, Anthony Quinn, Andy Garcia, Rita Hayworth, Raquel Welsh, Jimmy Smits, Raul Julia, Chita Rivera, and Rita Moreno; athletes like Nancy Lopez, Alex Rodriquez, Lee Trevino, Oscar De La Hoya, Roberto Clemente, Sammy Sosa, Keith Hernandez, David Ortiz, Manny Ramirez, and Jose Canseco; political pioneers like Representatives Loretta Sanchez, Ileana Ros-Lehtinen, Herman Badillo, Henry Gonzalez, and New Mexico's governor Bill Richardson; conservative intellectuals like Linda Chavez; singers like Jennifer Lopez, Christina Aguilera, Linda Ronstadt, Gloria Estefan, Joan Baez, and the Grateful Dead's Jerry Garcia; Nobel Prize–winning physicist Luis Walter Alvarez, astronaut Ellen Ochoa, Nobel laureate Severo Ochoa; and business leaders like Coca-Cola's late chairman Roberto C. Goizueta, tend often to be regarded as generically American notables rather than specifically Hispanic.

I know from my own experience that while the Latino community has always claimed me as their own (for better or worse, even after I opened Al Capone's vault on live television in 1986 and found nothing but an old stop sign and two empty Gilbey's Gin bottles, and despite my Jersey-born non-Hispanic Jewish mother or the fact that my career has had more ups and downs than the Cyclone roller coaster in Coney Island), most Americans don't think much about my ethnic background unless and until I make an issue of it, which has happened most vividly during this immigration debate.

But there is a growing consciousness among even self-professed liberals of the increasingly omnipresent Hispanics in certain aspects of American society. "I know all about Babe Ruth and Lou Gehrig, but today's baseball stars are all guys named Rodriguez to me," said Andy Rooney, then eighty-eight, resident geezer-commentator in August 2007 on *60 Minutes*. I laughed out loud when I heard about his painfully neo–Black Face remark. Surprised by the adverse public reaction, the reliably wry, self-confident humorist uncharacteristically apologized. "Yeah, I probably shouldn't have said it," he told the *New York Times*. If Andy meant to report on the increasing Latino dominance in Major League Baseball, he roughly succeeded. Unfortunately, he made it sound like, "To me, they all look alike."

There is no denying, though, that the country will be different as America continues into the brave new world of the Hispanic renaissance. For one thing, as I said on another program with my regular prime-time sparring partner O'Reilly, this one on the May day the census figures on rocketing Hispanic population growth discussed above were published, the country will eventually look more like me than it looks like him. Miami will not be Minneapolis. Salsa is not a jig and tequila is not whiskey. Not better, not worse, undeniably different, but ultimately just as American as the corner Irish pub, pizza parlor, or Taco Bell.

4

The New Hispanic America, from Sea to Shining Sea

I want to show how the demographic surge is actually affecting specific regions of the country. Because Spanish people, for various and obvious reasons, are usually more distinct and identifiable, you can visually register our surging population. We are easier to differentiate than, say, the Canadians from Clevelanders as they flow into west Florida. But we are part of the same churning migration to sunnier climes. When my longtime assistant, JoAnn Torres Conte, whose roots lie in Puerto Rico, announced she and her husband, Anthony, were leaving New York City to live near her mom in Orlando, Florida, she explained, "Who doesn't want to be warm?"

The explosive growth of the Hispanic population in the Sun Belt encompassing the Southeast and Southwest quarters of the country has been part of a larger movement of the American people, that vast internal shift of population and economic activity from north to south.

Take Phoenix, Arizona, as an example. Between 1980 and 2000, the Hispanic population there nearly quadrupled. Aside from the obvious issues a burgeoning population brings to any urban area—traffic, pollution, crime, school shortages, sprawl, and so forth—the town has not altered meaningfully in terms of its essential character. I went to college at the University of Arizona in the 1960s. The hills around Tucson or especially Phoenix may be scarcely recognizable from that rustic era, the once limitless vistas now reduced by haze. But while Phoenix is bigger in every sense, it is still a thoroughly modern, English-speaking, Anglo-dominated, All-American town, complete with crowded freeways, malls, fast-food franchises, retirement communities, spas, cowboys, and a passion for big-time sports.

Certainly, there are many more Hispanics. As part of the town's surging population, over that twenty-year period, 500,000 Latinos moved in. But they were only about one-third of the total increase. In other words, for every one new Latino, there were two non-Hispanic whites that left winter behind and moved into the Valley of the Sun. And most of the Hispanics who moved there during those two decades were citizen migrants from the Snow Belt, just like most of the other newcomers.

And in 2006 those new Phoenix Hispanic voters joined forces with progressive white and black suburbanites to oust a twelve-year congressman, J. D. Hayworth, who campaigned on how he was going to cleanse a state overrun by Mexicans, using as his noxious campaign slogan "Whatever It Takes." Also defeated in Arizona that year was Randy Graf, whose position on immigration was, improbably, even harsher than Hayworth's.

According to the Pew Hispanic Center, the same pattern of what you might call "They go where you go" migration holds for many other cities: Las Vegas, Denver, and Salt Lake, for example, all of which have changed dramatically during the last generation, but remained fundamentally the same. Vegas is still the desert gambling mecca boomtown, only bigger and glitzier with a burgeoning middle class, many of whom are unionized Hispanic hotel and casino employees who are able now to buy their own homes. Denver is still Rocky Mountain High, only it has spread east on to the Great

Plains, bringing Hispanics and everyone else into burgeoning new communities like Aurora. Salt Lake City remains the center of gravity for modern, striving Mormons, only now some of them are also Spanish speakers. There are more Hispanics in those places than there once were, sometimes a lot more, but there is also a lot more of just about everyone and everything else.

Take a closer look at Denver, Colorado's capital and the capital of the inland West. The Mile High City is a microcosm for much of the American and Hispanic experience, good and bad. After falling on hard times during the late 1960s through the early 1980s, when the population actually declined, the core city of approximately 600,000 in a metropolitan area of about 2.5 million has since shed most of its smog-choked, postindustrial shabbiness. Now young people pour into downtown, where 17th Street boasts the World Trade Center buildings often described as the Wall Street of the West. The high-tech and energy businesses, a sound economy, a huge new airport, a downtown baseball stadium, and that utterly alluring setting at the foot of the majestic Rocky Mountains are driving an enviable renaissance.

The Rocky Mountain "high" my dear pal the late John Denver used to sing about came closer to literal reality when the town in 2005 became the first major U.S. city to make marijuana legal for residents twenty-one and older. It is a fact the Republicans are sure to reference when Denver hosts the Democratic National Convention in 2008. In 1973, when he was the hottest performer on earth, John did a sold-out benefit Madison Square Garden concert to aid my charity for the mentally retarded. I'll always associate all things "Rocky Mountain" with John.

Aside from its booming economy, the old gold-mining, frontier town is now an integrated community in which half the population is white, about 35 percent Hispanic (of all races), 11 percent black, 3 percent Asian, and 1.5 percent Native American. An easy measure of the growing business clout of Hispanics and a barometer of future demographic trends can be found in Denver's radio ratings, where in fall 2006 Spanish-language KXPK 96.5 FM came in first among listeners ages eighteen to forty-nine and twenty-five to fifty-four, the two most important categories for advertisers.

While the percentage of Hispanics had until recent decades been relatively consistent, now it is surging, and with it the community is becoming more assertive. Hispanics long played third fiddle in a municipal orchestra directed by an uneven white-black coalition. Over the past half century Denver-area Hispanics have shed their traditional deferential invisibility in a slow, steady swelling of ethnic pride, which traces its origins back to the 1960s, when the town surprisingly became one of the epicenters of the Chicano Movement, that blend of Texas and Mexican cultural rhythms that is unique to the Southwest.

Called the Crusade for Justice and led by Rodolfo "Corky" Gonzalez, a boxer-turned-community-activist, the movement closely traced my experience with the Young Lords in New York during the same period. There were the same intense young Latinos holding rallies and staging demonstrations outside government buildings demanding social and economic justice, bilingual education, and an end to alleged police brutality and neighborhood segregation.

The rapid political evolution of the Denver Hispanic community from outsiders to players is easily traced. In 1983, just fourteen years after Corky hosted the First National Chicano Youth Liberation Conference in the tumultuous days of March 1969, Federico Peña became the first Hispanic mayor. I remember how proud I was to interview this accomplished young man (he is four years younger than I am) for ABC's *20/20* newsmagazine. An urban innovator, Peña went on to serve as secretary of transportation and later secretary of energy under President Bill Clinton, and today, the freeway connecting I-70 to the gigantic, futuristic airport he championed is called Peña Boulevard. "It's great to have a road named after you until one of your friends gets a ticket on it," he joked during a conversation.

Unlike many pioneering ethnic office seekers, Peña never felt the burden of the weight of history. He is a native of Brownsville, Texas, a community in which 90 percent are Hispanic; his family traces its roots to Tomas Sanchez, one of the fathers of south Texas and the founder of the important border town of Laredo. Peña's ancestors fought for the Confederacy during the Civil War. Politically inclined by his family's long tradition of leadership, Peña also did everything he could to assimilate into the majority culture. In the same way I was Gerry hanging out with my Irish and Italian buddies at West Babylon High School, Federico was Fred when he attended the University of Texas and its law school.

Ironically, when he announced he was running for mayor in his adopted town of Denver, many local Hispanics didn't support him because he was a long shot, he was too young, and he was from Texas. So instead, Peña assembled a broad coalition and surprisingly won the primary. It was at that point that Hispanics rallied to his candidacy. A voter registration drive garnered six thousand new voters in three days, many of them Latino. When a local reporter asked one new voter, a Señora Ayon, which party she was registering in, she replied, "The Peña party."

Peña unseated a fourteen-year incumbent, William McNichols Jr., a popular Irish American who voters apparently decided was an old-time politician. "I didn't run as a Latino candidate," Peña says, "but as an individual eager to serve all the voters and contribute to making the city better, who happens to be Hispanic and proud of it." Peña's success was later reflected in the mayoral elections of Hispanics in such majority white, politically conservative area towns as Colorado Springs and Fort Collins.

Denver now boasts Hispanic leaders in a wide range of fields. In spring 2007, Teresa Peña (no relation) was president of the Denver School Board, a challenging task given the troubling dropout rates among Hispanics, who comprise 60 percent of the student population. City Councilman Rick Garcia headed up DRCOG, the council of local governments comprised of thirty-eight municipalities spread over seven counties. Linda Alvarado is part owner of the Colorado Rockies baseball team, which went all the way to the World Series in 2007, and, perhaps most impressively, Timothy Marquez, the chairman of Venoco, an independent energy company with its headquarters in Denver, pledged a record $10 million gift for the construction of a new petroleum engineering building on the campus of his alma mater, the Colorado School of Mines. More recently Marquez and his wife, Bernadette, pledged another $50 million in college scholarships for graduates of Denver's troubled public high schools.

But neither the personal success of these leaders nor that of the Spanish-language radio stations suggests that the community's transition has been easy. Nor is it over. Tensions remain on issues as wide-ranging as immigration, police promotions, Spanish-language libraries, public education (with that astronomical Latino dropout rate), and gang violence. Four out of five of Denver's fourteen thousand gang members are Hispanic, according to one estimate from the city's Gang Rescue and Support Project. And a 2006 analysis by the *Rocky Mountain News* found that fewer than one in five Hispanic boys, just 19 percent of those enrolled in Denver middle schools, graduates from a city high school five years after starting eighth grade. For reasons as obvious as language proficiency and the even more pervasive need to make a living to help their families, these young men are not performing on a par with other groups of students.

The publication of the grim report designed to highlight the need for Denver's public education system to do more to keep these kids from dropping out was not universally well received. One letter to the editor of the *Rocky Mountain News*, written by a J. M. Schell of the suburban community of Arvada, was especially unsympathetic and laced with bitter sarcasm.

Apparently, my kids chose their parents very, very poorly. Had they only picked parents who were not born in this country, and/or are here illegally, taking advantage of the "free" education system, why then everyone and his tio *[uncle] would be bending over backward helping them get through the Byzantine college application process and navigating the financial aid minefield. Unfortunately, my kids picked parents whose grandparents were born here, who speak English like, well, natives, and who have told them all their lives how important education is.*

. . . Say, maybe they can get jobs mowing lawns or cleaning toilets for some of those "Hispanic" kids in the article?

If Hispanics are to be truly integrated into American society, much work must be done to overcome that kind of anger and resentment. For his part, Peña, who is now an investment banker, still spends much of his time on public service, including chairing an organization called A+ Denver, which seeks to focus attention on a public education system that has been in disrepair since an emotional tri-racial 1970s busing case attempted to parcel out white, black, and Hispanic kids but resulted instead in massive white flight to the suburbs with crumbling inner-city schools left behind.

"We also have to face the fact that Denver is now attracting larger numbers of immigrants from Mexico," Peña admitted. Keeping pace with the explosive growth of the community in the rest of the nation, Colorado's Hispanic population grew about 20 percent, from three-quarters of a million to almost 900,000, between 2000 and 2005 alone. And while the white population in Colorado increased even more during that time frame, those mainstream students didn't bring the same heavy baggage of poverty and language.

The immigrant children have poor English-language skills when they arrive. They can't compete initially and are a drain on teachers' time, support services and school resources. Our public schools are now 80 percent poor and minority. We need to do more for education if these people are to be absorbed and assimilated. And until we do, there will be tension, racial and otherwise.

Peña believes that as in the rest of the country, a strident media is exacerbating those tensions. "This harsh, anti-immigration rhetoric is really hurting the cause of integration," he says, pointing particularly at Denver's 630 KHO radio's Peter Boyles. Unlike Rush Limbaugh and Sean Hannity, Boyles is not normally a doctrinaire conservative. I worked with him on the JonBenet Ramsey case and found him clever and engaging. But in 2007, like many crowd-playing populists, Boyles found a convenient foe in Hispanic immigrants. "His rants just bring out the worst in people," Peña said.

And while Colorado did elect two Hispanics, the Democratic senator Ken Salazar and his brother, Congressman John Salazar, in 2004, the year President George W. Bush carried the state by 100,000 votes, a study by political scientists at the University of Colorado concluded the Salazar victories, like Peña's, came in part because neither emphasized their standing as Latino candidates, but rather in the Salazars' case their position as farmers and businessmen.

"In politics, you go where the numbers are," Jim Carpenter, Ken Salazar's former campaign manager, told the *Rocky Mountain News*. "While Colorado has seen a significant increase in Latino voters, and the Latino vote is a very important piece of the pie, they still represent (only) about 10% of the voter population."

Furthermore, the area south of the city overwhelmingly re-elected perhaps the nation's most virulent anti-immigrant crusader, the Republican congressman and Denver native Tom Tancredo. Nothing defines this tireless, pro-Minutemen, pro-fence agitator more than when he called on the Immigration and Naturalization Service, the INS, to investigate the family of an Aurora, Colorado, honor student, Jesus Apodaca. Jesus (pronounced *Hay-Zeus*) was featured in a front-page 2002 *Denver Post* story.

Emphasizing the challenges the young man had overcome since

arriving in the United States illegally as a small child with his family, the sympathetic newspaper portrayed Jesus as an example of rare success in a school system too often riddled by failure, an example of how hard work and strong character could still help someone starting with next to nothing achieve the American Dream. The honor student and longtime Colorado resident (but still illegal alien) then requested in-state tuition so that his impoverished family could afford to help him continue his education at a state school to study computer science.

That is when Tancredo struck, calling the INS and demanding to know why the agency's enforcers weren't scooping up this presumptuous family of Mexicans flaunting their illegal status and sending them back over the border. Another of the nation's most vocal anti-immigration crusaders supported him, the former Democratic governor Richard D. Lamm, who asked rhetorically, "Is there any moral or legal reason for illegal immigrants? Illegal immigrants jump the line, and anything we do to encourage illegal immigration is wrong." Even giving a kid with a 3.9 grade point and an unblemished record, who has lived almost his entire life in Colorado, in-state tuition?

Supporters of migrant workers came to Jesus's defense, unsuccessfully advocating passage of federal legislation, which would have given in-state tuition to illegals that graduate U.S. high schools. "The undocumented children who we've allowed to graduate from high school now want to better themselves and their communities," Estevan Flores, cochairman of Denver's Latino Campaign for Education, told the *Greeley Tribune* in 2002. "We believe this to be a rational, reasonable and humane way to proceed."

The effort to enact federal legislation failed, although ten states, including California, Illinois, and New York, have passed laws allowing long-term illegal immigrant students to become eligible for in-state tuition, if they meet certain other requirements. Colorado is not among them, although at the time of the Apodaca debate the newspapers there ridiculed Congressman Tancredo.

Even national Republicans (in that era before most embraced the philosophy of the Minutemen) distanced themselves from him, and yet Tancredo won reelection in a landslide. The loudest of the reborn Know-Nothings still plays a highly visible role in aggravating anti-immigrant passions. In a sobering display of the potency of his venom, wielding it in his improbable, one-issue campaign for the GOP presidential nod, he came in fourth in the Ames, Iowa, GOP straw poll in August 2007, far outpacing sane candidates, like ex-mayor Rudolf Giuliani, Senator John McCain, and former senator Fred Thompson.

It is also symptomatic of how widespread his once radical ideas have become since 2002 that five years later, Connecticut's notoriously moderate Republican governor M. Jodi Rell vetoed a bill that would have provided in-state tuition rates for illegal immigrants in the Nutmeg State's colleges and universities, saying she did not want to encourage the flouting of federal immigration laws.

"I understand these students are not responsible for their un-documented status, having come to the United States with their parents," the governor of the nation's richest and otherwise perhaps most liberal state said in a statement. "The fact remains, however, that these students and their parents are here illegally, and neither sympathy nor good intentions can ameliorate that fact."

When a Democratic state senator argued, "We're talking about young students who exhibit the best of what we expect from all of our children: academic success and the desire to succeed even more," the Connecticut governor countered that she was concerned the bill's passage would encourage "others to come to Connecticut in violation of federal immigration law," even mentioning its possible impact on national security, according to the *New York Times*.

I'll deal with the "national security" canard later. Suffice it to say that the emotional debate over immigration is distorting the political climate even in traditionally blue states like Connecticut.

Despite this spread of what I call "Tancredoism" and for all the work of noisy Peter Boyles or of angry former governor Lamm, who preaches that immigration, bilingualism, and multiculturalism are destroying America, metropolitan Denver Hispanics appear poised to become a more integrated, assimilated, English-speaking community in a growing town made more cosmopolitan by their presence. But if the prospects are optimistic, I asked Federico Peña, why the resentment?

"I don't think we've done a good job educating the broader community of all the talent and positive contributions we bring. We just sit back and expect people to recognize achievement. But we have to be more like the Anti-Defamation League, reminding people of the issues and challenges we face, some universal, but others unique to our ethnic group."

What about our responsibilities as successful Latinos? They are enormous and largely unfulfilled. For one thing, despite examples like Denver's Tim Marquez, Hispanics have yet to adopt the culture of giving back that so defines the national Jewish community, as one example. Perhaps because Latinos are relatively new to it, success seems to be held tightly and philanthropy usually limited to the family inner circle.

Mentoring has also been spotty, its successes gradual and measurable only over time. My buddy Cheech Marin is on the board of the Hispanic Scholarship Fund, which helps kids get and stay in school. Our favorite fighter, Oscar De La Hoya, has a foundation and a youth center in East Los Angeles, where I watched the multitalented Golden Gloves, Olympic, and professional champion mentoring inner-city youth and providing an alternative to gangs, juvenile delinquency, and drug abuse. I became deeply involved in an effort in New York City in 1989 during the last days of Mayor Ed Koch's administration. The charismatic "How'm I doing?" mayor initiated a program called Adopt a Class, which was designed to provide hands-on assistance to disadvantaged kids in troubled schools. The idea was that a role model would agree to make twice-monthly visits to a specific class to counsel and steer and encourage the students toward high school graduation and beyond.

I picked one of New York's worst performing schools, the Rafael Cordero Bilingual Middle School in East Harlem, where 80 percent of the kids were not graduating high school, let alone going on to college. Located in what was then a grim, inner-city neighborhood plagued by poverty, high crime, and unemployment, the school was one of those bleak and windowless urban fortresses designed to keep the neighborhood out and the kids in.

The twenty-four eighth-graders were all recent arrivals from either Puerto Rico or the Dominican Republic and spoke primarily Spanish. They were mostly poor; all were enormously needy. Many were from broken families, all living in Spanish Harlem in the era before gentrification that brought stability and routed the drug pushers. Seeing their intense needs, on impulse during my first visit I offered to send them all to college if they graduated high school. "I just blurted it out," I said when interviewed as some of them reached twelfth grade. "Later, I broke into a sweat when I started looking at the cost of it, but I had made them a promise."

"When we first met Geraldo, it was kind of a weird experience," one of the then high school seniors, Osvaldo Jiménez, whom we called O.J., told the local reporter as graduation approached. "We just stood there looking at him. We didn't know what to think except that he was a celebrity."

Over the eighteen years I was involved with the kids, I learned several important lessons from what was an inspiring and humbling experience. I found that keeping immigrant kids in middle and high school is a far tougher challenge than getting them into college. The distant promise of higher education is a weak lure to children whose lives are spent on the mean streets. Teaching them English and keeping them safe, drug-free, out of jail, their bellies full and their heads screwed on right is a far bigger priority than free college tuition a long way down the road.

I became "Uncle Geraldo" to the children, adopting them in ways I had never foreseen. My longtime assistant, JoAnn, the one who later moved to Florida because she was sick of the frigid North, became their twenty-four-hour hotline, helping them with issues ranging from emergency needs to family counseling. We took them on field trips to Washington, D.C., so they could learn about their new land, and back to Puerto Rico so they could touch base with their old.

On one memorable trip to the island in 1993, the kids got to visit the elegant governor's mansion and meet the sixth man to hold that position, Dr. Pedro Rosselló, and his wife, Maga, one of Puerto Rico's most stylish and graceful First Ladies. Fresh from El Barrio, the youngsters marveled at the elegance of the luncheon she had ordered prepared for them. I befriended Rosselló, as I had his three immediate predecessors, Luis Ferre, Rafael Hernandez Colon, and Carlos Romero Barcelo, and later joined him in a massive, virtually universal protest of the continued use of the offshore Puerto Rican island of Vieques as a U.S. Navy bombing range. The bombardment ceased in 2003. Emerging from semiretirement and a stint in the island's Senate, Rosselló, a member of the pro-statehood party, has announced his 2008 candidacy for reelection to governor.

"I learned there's more to life than hanging out on a street corner," then seventeen-year-old O.J. was quoted as saying as he approached graduation en route to the Mohawk Valley Community College in Utica, New York. "Without him, I might have dropped out of school." Many did anyway. Of the twenty-four, only eighteen were still in school when it came time to think about college. Of that group, just ten graduated on time, nine going on to some higher education, with four actually earning degrees. "These were kids from the community who had already been through rough times at home and school, who were fighting the odds when he [Geraldo] stepped in," JoAnn said. "Hopefully, all of them are in a good place today."

While several of the kids have done well in fields as far-ranging as television news production and the military, we had one big star, thirty-two-year-old Brenda Natal. Already a registered nurse and the mother of a small child, she is now Doctor of Emergency Medi-

cine Brenda Natal, MD, having graduated from the Medical School
of New Jersey in May 2007. In keeping with the core idea of giving
back that Federico Peña spoke about, Dr. Natal and her husband,
Dr. Carlos Meletiche, who is also an MD whose roots lie in Puerto
Rico, have established an annual scholarship in my name at Brenda's
medical school. My wife, Erica, and I were present at her graduation
when this generous gift was announced by the dean. It brought me
to tears, tears both of pride at her achievement and of melancholy
for the many students who fell by the wayside along the way.

"We have to remind our own community that, 'Hey, our kids
have to learn English,'" says Peña. "We have to tell our children that
they have to work hard in school. Too many have forgotten that it
takes hard work to succeed. [Ex-Governor] Lamm actually called Hispanics 'culturally deficient' and 'lazy.' What he is preaching now is
the same stuff the anti-immigrant forces were saying a hundred years
ago. 'Here come these poor, oppressed, untrained ghetto dwellers to
drain our economy.' Three generations later those Irish and Polish
immigrants are leaders. By 2030 it will be our turn.

"Already in this town no matter where you are there is a Hispanic person, maybe an immigrant mowing your lawn, building
your house, and working in the restaurant kitchen or the ski resort.
Every afternoon when those shiny offices downtown empty out, the
executives and secretaries walk past the almost invisible Spanish
lady who is going to clean out their office. How is that lazy?

"What we have to do is ask people to check their real experiences against the negative rhetoric. Give these people an opportunity
and an education and someday they'll have a street named after
them, too."

Peña's point is worth repeating. "Ask people to check their real
experiences against the negative rhetoric." I believe that most of
those vehemently opposed to immigration reform have never had a
real-life negative experience with an illegal alien. They have never
lost a job to one, never been victimized by a crime committed by

one, and never in any way been disadvantaged by one of them. Because so many opponents of immigration reform are already of a certain age and are often already collecting Social Security, they are obviously not put at risk of impoverishment in their old age by these new arrivals. If anything, the immigrants are the young strong backs that will ensure the system's viability going forward. No, it is not facts but the fear of change that incites the rage and loathing.

The Pew Report on the surge of Hispanics into cities in the burgeoning West and South makes another interesting point. Many cities that are down on their luck today have had only minimal Hispanic population growth. "Places like Cleveland, Philadelphia and St. Louis look to the west with envy," concludes the report.

In the twenty-first century you can almost track the spread of prosperity in America by charting the pattern of settlement of the Hispanic migrants. My sister Sharon lives in Pittsburgh, a town long down on its luck that has in recent years overcome the loss of industry and sour black-white race relations that for a time caused the federal government to take over the city's police force. I spent weeks there doing a scathing report for NBC *Dateline* in 1999, called "Blacks and Blue."

Now, a brilliant downtown renewal has breathed new life into a smooth-functioning, growing, and vibrant community. And guess what? Here come the Latinos. Connected by the light-rail line that runs right down Broadway, the still hard-luck neighborhood of Beechview offers lower rents than most and a hospitable environment for newcomers. And they are coming. Mexican restaurants and other Spanish-oriented businesses catering to the new arrivals from south of the border have rejuvenated the vacant storefronts along Broadway.

In 2000, Beechview had 147 Latinos. By 2005, there were at least 747, according to a survey conducted by the *Pittsburgh Post-Gazette*. The newspaper noted the presence among the many still-vacant storefronts along Broadway of vibrant stores with names like *Maya*, *Tienda La Jimenez*, and *La Azteca*.

In July 2005, Beechview celebrated its one hundredth anniversary and the St. Catherine of Siena Catholic Church held its first-ever Spanish-language Mass. "They remind me of the people, like the Italians, who came to America and were hard workers who never said 'no' to work, and saved and improved their lot," Palmo Cicchino told the *Post-Gazette* reporter Diana Nelson Jones. Cicchino, who owns P.C. Auto Repair on Broadway, himself emigrated from Italy twenty-six years ago.

Additionally, it is important to look through the fog of the harsh debate over immigration and see the real impact Hispanic population growth is having on areas of the country not usually seen as particularly affected by shifting demographics. There are many depressed cities and towns, particularly in rural areas, that have been saved by the influx of Latinos both native-born and recently immigrated.

There might be more store signs in Spanish in these towns than before, but over time even those will morph into English. Yet there is also no doubt that in the meantime the changing face of certain communities is causing alarm and overreaction among some longtime residents. Listen to this quote from the nephew of an Alabama man, who alleges his uncle planned to commit violence against area Mexicans. The nephew told law enforcement that his uncle threatened that "he needed to make up his mind whose side he wanted to be on, the Mexicans or Americans. The main thing he always told me was there was going to be a war between the Mexicans and whites."

This exchange took place in Collinsville, a small Alabama town, where in May 2007 federal agents and local police confiscated an arsenal of weapons, including homemade grenades, and arrested six members of the Free Militia, who allegedly planned to target Hispanic immigrants who have recently surged into the area. The town includes an old rail depot and is located about halfway between Birmingham and Chattanooga. Fewer than two thousand people live there. Downtown is a forlorn strip about two blocks long, holding a handful of businesses, vacant storefronts, a shut-down theater, and a closed feed mill. Challen Stephens chronicled the arrest of the alleged anti-immigrant extremists and the subsequent guilty pleas of most of them for the *Huntsville Times*. Stephens wrote, "Some new businesses thrive. They have names such as *Los Reyes Carneria y Panderia*, *La Princesa Boutique* and *San Martin Tienda*."

"There would be very few businesses even operating in downtown without the influx of the Hispanic immigrants," Stephens, who reported the Collinsville clash in the style of William Faulkner, told me. "It's the same story throughout the South. The tide goes out, and the tide comes in. As the locals leave, heading for the big cities, the immigrants have come in behind them, preferring small-town life."

If not yet prosperous, Collinsville is at the moment being sustained by the recently arrived Hispanic families who came to work at places like Cagle's Poultry Processing, by far the largest employer in town. Stephens points to how these recent arrivals "have swelled the school rolls. Collinsville High, which runs kindergarten through twelfth grade, climbed from 476 students in 1975 to 643 last year." In 2006, half of all third-graders were Hispanic. And remember, this is in Alabama. Among the many fringe benefits of these new arrivals, Hispanic athletes propelled the Collinsville High School soccer team through the state playoffs. "If it wasn't for the Hispanics, we wouldn't have a soccer team," said Roger Dutton, the town's barber, as he clipped hair at Cook's Barbershop. "They helped the town a lot, as far as the economy goes," he told Stephens.

The positive Collinsville migrant experience is reflected throughout rural America, which makes up fully 75 percent of our national territory but holds only 17 percent of the population. The Carsey Institute at the University of New Hampshire has noted in a report how our rural communities experienced dramatic population loss as millions of mostly white residents, particularly those in their twenties, left for the opportunities in booming cities. The report goes on to say that otherwise depopulated or even defunct towns have been recharged by Hispanic population growth, which "grew at the fastest rate of any racial or ethnic group during the 1990s and the post-2000 period."

In other words, as whites flee the rural Midwest and Heartland communities, and in the South white and black young people empty rural Dixie, Hispanics are moving in at a far faster clip than any other group. Some are obviously farmers and farmworkers. The "family farmer" so often idealized by politicians looking for support for subsidies or campaigning against the death tax is increasingly likely to be named Pedro or Pablo rather than Peter or Paul.

But most residents of these rural communities no longer farm the land. In fact, the Carsey report makes clear that only 6.5 percent of the rural labor force these days is engaged in planting and harvesting. Twice as many rural workers are employed in factories like Cagle's Poultry Processing or in service industries, often related to tourism or retirement communities.

In Arkansas, perhaps surprisingly, the Hispanic population grew at a rate faster than in any other state between 2000 and 2005—48 percent. They had an after-tax income of $2.7 billion in 2004. And contrary to the claims of critics who allege the "selfish" Mexicans are just taking our money and sending it all back to Mexico, while about 20 percent of the $2.7 billion was indeed sent home to families abroad, or was saved or used to pay off loans, "the remaining spending reverberated throughout the state's economy." And, according to a study by the nonpartisan Urban Institute, "this spending could generate as many as 84,700 spin-off jobs (in Arkansas alone), contributing $303 million to state and local taxes."

A study by the Kenan Institute of Private Enterprise at the University of North Carolina assessed the economic impact of that state's rapidly growing Latino community and similarly found a net positive. Latinos filled one in three new jobs created in the state between 1995 and 2005, 29 percent in the construction industry alone. "North Carolina's rapidly growing Latino population contributed more than $9 billion to the state's economy in 2004 through its purchases, taxes and labor," according to the study.

Surry County, North Carolina, is located on the Virginia line, twenty-five miles north of Winston-Salem. Once a beehive of economic activity centered on furniture making, tobacco, and textiles, the region has been hit hard by globalization. Bassett, its last remaining furniture factory, was closed by 2006, as jobs got exported to cheaper Central America and Asia. But jump-started by a dramatic influx of mostly Hispanic migrants, even real-life Mayberry RFD is on the rebound.

Mt. Airy, population eight thousand, is the county's commercial hub. Julie Ardery, one of the Carsey Institute report's authors, writes how:

Andy Griffith was born here, and with only occasional hints of embarrassment the myth of "Mayberry" hangs heavy: there are statues of the actor and fictional son "Opie" toting fishing poles, "Aunt Bea's" barbeque restaurant shaped like a barn, "the Goober" (a specialty drink at the local coffeehouse), and Floyd's Barber Shop replicated in a storefront downtown.

And many of the service workers in those tourist-related businesses are Hispanic. The community has astutely made an asset out of the enduring popularity of *Mayberry RFD*, a pop-cultural phenomenon other places might have been embarrassed about. Like Collinsville, Alabama, Surry County, North Carolina, is big on poultry processing. Jobs in these plants are some of those unpleasant positions traditional residents have in recent decades been increasingly reluctant to fill. Not so the migrants. Wayne Farms, one of the county's largest employers, processes 650,000 birds each week; 80 to 85 percent of the company's workforce is Hispanic, who now outnumber African-Americans in Surry County.

And as in Collinsville, Hispanics have reenergized the community. The fading school population surged 23 percent since 1996.

Hispanic high school enrollment leaped from 40 students in 1996 to 227 in 2005. "Every time you blinked your eyes, ten Hispanic children would be here at the school to enroll," the principal of Dobson Elementary, Jan Varney, told the report.

And how are those students doing in terms of learning English and becoming "real" Americans? A lot better than Samuel Huntington or Tom Tancredo would have us believe.

One of the historic obstacles to the linguistic assimilation of immigrant children has been the traditional reluctance of Hispanic parents to become involved in their children's education. Whether because of the more authoritative educational model in Latin countries or just immigrant shyness, many parents expect schools to assume complete responsibility for their children's education. Surry County has worked hard, setting up Hispanic Parent Teacher Organization meetings and using an educational model that focuses on Principal Varney's philosophy as expressed in the report. "If I can teach you to read, you'll succeed."

In eight years, with a rapidly changing and increasingly diverse student body, Dobson Elementary English-language proficiency scores have risen from 70 percent to 90.3 percent. As has been the case with immigrants since this nation began, the children are learning the language of their new country. Likewise, church attendance is way up, as the deeply religious newcomers swell the ranks of the faithful that had been depleted by the flight of white and black youngsters to the big cities.

And as in many communities, in Surry County the growth of the Hispanic population is becoming increasingly driven not by immigration but by native births. "The families that we have now have pretty much settled in," Varney told the report. "These people are here to stay."

And still, Mayberry RFD remains Mayberry. Andy, Gomer, Goober, and even famously blundering Barney would be proud. Maybe they can all grab lunch down at the new burrito joint.

5

Will Hispanic America Be Like French Quebec?

"We have no room for but one language in this country, and that is the English language, for we intend to see that the crucible turns our people out as Americans, of American nationality, and not as dwellers in a polyglot boarding house."
— President Theodore Roosevelt

"This is America, please order in English"
— Sign in the window of Geno's Steaks, Philadelphia

When Joey Vento, the owner of Geno's Steaks, defiantly posted that sign in the window of his restaurant, a popular destination for lovers of the City of Brotherly Love's trademark cheesesteak, he made national headlines as a champion of real Americans taking a stand against the immigrant onslaught. Vento quickly became a fixture on cable news programs with his militant stance against customers who didn't speak English. Vento is, ironically, the grandson of the wave of early-twentieth-century Italian immigrants who changed the face of South Philly. He told reporters, "If people want to come here, that's their choice, welcome to America, but they have to adopt the ways and means of people here."

With his in-your-face bluster, Vento was giving voice to one of the most immediate issues regarding the boom in our Mexican and Hispanic population, the perceived threat to the dominance of the English language. "The American people are speaking out. They found a guy finally who said what he meant. I backed it up. I put my money where my mouth was. They threatened me with lawsuits. Bring it on! The sign's not coming down," Vento told the BBC in 2006.

"Acceptamos Pesos"

—Sign in the window of Pizza Patron store in Dallas, 2007

The counterpoint to Joey Vento's English-only rant is the move made by Dallas-based Pizza Patron, a chain of sixty-four stores located in strip malls across five states with significant Hispanic populations: Texas, Colorado, Arizona, Nevada, and California. In January 2007 the chain rolled out a new promotion. They announced they would accept Mexican pesos as well as U.S. currency as payment for a slice and a Coke. Begun as a postholiday promotion for customers returning from their Christmas trips to Mexico with unused pesos, Pizza Patron told ABC's *Nightline* program in June 2007 that the idea had become so popular it had been made a regular feature.

"We wanted to say to our customer, 'Look, we understand you,'" Antonio Swad, the CEO and founder of the chain, told the program. "We understand that you might have some pesos that you want to exchange for pizza and we're the place to do that." He added that the idea became as red-hot as his pies, immediately attracting new customers. "Yeah, it was exactly the right thing for our customers," he said. "It was a way for us to reach out and to do a better job of serving our customer than maybe some of our competitors."

These days, at every cash register, store employees in the usually tiny restaurants consult a chart to fairly convert the currency based on the official exchange rate, which is roughly twelve pesos to the dollar. But unlike Joey Vento's English-only idea, which was warmly received by a wide range of commentators, like my Fox News colleague Neil Cavuto, the owners of Pizza Patron complained of death threats and hate mail pouring in almost from the moment their pesos-for-pies promotion began. While the move by Pizza Patron was interpreted by anti-immigrant activists as encouraging foreigners to flaunt their foreignness, Vento's action was widely perceived by them as almost patriotic, just one of the more flamboyant incarnations of the "English-only" movement that swept much of the country in the 1980s, attempting for the first time in American history to restrict the public use of minority languages.

Adopted by at least two dozen states, the high-water mark of the English-only movement came in 1996 when Congress, under the leadership of Newt Gingrich and his new Republican majority, attempted to designate English as the federal government's sole official language. Happily, Gingrich and his linguistic revolution failed. Threatened with a veto by President Bill Clinton, the legislation stalled and never made it to the floor of the Senate. Still, the debate is now as widespread and urgent as ever, encompassing both the symbolic importance of everyone speaking the same language and the more practical need to avoid immigrant America becoming an unholy Babel.

Gingrich in 1996 and Vento in 2007 both understand the potent fear many people have that the social glue that English provides our diverse national community could come undone, that outsiders speaking in foreign tongues and refusing to be assimilated threaten our founding and de facto national language. These fears are misguided and uninformed. The data shows that with only temporary and reasonable lapses, principally among first-generation immigrants or physically isolated communities of Native Americans, English remains the overwhelming dominant language of government, business, education, and even fast-food joints like Geno's Steaks and Pizza Patron. Yes, you can find the occasional Spanish-language ballot and in select cities you can press "2" when you call 411 to hear Spanish, and we do sometimes celebrate Cinco de Mayo along with St. Patrick's Day and Chinese New Year, but my God! Are we so afraid of linguistic pollution that we want to stamp out bilingualism? What will we call a taco in the post-multilingual world—a "hard shell sandwich"?

It is easy to prove that the linguistic assimilation so crucial to cementing our uniquely blended American society will continue. Look around. I know a lot of Hispanics, but not a single, second-generation immigrant child who doesn't speak English. In researching this book, I polled my father's surviving siblings or their children. In order, my *abuelos* (grandparents) Juan and Tomása produced Ramón, Manolo, Panchita, Gregoria, Juanito, Cruz (my dad), Pedro, Júlia, Maria, Carlos, Augustín, Ana, Lucy, Ophelia, Angie, Mercedes, and Elizabet. Together, those seventeen produced a tribe of at least sixty children. And every one of those first cousins who ever lived in the States, plus most of those who never left or who have subsequently returned to Puerto Rico, speak English as either their first or second language.

Indeed, by the third generation—that is, the cousin's children—most either do not speak Spanish at all or have had to learn it as a second language in school. My Puerto Rican cousins work in city or state government; they are lawyers, doctors, educators; they own bodegas, a Coca-Cola distributorship. One of my favorites, Lilly, who is named for my mom, is an ordained Pentecostal minister who preaches bilingually to a diverse congregation in a racially mixed neighborhood under another elevated subway, this one in the Bronx.

I am reminded once again of my dear friend Cheech Marin. Cheech is best known as the Mexican half of Cheech and Chong (who is half Chinese). I've known Cheech since 1972, when he and his partner first ridiculed my sometimes larger-than-life persona by creating a character on their first comedy album called "Horrendo Revolver." Later we lived next door to each other in Malibu and each got married, had kids, got divorced, remarried, had more kids, and went up and down and up again professionally more or less in tandem. For thirty-five years we've been like a couple of synchronized swimmers. Cheech is a gifted actor and writer. He made a solo movie relevant to this work called *Born in East L.A.*, which chronicled the misadventures of a U.S.-born Chicano who gets swept up in an INS raid. Devoid of money or identification, the character gets wrongfully deported to Mexico, a place he has never been. Forced to live the life of the undocumented and seeing how they risk everything just to get into this country to work, his clueless character begins to care less about his own plight and more about theirs. Funny and poignant, Cheech's comedy may be one of the best films ever on the subject.

The movie ends with Cheech leading a group of undocumented workers over a hill from Tijuana into San Diego, a scene set to our mutual friend Neil Diamond's song "Coming to America," which Neil wrote to celebrate the Jewish immigrant experience a century earlier. Asked if he understood the deep social significance of the film at the time, Cheech admitted to me, "Not really. It has gained resonance over the years because it was based on a real incident that just keeps happening," citizens or legal residents without access to lawyers or a good command of the English language who get swept up by Immigration and Customs Enforcement's broad brush.

Cheech cultivated the old doper-dropout image in his classic buddy films with Tommy Chong, movies that will live forever as they get discovered by generation after generation of college kids. Contrary to his film persona, my pal is the Phi Sigma Kappa college-educated son of a high-ranking L.A. County Sheriff's Department official. His traveling art show, "Chicano Visions, American Painters on the Verge," a collection of eighty-four paintings, has appeared to record-breaking crowds across the country, including at the Smithsonian National Museum in Washington. But this winner of *Celebrity Jeopardy!*, renowned Chicano art collector, pillar of the Hispanic celebrity establishment, like me and many other proud Latinos, has never quite mastered Spanish.

To poke fun at the widespread lack of Spanish-language skills among the second- and third-generation Chicanos, Cheech wrote a song about bilingualism. Delivered in an intentionally off-key, sing-song cadence, it goes:

> *Mexican Americans love education*
> *So they go to night school*
> *And take Spanish*
> *And get a B.*

Putting aside the anecdotal for the scientific, statistically there was a 25 percent increase in English-speaking ability between Mexican immigrants and their American-born offspring living at home, according to the 2000 Census. That is 7 percent greater than the equivalent generational change in 1980. In other words, the children of Spanish-speaking immigrants are learning to speak English and they are learning English at a faster rate than did previous generations. In many Hispanic families, particularly second- and third-generation immigrants, the problem isn't that they don't speak English, it is that they have forgotten or never learned Spanish.

Of my four brothers and sisters, only Willy and I are reasonably bilingual. Willy speaks Spanish because he was born in Puerto Rico. I was born in Beth Israel Hospital on New York's East Side and couldn't utter more than a *Como está?* until my parents sent me to live with my dad's family in their hometown of Bayamon in Puerto Rico the summer I turned sixteen.

My grandparents were an extraordinary couple who not only raised their own seventeen children, but also informally adopted several other kids. All the children were equal in the hearts of the matriarch and patriarch, both of whom lived well into their nineties. And they used their bountiful charm to make me fall in love with being Puerto Rican.

Until I stepped out of the door of the four-prop Eastern Airlines DC-6 on the tarmac of what was then called San Juan International, the Puerto Rican side of the family had taken a backseat to my parents' ongoing efforts to make their life on Long Island. They were handicapped in their attempts at social integration by being not just the only Puerto Ricans in heavily Italian and Irish West Babylon, but also the only Jews. Having been Bar Mitzvahed and confirmed, I went both ways, religiously speaking. With a huge Spanish side of the family and a relatively tiny Jewish side, I was brought up with a healthy dose of my father's Catholic upbringing. That included occasional confession at the local church with best friends, the brothers Vinnie and Frank Simone and Frankie DeCecco, my Italian buddies. It seemed the more efficient way to purge guilt. Obviously, I was confused about my particular multiculturalism.

Living the summer I turned sixteen in Puerto Rico in an all-Spanish-all-the-time environment, I at first came unglued, unstuck in time in a way reminiscent of my late, great, former father-in-law Kurt Vonnegut's most unforgettable character, *Slaughterhouse-Five*'s Billy Pilgrim. I could no longer charm or spin yarns. I was disoriented and linguistically forced down to basics like, "I'm hungry," "I'm sleepy," "Let's go to the beach." Nuance in Spanish was far beyond my just emerging capacity.

It was a humbling time. I remember waking up my first morning back in the States three months later realizing how expansive my ability to express myself was. English, and the baloney with it, were back. But the experience made me recognize the importance of bilingualism. My dad used an Old Spanish proverb: *Si tiene dos lenguas, tiene dos almas*, essentially, If you can speak two languages, it's like having two souls. To me speaking Spanish was also the appropriate thing to do, especially when in Spanish lands. It has certainly stood me in good stead in my travels as a news correspondent throughout the region, even though I'm stuck in the present tense. I just wish I were better at it, because Spanish is such a beautiful language.

Many Americans are apparently suspicious of bilingualism, fearful perhaps that it is decadent evidence of the truth of Colorado's former governor Lamm's paranoia about pending national doom and his theorized plot "to destroy America." I have tried to emphasize the importance of language training to my own children. I sent my second son, Cruz, to Mexico and to Spain for language immersion similar to my stay in Puerto Rico. As a result, his Spanish is better than his siblings'. Sol Liliana, our two-year-old daughter, attends La Escuelita, where only Spanish is spoken. Since her entire world outside that preschool is an English-only environment (with the exception of *Dora la Exploradora* and occasionally *Sesame Street* in Spanish), Erica and I figured that it was the best way to get her started early on second-language skills. I wonder if Samuel Huntington would approve, although I hope even he would be hard-pressed to say my clan wasn't as red-bloodedly American as his own.

When California's colorful immigrant governor Arnold Schwarzenegger said at the annual convention of the National Association of Hispanic Journalists in San Jose in June 2007 that the Spanish community would do well to turn off "dah Spanish-language television" and learn English, I agreed with him to a certain extent. Immigrants do have to learn English (and happily they are, at historic rates). Media affects that process, and total immersion in English media for native Spanish speakers is one good way to learn hard and fast.

But suggesting that immigrants turn off Spanish TV completely is a lame idea. There are the requisite burlesque and tawdry programs, but there are as many good shows on Spanish television as there are on English, shows like *Fea Más Bella*, aka *Ugly Betty*, the hit English-language show on ABC that is derived directly from the original hit on Spanish TV.

When he came home from his job in the kitchen of that defense plant, my dad used to love to watch the *telenovelas*, the Spanish-language soap operas. Because everybody around him on Long Island, with the exception of his brothers Ramón and Augustín, who also worked at the plant, spoke English, later in life he missed hearing his native tongue. It certainly didn't impair his ability to speak

English, which he did with barely an accent (except, remember, when he was on the phone).

According to a report published by the American Political Science Association in March 2007 called "Testing Huntington: Is Hispanic Immigration a Threat to American Identity?," while Mexican immigrants may know less English than newcomers from other countries when they get here, the trajectory of their kids' assimilation resembles that of their European predecessors of a century ago.

"Hispanics acquire English and lose Spanish rapidly beginning with the second generation, and appear to be no more or less religious or committed to the work ethic than native-born whites," the report says.

But is the current tension really about language or is language just the most obvious symbol of something deeper? Is there a suspected, semisecret refusal by Mexicans and other Hispanics to see ourselves as wholly American? That is certainly what the man who made a long-shot, one-issue candidacy for the Republican presidential nomination, Tom Tancredo, believes. "The impact of immigration, legal and illegal, on jobs, schools, health care, the environment, national security, are all very serious problems," he told the *New York Times*. "But more serious than all of them put together is this threat to the culture. I believe we are in a clash of civilizations."

A clash of civilizations? If this guy is for real, on what side of that clash does my Rivera clan fall? Does the congressman from suburban Colorado really believe that Hispanics harbor and nurse the desire to secede from the United States or otherwise undermine the Constitution of the United States? If so, his fears are as misguided as his politics and rhetoric are extreme. And there seem no bounds to how far he will go to insult Latinos. Here is how Tancredo described Miami, Florida, in November 2006:

Look at what has happened to Miami. It has become a Third World country. You just pick it up and take it and move it someplace. You would never know you're in the United States of America. You would certainly say you're in a Third World country.

Outgoing Florida governor Jeb Bush called the inflammatory remarks "disappointing" and "naïve." "Miami is a wonderful city filled with diversity and heritage that we choose to celebrate, not insult," Bush wrote.

After citing the city's role as America's "murder capital," Tancredo's reply was defiant and in keeping with his vision of an America overrun by Hispanic people. "I certainly understand and appreciate your need and desire to create the illusion of Miami as a multiethnic 'All American' city," Tancredo wrote. "However, it is neither naïve nor insulting to call attention to a real problem that cannot be easily dismissed through politically correct happy talk."

What exactly is Tancredo's "real problem"? Too many Spanish people? I don't know if Tancredo has ever been to Miami. Perhaps, like certain hip-hop stars, he is fixated on the garish image of the city portrayed in Brian De Palma's classic 1983 remake of *Scarface* starring Al Pacino as refugee-turned-coke-dealer Tony Montana. Or maybe Tancredo is stuck on *Miami Vice* reruns. But despite the congressman's typical bluster and fearmongering, in truth, any Third World country would covet a thoroughly modern, salsa-flavored burg like Miami.

Since the 1960s, the sultry, ever-stylish subtropical city's population has experienced explosive growth, almost doubling in size. Around 400,000 people now live within the city limits, part of a burgeoning, booming metropolis of about 4.3 million, excluding the Palm Beaches, almost half of whom are already Hispanic, with the percentage growing. Cuban Americans are far and away the largest group among the relatively recent arrivals, followed by substantial numbers from Colombia, Puerto Rico, Mexico, Nicaragua, the Dominican Republic, Venezuela, and Argentina. Once limited to traditional Hispanic neighborhoods like Calle Ocho, Hialeah, and Little

Havana, Latinos have spread throughout Dade and southwestern Broward counties. Adding to the melting pot, longtime African-American neighborhoods have since the 1980s been flavored by substantial immigrations from the Bahamas, Haiti, and Jamaica. Add to the colorful mix more than seventy thousand Brazilians and you get an idea about why the town is a fast-bubbling cultural brew.

The town's significance as an international financial, trade, and cultural center has also grown exponentially in recent decades. Virtually every foreign nation now has a consulate in the Big Orange. With its soaring office towers and condos, its ever-expanding harbor and cruise ship port, its beaches, restaurants, and club life, it also remains a magnet for tremendous internal, multiethnic migration within the country. Anglos, Jews, and others across the American spectrum are still searching for paradise, as they have been since the first great Florida land rush of the 1920s, adding to that later wave of pan-Latin immigration from abroad.

Traffic along the I-95 corridor is an ever-increasing pain, and the bloom may be off the building boom as many newly built condos wait unsold or go for reduced prices in 2007's general nationwide real estate slowdown, but the town and environs remain generally flush, hip, and enviable. Nor is it the "murder capital of the world," as the congressman falsely asserted to back his claim that the city represents a threat to the American way of life. Stabilizing after the *Miami Vice* years in the 1980s, when it was indeed the country's cocaine-import capital, Miami's aggressive law enforcement and reduced or at least changing domestic demand for drugs like cocaine have helped restore the city to normalcy. According to the 2005 FBI Uniform Crime Reporting data, of the twenty most populous cities in the United States, there were nine with higher murder rates: Baltimore, Detroit, Philadelphia, Memphis, Dallas, Houston, Chicago, Phoenix, and Columbus.

Tancredo is right about one thing. Miami is America's most pervasively and uniquely Caribbean Latin–flavored urban center. The expanding dominance of Spanish-language media illustrates the cultural penetration of Latinos. The television networks Univision and Telemundo compete with three independent stations for the Spanish-language crowd, along with a wide array of ratings-dominating AM and FM radio stations. "That's why I still do plenty of Spanish songs," the heartthrob singer Enrique Iglesias, son of Julio, told me during a 1999 interview at his lavish waterfront home. "The biggest television stations and the biggest radio stations around here are in Spanish."

Miami's news-reading public is served by *El Nuevo Herald*, the twenty-year-old daily, which is owned by McClatchy, the Sacramento-based company that also owns the *Miami Herald*, and by *Diario Las Americas*, another daily newspaper. There is a big weekly paper called *El Sentinel*, another biweekly called *El Popular*, plus at least fifteen smaller weeklies, like *El Colombiano* and *La Estrella de Nicaragua*, aimed at specific nationalities.

Los Angeles also boasts powerful Spanish-language media and areas of town where you are more likely to hear Spanish than English. The fundamental difference in the tale of the two cities is that in Miami, Latinos, led by those of Cuban descent, are already part of the power structure. They are bilingual, upwardly mobile, middle class, and with strong emotional and economic ties to Latin America. The city and surrounding region is perhaps the most important trade and cultural center in the Hispanic world outside of Madrid or Barcelona, surpassing even Mexico City and Buenos Aires. Unlike Los Angeles, where, despite the election of the first Latino mayor in modern times, Hispanics are working their way up the political and economic food chains in a postmodern, still mostly Anglo-flavored town, in Miami they already dominate the upper echelons of municipal life.

Miami, like L.A. before it, is edging ever closer to becoming majority Hispanic, with a Latino population growth of 21 percent between 2000 and 2006, according to Geoscape American Marketscape DataStream (2007). Of more structural significance is the fact Miami has also become the de facto financial capital of Latin America, its go-to economic and banking hub. And as I reported in two news specials on the city's dramatic ethnic transformation, one in the 1980s for ABC's *20/20* and the other in 1999 for NBC's *Dateline* called "Nueva America," Miami's destiny as a Spanish-accented world city has been sculpted by geography and twentieth-century politics.

The modern political history of the city is BC or AC, as in Before Castro or After Castro. As of this writing, the once-dashing bearded rebel who overthrew Fulgencio Batista, the last in a sad chain of Cuban, mob-schmoozing dictators in 1959, is ailing, but stubbornly resilient. After a brief but impassioned romance with the *New York Times* and other mainstream U.S. lefties in the 1959–61 period, Fidel revealed his true hardcore commie colors soon after Batista's overthrow with seizures of property, expulsion of political opponents, and the installation of a Soviet military presence, including intercontinental ballistic missiles that almost led the planet into an apocalyptic nuclear war. But his excesses and repression provided the United States with an immigrant bounty. Unlike other exceptional migrations, the first wave of Cuban refugees was extraordinary in the social and economic resources of it members. It may stand as history's sole white, middle-class, and upscale population transfer. Rather than "Send us your huddled masses," it was more like "Send us your dentists, your doctors, your lawyers, property owners, and bankers yearning to breathe free."

Only the pro-Israel lobby rivals Cuban Americans in terms of cohesion, organization, and political and social clout, as witnessed by their decisive impact on the contested 2000 presidential election. The new Cuban Americans morphed into a Florida powerhouse soon after they arrived, strong enough to steer the Cuban Adjustment Act of 1966 quickly through Congress. The act legalized the presence of all Cubans who had flocked to the United States since Castro and established the dynamic community as central to the life of Miami, the state's most important city. Quickly seizing the reins of power, the Cuban-American juggernaut was able to endorse expanding citywide bilingual education, even as California struggled with anti-bilingual initiatives like Proposition 227, which effectively ended most such programs in the Golden State.

Coral Way Elementary School on Cuban Memorial Boulevard in the Little Havana district sits just south of the shrine to those who died during the ill-fated CIA-sponsored Bay of Pigs invasion in 1962. Last time I checked, all students there were spending three hours a day learning English in one classroom and two hours learning Spanish in another. The expansion of bilingual education was propelled in part by a 1995 study of local businesses that found in Miami and surrounding Dade County that more than half did at least 25 percent of their work in Spanish.

The rapidly expanding Cuban clout did not come without cost to either the old Anglo-Jewish municipal aristocracy or the blacks. African-Americans made up less than 20 percent of the population but they had long held sway as the most important minority, a position that had existed since Overtown was called Colored Town. Blacks provided the sweat that harvested Florida's crops and built Florida's railroads, mansions, and hotels and later provided the maids, porters, gardeners, and waiters to staff them. But in traditional African-American enclaves like Liberty City and Overtown resentment festered. The federal highway program aggravated and accelerated the process of black disillusionment by cutting a substantial slice out of Overtown's urban heart to make room for Interstate 95 and the massive I-395 connecting highway.

The black minority's ascendancy began its final chapter on December 17, 1979. That is when an African-American insurance agent named Arthur McDuffie was killed in an encounter with cops during a traffic stop. Then, in an urban catastrophe that presaged the Rodney King riots in Los Angeles, after a change in trial venue, an all-white jury in Tampa acquitted the cops on May 17, 1980. Miami was subjected to its worst-ever rioting. The riots were later blamed in part on a malignant feeling of powerlessness, resentment, and perceived injustice among African-Americans. Eighteen people died, 371 were injured, $80 million in damage was done, and the community was left shattered.

The riots came around the time of the Mariel boatlift, which brought tens of thousands more Cubans (much darker and poorer and less connected than the Cuban immigrants who had preceded them), to the shores of South Florida in the last great wave of migration. Many believed then and now that the riots were exacerbated by the justified perception among black Miamians that Cubans were taking over.

"After that spring [1980], you saw the evaporation of goodwill and the sense of community. It all went up in smoke." In 2000, the Ft. Lauderdale *Sun-Sentinel* reporter Vanessa Bauza interviewed Marvin Dunn, a professor of psychology at Florida International University and an expert on the history of blacks in Florida. "Any sense of community between Hispanics and blacks that had been established was nearly destroyed," the professor told her.

That process was fatally accelerated by two further cataclysms, one in the black and one in the Hispanic community. First, there was America's last major race riot, in what was left of Overtown, in January 1989. Like the death of Arthur McDuffie, the proximate cause of the four-day orgy of looting, fires, and generalized violence was a traffic-related police shooting. What made the deaths of motorcyclist Clement Lloyd and his passenger, Allan Blanchard, even more destabilizing was the fact the shooter, Miami police officer William Lozano, was Hispanic. Rebecca Wakefield, writing in the *Miami New Times*, attributed the sharpness of the violence to "the pent-up frustrations of a marginalized populace . . . an insular community poorly understood by outsiders."

Lozano was initially convicted of manslaughter, but in 1989 that verdict was overturned on appeal and Lozano was acquitted after a 1993 retrial. The festering ethnic division the saga left behind was made raw by a later story I covered in-depth in 2000, the Cuban community's muscular, emotional, and perceivably wacky overreaction to the Elián González affair.

The poor kid, who had survived the nightmare crossing of the Florida Straits that killed his mother and ten of the twelve others on board his small boat, became the centerpiece in an epic municipal civil war between those who wanted him to remain in the United States with Miami relatives and those who wanted him returned to his father in Cuba.

Most non-Cubans, including the Clinton administration and the federal courts, believed the six-year-old should be returned. Most Cuban Americans, including the actor Andy Garcia and the singer Gloria Estefan, but particularly the older, island-born generation of exiles, reflexively anti-Castro in all things, felt strongly that Elián should remain in this country. When a federal judge dismissed the Miami relatives' petition for asylum filed on Elián's behalf, the mayor of Miami-Dade, Alex Penelas, joined twenty-two other officials and went so far as to announce that the municipality would neither cooperate with federal authorities in the child's repatriation nor allow the local police to assist in any way in the boy's removal.

When Elián was forcibly removed in the predawn dark of April 22, 2000, despite the threat of violence from his Miami relatives, protestors taunted the feds with cries of "Assassins!" Civil unrest boiled in Little Havana as hundreds of enraged protestors burned garbage and jammed the streets of the neighborhood.

Elián González was returned to Cuba after the U.S. Supreme Court refused to get involved. The boy's departure on June 28, 2000, left behind a severed connection between blacks and Cuban Americans. "Everything is about Castro," Pastor Victor Curry, the president of the Miami-Dade NAACP, told PBS's *Frontline*. "It just tears up the whole community, fighting against that one man ninety miles away. Go fight him, go back to your homeland, and do whatever you have to do. But don't cause chaos in this country. Move on. You are an American now, you have to assimilate."

The Cuban community went on to exact terrible revenge on state, local, and national Democrats for the Elián affair by overwhelmingly backing George W. Bush against Clinton's successor, Al Gore, in the contested 2000 election, and then politically and even physically defending the disputed vote count. To me, it seemed that many younger Cuban Americans seemed almost embarrassed by the shrill tone of their community's politics. And while the automatic and fierce anti-Castro ethic persists among their parents' generation, it seems much less raw now than it did in 2000.

The progress of inevitable assimilation is evidenced by the lack of specific recent conflict between the various ethnic communities in the years since 2000. A new equilibrium has apparently settled in, in part a consequence of white and middle-class black flight from downtown Miami in the last two decades, which has yielded the dominant role in governance of the city to the eager Cuban and other Hispanic strivers. Local elections have since solidified their dominant political role, as store and street names changed and concerts, clubs, and cultural events have taken on a distinctively Latin flavor. For probably the first time since Juan Ponce de León sailed into Biscayne Bay in 1513, Latinos are in charge of Miami.

What has this wrought? On the downside, an African-American community that continues to feel marginalized and segregated at the lower economic margins. African-Americans are concentrated in what is left of Liberty City and Overtown, while an Anglo and celebrity elite has hunkered down in places like Boca Raton and Fisher's Island or up the coast in the Palm Beaches. A Jewish community continues to thrive in Miami Beach, and there is a burgeoning, often Latin-flavored, middle class everywhere else in the still expanding metro area, which boasts a remarkable concentration of ostentatious wealth, fast cars, big houses, mandatory swimming pools, loud boats, cool clothes, and gays and tanned boldfaced names.

And while many old-timers in the Cuban community still dream of invading the home island and returning the Pearl of the Antilles to democratic government, their offspring are more likely to be dominated by the English culture than not. They watch English TV channels, speak English at work, play, and school, and worship at the same altar of pop culture as the young adults in New York or Chicago. They probably speak Spanish only to their parents and family. Their allegiance is to the United States, most have never even visited Cuba, they eat McDonald's when they get tired of rice and beans, and they think of the Castro brothers as relics from the era of their *abuelos*.

Ironically, given Congressman Tom Tancredo's staunchly conservative Republican credentials, Miami Cubans have also become one of the most loyal, consistently bankable GOP voting blocks in the country. Aside from Congressman Mario Diaz-Balart's Cuban heritage, it would be difficult to determine what problem Tancredo could have with Diaz-Balart, a fellow conservative and member of the Republican Study Committee. Diaz-Balart's insistent support of the embargo of Cuba is perhaps the most formidable obstacle facing any reform.

Over the years, I've interviewed Mario and his older, politically more moderate brother Lincoln and have enjoyed the newscasts of third brother Jose, a popular host and news anchor for Telemundo. What is striking is how accomplished they all are, proud sons of Cuba and, now, the nation that welcomed them as immigrants. Their dad, Rafael Diaz-Balart, was a Cuban senator and an anti-Castro hero who died at his home in Key Biscayne a couple of years ago. To complete the family's uniquely Cuban circle of life, Rafael was the brother of Mirta Diaz-Balart, Fidel Castro's first wife.

Significantly, as a subsequent chapter will make clear, Florida is unique, the only Republican success story in an otherwise gloomy electoral picture that could spell permanent national minority status for the GOP, with Hispanic Democrats rising everywhere else.

The larger point is that Hispanics want to be part of all the American processes of government and life. That is not to say they lose interest in the affairs of their homeland. Aren't Italians and Irish still interested, even multiple generations removed from the old country? Jews certainly follow the triumphs and travails of Israel and root for the home team, even those Americans who have never been there. The significance lies not in whatever attention they pay to what's happening back over there, but in whether their primary allegiance and attention are here. And happily, again according to the American Political Science Association report, "A clear majority of Hispanics reject a purely ethnic identification and patriotism grows from one generation to the next. At present, a traditional pattern of political assimilation appears to prevail."

In other words, Latinos are now and will be in the future just as American as previous immigrants. "It's not like we haven't seen this script before," Matt Szabo, the press secretary for Los Angles mayor Antonio Villaraigosa, told me, quoting his boss appropriating an entertainment business metaphor. "We know how this one ends, just like it has always ended."

It has always ended in immigrant assimilation with hybrid vigor helping forge a stronger America, but between English and Spanish, white and Hispanic, which will prove the dominant culture in a world city like Los Angeles in which half the 4 million residents are already Latino?

In 2005, Matt Szabo's boss, Antonio Villaraigosa, became L.A.'s first Hispanic mayor in 133 years. Villaraigosa won in a landslide, unseating the mediocre incumbent James Hahn, whose family has been active in Los Angeles politics for decades, and whose father was especially adored by the black community. The last time a Hispanic sat in the mayor's chair the town was a dusty pueblo of less than six thousand souls, then as now roughly divided between Mexicans and others, and still at least a decade away from the beginnings of the explosive growth that would ultimately propel Los Angeles to become the world-class capital of the global entertainment and other industries.

The former Speaker of the California Assembly, who lost his first try for City Hall in 2001, Antonio Villaraigosa succeeded this time by putting together a grand coalition that added Jews and African-Americans to the, as he put it, "Latino, labor and white lefties" who had supported him the first time around. And he won despite an environment of resentment, especially among African-Americans, that the Mexicans were taking over the town. South Central, including historic Watts, which was overwhelmingly black, had become 60 percent Hispanic. There was racial and gang violence in the public schools and tension on the streets of a city that aside from the mosaic of the Valley could roughly be divided as affluent and white on the West Side, African-American on the south, and overwhelmingly Latino on the East. Yet Villaraigosa easily beat the veteran incumbent, whose lackluster term had been tainted by corruption, by convincing more than enough voters that he wanted to represent everyone equally.

"Many of the black leadership did not support Villaraigosa the first time," the Reverend Al Sharpton told me in an expansive conversation on the current immigration situation. "They loved Hahn's father, not even the guy running. And he screwed them badly. When there was the second time around, everybody got together and Villaraigosa became mayor. That was a victory for all of us, because Villaraigosa not only has an inclusive administration, he has a fairer policy in terms of things like racial profiling, economic justice, and health care."

Villaraigosa's first two years in office have coincided with a surge in Hispanic political activity that brought hundreds of thousands of mostly Mexican and other Latino demonstrators onto the streets of his city. The shows of strength heartened Latino activists, particularly young people, uncovered the deep Latin roots of the City of Angels, but also helped terrify and motivate those opposed to further Hispanic immigration. This opposition includes a lunatic fringe for sure, but sadly also grassroots social conservatives who later rose up to quash any hope of immigration reform.

The gathering storm began a continent away in Washington, D.C., where on December 16, 2005, the GOP-dominated House passed a draconian anti-immigration measure sponsored by the Wisconsin Republican Jim Sensenbrenner. The ugly essence of the harsh measure that passed in the distracted atmosphere just before the Christmas break was a proposal to raise penalties severely for unauthorized immigration. The bill proposed making felons of every illegal alien, man, woman, or child. It also proposed making felons of all who helped them enter or remain in the country.

Since being in the United States illegally was and remains only a rarely enforced, low-level federal misdemeanor punishable by up to six months in jail and/or a fine of $50 to $250, the bill grossly escalated the severity of the offense, making federal felons of all 12 million people already in the country illegally. Furthermore, the fact that it is technically a misdemeanor does not reflect the fact that the criminal charge is almost never brought. To prevent the overwhelming of courts and detention centers, most illegal aliens apprehended are deported or simply allowed to leave the United States voluntarily. According to a Congressional Research Service 2006 report, the most common charge against those caught without authorization in the United States is "unlawful presence," a civil rather than criminal offense. The penalty is removal from the country. When anti-immigrants say that illegal aliens are "criminals," they are stretching the bounds of reality big-time.

The Sensenbrenner bill not only created this new class of federal felons that is six times larger than the entire current U.S. prison population; more alarmingly, it made potential felons of their landlords, teachers, clergy, employers, doctors, nurses, social workers, or anyone else deemed to have helped them get or stay here. It changed the definition of who is a criminal, and they potentially numbered in the millions.

It was dumb and merciless and the fact H.R. 4437 passed the House by a solid 239–182 vote showed how far down the road to illogic its mostly Republican proponents and supporters had traveled.

As the Senate took up the odious measure following the holidays, a grassroots movement stirred across the nation, mobilizing to ensure its defeat. Beginning in February in Philadelphia and spreading to D.C., Milwaukee, Denver, Reno, Atlanta, and Phoenix, the movement hit its stride surprisingly in Chicago, a town not immediately associated with having a large Hispanic population. But on a March day in the Windy City over a half million marched from Union Park to Federal Plaza. I remember being thrilled by both the enormous size of the Chicago march and its respectful nature, both peaceful and mature. The stage was set for *La Gran Marcha* in Los Angeles.

The marchers were drawn from three constituencies that are all fundamental segments of modern Los Angeles: those here illegally and their close family members and friends, most of whom are Spanish-speaking; Internet-savvy Hispanic high school and college students, most of them predominantly English-speaking; and white and black sympathizers and activists, ranging from union members and clergy to socialists and followers of the long-dead but ever-charismatic Che Guevara.

But the largest component of the L.A. demonstration on March 25, 2006, was those Spanish speakers, many of them undocumented. As the group most directly affected by the Sensenbrenner scheme, their urgency was understandable. What was surprising and unprecedented was the crucial role played in their mobilization by Spanish-language media. It began on a wildly popular morning show hosted by a former illegal alien named Eddie "Piolín" Sotelo.

"Piolín," which roughly translates as "Tweety Bird," began lambasting Congress shortly after the bill passed the House. With his deceptively down-home delivery, Piolín brought tears to his audience's eyes with his dramatic retelling of his own family history, their walking across the border, hiding from the Border Patrol and later the *Migra*, the INS agents on the prowl. Piolín spoke of getting a green card indicating legal, permanent residency and a job on the Spanish-language station KSCA radio after the Reagan-era amnesty of 1986, ultimately becoming by far the highest-rated morning radio personality in town, far outpacing Howard Stern or Don Imus.

Perhaps sensing that the issue's time had come, making it acceptably mainstream, personalities at the big Spanish TV networks, Univision and Telemundo, also joined Tweety Bird in promoting the demonstration that was the central focus of the DJ's campaign. Their involvement was made easier when Cardinal Roger M. Mahony, the archbishop of Los Angeles, energized and encouraged participation by his increasingly Latin-flavored archdiocese. When the time came for the spirited but peaceful march as many as a million or more showed up. Many of the vast throng wore white to symbolize peace and waved American, Mexican, and several Central American flags and chanted *"Sí, se puede!"* ("Yes, it can be done!"). They marched on City Hall from their gathering point in downtown.

When they arrived, Mayor Villaraigosa greeted the mass rally. Then in a short but historically significant speech in Spanish, the mayor said of the pending legislation, "We are in favor of an immigration reform, but not in criminalizing our children. We cannot criminalize people who are working, people who are contributing to our economy and contributing to the nation." The first Latino mayor of a newly majority Latino town in the modern era had, while speaking in Spanish, sided with the mostly Hispanic demonstrators in their protest against officials in Washington. Piolín and I were proud.

Antonio Villaraigosa is a third-generation Mexican American and former high school dropout who as a youth wore a "Born to Raise Hell" tattoo. His impassioned stance on the immigration issue aside, like Federico Peña in Denver, Villaraigosa has worked to calm constituent anxieties about the changing face of his community. He did it when he was unhesitant about using law enforcement to stop protesting students from blocking traffic, roaming the streets, and even marching onto the freeways during the emotional height of the pro-immigration demonstrations. "When kids are walking on freeways, that's not free speech," he told me. "They had to get back to school."

Villaraigosa has also reached out to L.A.'s entertainment and sports communities, the West Side's middle and upper classes, and, perhaps most important in political terms, African-Americans like the veteran congresswoman Maxine Waters. Reverend Sharpton wonders almost wistfully what domestic politics would be like if other minority politicians were as astute as Villaraigosa in reaching out to blacks.

"We would be controlling a lot of things if we had that kind of coalition. What I think people have not realized, Geraldo, there was a time not long ago, when the mayor of Atlanta, the mayor of New York, the mayor of Chicago, the mayor of Philadelphia and the mayor of Detroit were all people of color. Without a coalition with Latinos, Hal Washington wouldn't have won in Chicago, Andy Young wouldn't have won in Atlanta, and [David] Dinkins wouldn't have won in New York. Now, if you look around the country, the coalition has fallen apart. We have gone backward. Our parents did better than we did with less to work with. So, who changed the script? What meeting happened where we said, 'Let's divide and give it back to those who are adversarial to us'? I missed the memo." Pointing to the success of Villaraigosa in reconstituting the old minority coalition, Sharpton said, "We've got to remember our common interests."

Under Villaraigosa's watch, crime rates in L.A. have fallen to historic lows, and racial tensions have eased away from the rawness of the recent past, although they still simmer below surface civility, despite Al Sharpton's reassuring words. The town is enjoying

another gigantic building boom, and, despite a bulging population, smog and air pollution are greatly reduced. Freeway traffic,
though, is still the worst in the nation, public education seems to
lurch in perpetual crisis mode, and gang violence stubbornly persists. Yet there is a feeling of exuberant optimism and vitality such
that Villaraigosa's approval rating remains in the 70 percent range.

I have known Antonio Villaraigosa since he was a state assem-
blyman in the 1990s. His personal story is hopeful and dramatic.
His clout has been growing steadily as Latinos figure ever more
prominently in national politics. By early summer 2007, every Democratic presidential hopeful from Barack Obama to Hillary Clinton
hungrily coveted his endorsement, and he is widely favored to succeed Arnold Schwarzenegger as California governor in 2010. But
his career was staggered in 2007 by the exposure of a marriage-
ending affair. The mayor was further embarrassed by the news his
admitted paramour was lovely thirty-five-year-old Mirthala Salinas, a Spanish-language anchor and reporter who had covered the
mayor on a regular basis. Aggravating the fallout, she was on the air
and even announced the rumored but unsourced news of the may-
or's separation from his wife (and mother of two teenagers), saying,
"The rumors are true." Complicating Villaraigosa's political recov-
ery was Ms. Salinas's subsequent suspension from her job for violating network conflict-of-interest policies.

Many of his most ardent supporters are furious with the mayor
for lack of personal discipline, which put his years of hard work and
enormous political promise at risk. I am just rueful that over the
years when confronted by both challenge and opportunity, men like
the mayor and I have seemed prone to living the stereotype of the
Latin lover.

Another example is Henry Cisneros, the pioneering golden-boy
mayor of San Antonio, who became a Clinton-era cabinet secretary
and was on the fast track toward national prominence. He was forced
out after being indicted for covering up the payment of hush money

to his former mistress, a woman named Linda Medlar. Lingering embarrassment over that melancholy end to his political career is probably why he was the only requested interview who declined to participate in this book. Cisneros pled guilty to a misdemeanor, never did any jail time, and was pardoned by President Bill Clinton in January 2001. He later shook off any residue from the incident and became a community-oriented philanthropist and successful real estate tycoon, inducted in 2007 into the National Housing Hall of Fame. Cisneros and I aged out of the trick Romeo gene, Villaraigosa will, too, and without any more self-inflicted distractions Golden State voters will hopefully focus on the mayor's impressive abilities because he is a terrific, rags-to-riches leader and an inspiration.

Antonio Villaraigosa's family was deserted by his father, an alcoholic and abusive Mexican immigrant. The family lived on the edge of economic despair in a run-down neighborhood called City Terrace in heavily Hispanic East L.A., which for better and worse can be indistinguishable from Tijuana, Mexico. Raised by his hardworking mom, at seven he started earning his own way hawking the Spanish-language daily newspaper *La Opinion* on street corners. The young Antonio's shoes were so worn they were lined with cardboard. At age fifteen, he worked to support the first grape boycott organized by our mutual hero, Cesar Chávez.

In July 2005, in his inaugural address as mayor, he talked about his mother's struggles and told a rapt audience that there were stories like hers everywhere. "We see them in the faces of people who clean homes and offices. Who work the night shifts and who empty bedpans. We see them in the faces of people who sweep the floors and load the freight."

Villaraigosa brought it all home for Tinsel Town. "Even though we live in the entertainment capital of the world, it is not hard to see who the real stars are."

Like Federico Peña and me, he adopted the Spanish version of his given name later in life, in his case Tony becoming Antonio. His original family name is Villar, which he blended when he married Corrine Raigosa, then a schoolteacher, in 1987. She is the scorned woman and mother of his children from whom he is now separated. There is minor curiosity over whether he will change his name back to Villar.

A former student activist, board member of the ACLU, and union organizer, Villaraigosa is charming, ambitious, and competent. His English is better than his Spanish, but his Spanish is good enough to be widely appreciated by constituents who are newly arrived or stuck in their native tongue. And it doesn't take Karl Rove to know that any truly bilingual politician has an advantage, even if half or less of those predominantly Spanish-speaking but otherwise qualified voters actually exercise their franchise. That demographic, in addition to his high approval rating among crossover voters, is why he is an early favorite to succeed Arnold.

In the context of race politics and Hispanic evolution, some of Villaraigosa's speeches are electrifying, like the 2005 inauguration and the one he delivered nervously to that mass rally at City Hall in 2006. But if recent polls are to be believed, his liberal-activist credentials work against his efforts at consensus politics. His popularity, especially among Republicans, has dropped dramatically during this polarizing immigration debate, and local reporters in L.A. say he doesn't like to talk as much about the issue as he did. Still, when he does, his energy and idealism swell into optimism that his multicultural city will be a beacon and role model for a changing nation.

I was a reporter-cheerleader for a May Day 2006 rally in Los Angeles, attended by perhaps fifty thousand demonstrators. The event was memorable for me because I did a live shot for Bill O'Reilly's program and argued immigrant rights and the need for reform from a position in the midst of a sea of Spanish people who enormously enhanced the power of my arguments by remaining peaceful, dignified, and orderly.

When the smaller second-anniversary May Day 2007 immigration-rights rally in Los Angeles turned violent, Mayor Villaraigosa needed all of his legendary energy and optimism to calm his troubled town. His cops had mishandled a melee originally involving a small group of isolated agitators, and twenty-four protestors and reporters were badly roughed up in the ensuing police roundup. After promising a full, fair investigation of the ugly incident, Villaraigosa tirelessly walked the east side of town telling residents in English and Spanish that he would get to the bottom of it and hold wrongdoers responsible, even if they were cops. "We are one L.A.," he says proudly.

A month later, I met up with the now fifty-five-year-old mayor of L.A. in Washington, where he had come to try and breathe life into the much-altered immigration reform bill even as it was going down to ignominious defeat in the Senate. Alerted to the problems it faced by two of the bill's sponsors, Colorado's Ken Salazar and Ted Kennedy of Massachusetts, Villaraigosa hurried to Washington, but was disheartened by the tone of the debate.

"Unfortunately, too much of the debate that takes place here in Washington is acrimonious and partisan, all finger-pointing and vitriol," he told me over lunch. "It's the nature of the place, frankly. And there is no question the demagogues have tried to foment fear and anger on this issue."

But what about their concerns? I asked as we walked toward the Capitol. After reminding the mayor of the outcry that followed the waving of the Mexican and Central American flags during the L.A. immigration marches, I asked, "Don't the critics point to Los Angeles as the capital of Mex-America, the city that sold out to the Hispanic side? Because of the sheer numbers involved, because of the proximity to Mexico, the fact that people come and go, that there are divided loyalties somehow?"

"That's not been my experience," the good-looking, dark, slender man said, smiling almost sadly. "I represent the second largest city in America, a city that's forty-six percent foreign-born. A city that's nearly half Latino. A city of great vitality and energy. A city where there are thirty-six different nationalities that have their largest population outside their country of origin. I can tell you that Los Angeles is dynamic as it is today because of the immigrants who have come here. They have infused us with new blood. They're focused on making it, on achieving that American Dream."

But what about Samuel Huntington's fear, picked up and amplified by screamers like Tancredo, Dobbs, and Malkin, the perception that Mexicans are different from previous immigrants because there are so many of them, their country of origin is so close, their subculture so pervasive, their historic claim to our national territory so strong?

"There are always going to be the Huntingtons of the world. There have been others like him in history. They'll be forgotten. And the hard work, the contributions of these immigrants, won't be."

As the mayor said when he addressed the congregation at the end of Mass at the Cathedral of Our Lady of the Angels days after the May 2007 melee, "There are many who have forgotten how they got here and seek to demonize the immigrants among us. I ask Angelinos to come together. Now is not a time to point fingers but to come together."

Villaraigosa's demeanor and message should be soothing to those worried about a state within a state. He is on target. Based as it is on data rather than ideology, the American Political Science Association report concludes, "With each successive generation, social, economic, and emotional ties to Mexico diminish." And finally, "Mexican immigration is not the threat to American national identity that Huntington and others assert."

And insofar as which language will dominate, whether in La-La Land or elsewhere in America, according to the report, ". . . learning English is virtually inevitable for the children and grandchildren of immigrants," like Mayor Antonio Villaraigosa. Tomas R. Jimenez, an assistant professor of sociology and a visiting research fellow at the Center for Comparative Immigration Studies at UC San Diego, writing in the *Los Angeles Times*, put it this way:

> According to a recent study by social scientists Ruben Rumbaut, Douglas Massey and Frank Bean published in the *Population and Development Review*, the use of non-English languages virtually disappears among nearly all U.S.-born children of immigrants in the country.
>
> Spanish shows more staying power among the U.S.-born children and grandchildren of Mexican immigrants, which is not surprising given that the size of the Spanish-speaking population provides near-ubiquitous access to the language. But the survival of Spanish among U.S.-born descendants of Mexican immigrants does not come at the expense of their ability to speak English and, more strikingly, English overwhelms Spanish-language use among the grandchildren of these immigrants.

But while Professor Jimenez accurately cites the *Population and Development Review* research of the primacy of English, many Latinos remember when the former Speaker of the House Newt Gingrich said this in March 2007 to the National Federation of Republican Women to a standing ovation: "We should replace bilingual education with immersion in English so people learn the common language of the country and the language of prosperity, not the language of living in a ghetto."

Gingrich was surprised when, after his supposedly nontelevised speech was broadcast on YouTube, he was reamed by critics who blasted him as racist and even ignorant to suggest that Spanish was only spoken in the ghetto. The outrage forced Gingrich, who at the time was still engaged in his long-shot run for the Republican presidential nomination, to go back on television to apologize for his offensive remarks. To his credit, Gingrich delivered his act of contrition in Spanish. Mayor Villaraigosa's reaction to Gingrich was more measured than most, but he does seem offended by the not-so-subtle suggestion by the former Speaker and others that there is something almost disloyal with foreign-language proficiency.

"Look, there's nothing wrong with saying that we want people to learn the language of commerce in this country," Villaraigosa, who frequently gives press conferences in both languages, told me. "If you want to be successful in the United States, you have to know English, the language of commerce and success. But by the same token, we in this great country understand that in a global economy, we want our kids to speak English, Spanish, Korean, Mandarin, and the many other languages of commerce in the world. The real point is we want our kids to learn English, but we want them to be bilingual and trilingual as well."

Just as I believe the vast majority of Americans most emotionally opposed to amnesty for immigrants have never met one, I also suspect that those most offended by the public use of Spanish and other languages speak only English and have not traveled extensively. Nativism is an ugly brew best savored in cultural isolation. I was going to say "ignorance," but that is too French. And while it is a recurring theme in our national history, there is also a more honorable tradition of open-minded welcome.

There are millions of stories out there, and countless vignettes I could use to illustrate our instinctive hospitality to new arrivals. How about one from my mother-in-law? Nancy Levy is an educator in Cleveland Heights, Ohio. While much of the area has staggered economically in the postindustrial era, curtailing large-scale immigration, she remembers another era when the neighborhood absorbed succeeding waves of new arrivals, mostly Eastern Europeans. In the following excerpt, Nancy is responding to an article in the *Cleveland Jewish News* about how her old school, Coventry Elementary, which had absorbed the children of those immigrants, was finally being closed. Here is Nancy's letter:

Arlene Fine's wonderful cover story about Coventry Elementary School triggered so many feelings and memories for me. One of the strongest memories I have is of the many immigrant children who came to the Coventry neighborhood and school throughout the 1950s. At one point, there were so many foreign-speaking students the teachers would give us individual assignments to teach the children how to speak English.

I remember a group of my friends deciding the best place to learn English first would be on the playground . . . and we were right! Also, in fourth grade, I was selected to be the Statue of Liberty for an all-school assembly where children dressed in the respective countries of their birth, and a representative of that country would give a brief speech about his or her first homeland.

Working for the assembly was a great unifier, as we students were all involved in the artwork, learning about the other countries and, consequently, appreciating our new friends.

I now work as an ESL [English as a Second Language] teacher for young children, and I often draw on my memories of those years. How lucky I was to be a student at Coventry.
—Nancy Levy
July 2006

Trust the wisdom of the Jewish mother-in-law. With guidance from educators and exposure to the dominant culture, children adapt to their new country. And they do it regardless of their parents' continuing loyalty to the old. Despite the vast spread of Spanish-language media in this country, and the obvious trappings, especially in towns like Los Angeles or Miami, of a society within a society, by the second and third generations, whether they live in the Barrio of East L.A., the Latin heart of downtown Miami, or attended Coventry Elementary in Cleveland Heights, Ohio, most of their children speak English and are becoming as American as Philly cheesesteak's Joey Vento.

6

Importing Terror

"It is possible to argue back and forth about the economic and social impact of illegal immigration into the United States. But surely there can be no argument about the undesirability of terrorism."

—James P. Pinkerton, "The Fort Dix Plot and Illegal Immigrants," *Newsday*, May 2007

"The foiled terrorist plot in New Jersey further highlights the need for tighter border security and stricter immigration controls."

—Congressman Tom Tancredo, until 2006 Chairman of the House Committee on Immigration Reform (May 2007)

Congressman Tancredo and *Newsday* columnist Jim Pinkerton are doing something distressingly common in the post-9/11 era, making a connection that is upon inspection demonstrably false and unfair. They are linking illegal immigration to an attempted act of terrorism, in this case a plot by the so-called Fort Dix Six, who allegedly conspired between 2005 and 2007 to commit mass murder of U.S. soldiers serving in the large army facility in New Jersey and, according to federal prosecutors, to "kill as many American soldiers as possible" in attacks with mortars, rocket-propelled grenades, and guns.

Without passing judgment on the alleged conspirators' guilt or innocence, or their ability to carry out these wicked attacks, this was a hapless crew of rank amateurs who allegedly trained by playing paintball in the woods in New Jersey. They included a pizza deliveryman suspected of using his job to scout out the base. A clownish gang, the coconspirators were sufficiently incompetent to get caught by the photo tech at Circuit City, who could not help but notice their jihadist training on a home video one of them had asked him to copy onto a CD.

The total factual disconnect between this case and immigration control is obvious and easily demonstrated. More insidious is how the combination of official exaggeration and sloppy or lazy journalism has allowed the fake relationship between terrorism and immigration to fester and become a common misconception. The perhaps surprising headline is that among the most severely affected victims of the 9/11 bombings count America's immigrant community, particularly undocumented Hispanics who don't have a terrorist bone in their bodies.

In the era before terror, an air of benign official neglect had settled over even the most recently arrived migrants. The atmosphere in many communities, like New York, Chicago, Los Angeles, and Miami, was such that local officials made it a point of pride not to cooperate with the INS. When Congress attempted to force local cops to cooperate with federal immigration officials, in New York City, Mayor Rudy Giuliani filed suit against the feds. Even after losing in two federal courts and being rebuffed by the Supreme Court, Rudy vowed not to enforce the law. And he never did. Even today, the Big Apple refuses as a matter of policy to enforce immigration laws.

Leading in the race for his party's presidential nod in all national polls, Rudy was assailed as "soft on immigration" by his bitter rival for the nomination, the former Massachusetts governor Mitt Romney. In a response I find disappointing from my open-minded former mayor, and not a little hypocritical, Giuliani announced a new get-tough immigration policy featuring enhancing enforcement and the construction of a new border fence, both physical and virtual. (I assume that means one enhanced by cameras, radar, satellites, and such.) As of this writing he had not yet denounced his former "sanctuary" policy, although the writing is presumably on the wall.

I interviewed New York City's tough police commissioner, Ray Kelly, at the June 2007 National Puerto Rican Day Parade. How does he respond to critics who say that New York is too easy on illegal immigrants? I asked Kelly this question Sunday morning, as we stood on the corner of 44th Street and Fifth Avenue waiting for the world's biggest, noisiest parade to begin. The granite-jawed cop and ex-marine is probably running for mayor in 2009 with the encouragement of the current term-limited incumbent, Michael Bloomberg (and this correspondent). Kelly was enjoying a weekend *New York Times* story lauding the fact that there had been a 28 percent drop in serious crime during his six-year watch. As he looked around at the spangled floats, exuberant marching bands, and excited baton twirlers, the straightforward commissioner answered with quiet confidence.

> We have a policy here that we serve everybody, irrespective of their immigration status. We don't ask that question. It's not an issue for the city police department or other city agencies. This is a city that's focused on servicing the people who live here and come here and we're not a federal immigration agency. We don't enforce those rules.

Newly elected New York governor Elliot Spitzer was also attending the parade, and he backed the commissioner's position. "We are sanctuaries for the lifeblood of creativity, ingenuity, economic activity, and everything that has made this nation great. As I love to say to every person in this nation, we are all immigrants." A former white-collar-crime-busting state attorney general, Governor Spitzer had a rude awakening to the bare-knuckled politics of immigration when he got buffeted for proposing that illegal immigrants be allowed to obtain drivers' licenses. Even that consummate veteran of hard knocks former First Lady and leading contender for the Democratic presidential nod Hillary Clinton also got her political nose bloodied when she awkwardly tried to support Spitzer's move in late October 2007.

In the bigger picture, New York and every other city with the "don't ask, don't tell" policy of servicing everybody regardless of immigration status came under extreme pressure following the catastrophe of September 11, 2001. Then, alongside many noble actions taken by the federal government, came what was arguably one of history's most misdirected retaliations.

It started righteously when President George W. Bush brilliantly called for "a broad and sustained campaign" against the "terrorist organizations and those who harbor and support them." In drawing that big *X* over Afghanistan, he made sure that the attacks on the World Trade Center and Washington had a return address and that the renegade Taliban government was about to pay with its life for the transgressions of its al-Qaeda guests and allies.

I remember a conversation I had in December 2001 in just-liberated Kabul, Afghanistan, with Dr. Abdullah Abdullah, then foreign minister for the rebels' government-in-waiting, the Northern Alliance. Sitting on a rug before a large table from which we were eating lamb and rice, I asked the sharp, war-hardened diplomat whether one of his reactions that awful September day included some secret relief that now his enemy was the enemy of the United States.

"But how did I know?" he asked quietly, smiling sadly through a well-trimmed goatee. A quarter century of war and deep personal loss, including the assassination of his friend the charismatic leader Sheikh Ahmad Shah Massoud two days before the Trade Center attacks, have made him weary and wary of optimism. "The attacks could have been carried out by some crazy homegrown militia, like in Oklahoma City! Of course, when it quickly became clear that the attacks had originated from here, then I knew help was on the way."

Help came to Afghanistan, and by the end of 2001 the Taliban government had been ousted and al-Qaeda displaced and scattered, though not defeated. But in the mobilization to fight the terrorists who had attacked us that day, we made some harsh legislative and law enforcement adjustments at home, passing the Patriot Acts, enormously enhancing domestic surveillance, and looking with hard new eyes at our resident Muslim population. It was as if authorities at every level of government suddenly discovered the Muslims among us, hugely accelerating a process that really began after the first Trade Center bombing in 1993. Selective scrutiny of mosques was suddenly intensified, surveillance watch lists were expanded, and Islamic charities were subjected to intense scrutiny as terror-fighting agencies geared up to battle what was perceived as the enemy within.

Whether racial profiling of Arabs in this or any situation is justified is an often-debated question. What is not debatable is how our nation's understandable fears in part became misdirected paranoia that absolutely dropped the hammer on Hispanic immigrants, the southern border, and life all along the Mexican frontier.

It was a brutal and jarring turnaround. In the spring and summer of 2001, the picture for the undocumented had been relatively rosy, and not just in immigrant-friendly towns like New York or Los Angeles. A popular, border-savvy former Texas governor was in the White House and Spanish-speaking *Presidente Jorge* had essentially agreed with Mexico's fellow cowboy, the charismatic and seemingly competent new president, Vicente Fox, that fast-tracking immigration reform—that is, further liberalization—could help the profoundly linked economies of both countries (and Canada). Liberalization would be the logical next step in the NAFTA process, creating a freely moving cross-border labor force, which would relieve social pressures in Mexico and nearby Latin America and fuel the surging engine of American enterprise. Driven by tried-and-true laws of fundamental free-enterprise economics, the de facto globalization of the workforce, which had already existed for decades, was about to be given a legal framework.

The attacks changed everything. The Saudi Arabian attackers had all entered the United States legally and then overstayed their legally obtained tourist visas. So they neither snuck across our southern border nor were they Mexican. Still, it was along that twenty-one-hundred-mile southern border with Mexico that federal reinforcements mustered. Did open Mexican migration represent a threat to our national security? No, but who knew? Certainly most of the nation thought at the time that it was better to be safe than sorry. As Jim Pinkerton wrote more recently:

> Let's simply recognize that the most dangerous elements in our society, by definition, are those who are illegal and unknown. Those unknown illegal immigrants might be honest and hardworking busboys. But they also could be mass murderers: The point is we don't know.

Well, we do know. As you will see, only a minuscule percentage, much less than 1 percent of the immigration cases brought by the feds, involve charges of terrorism. But the association is firmly and perhaps forever made. Just as many people today still falsely link Saddam Hussein to 9/11, the issue of immigration is permanently linked to terror. Gone in a bitter heartbeat was any notion of open borders or immigration reform. Instead, we did as we have always done when facing a foreign-made crisis in our country: we hunkered down. And as our armed forces mobilized to track, find, and kill the 9/11 murderers, a new cabinet-level federal agency was bulking up in Washington.

Grandiosely named the U.S. Department of Homeland Security (DHS), much of the agency's luster comes from its assumed role as our national protector. Former Pennsylvania governor Tom Ridge, another of those tough, Mt. Rushmore–faced lawmakers, was selected as its first secretary, although he stumbled right out of the gate by introducing a color-coded alert system that managed simultaneously to frighten and confuse the entire country. Red, orange, yellow, green? What are we supposed to do with these alerts? Look under our beds? Call our mothers? I was waiting for a code pink signifying an imminent invasion by gays, or code black (with the skull and crossbones) for a pirate attack.

History will prove that combining disparate agencies into this mammoth creation succeeded mostly in adding yet another expensive layer of bureaucracy, yielding no meaningfully enhanced security. The result was embarrassing, bureaucrat-induced tragedies like the botched Hurricane Katrina relief, providing the opportunity for national security pimps to get rich dipping into its virtually unlimited terror-inflated coffers. At its heart the Department of Homeland Security is a monumental waste of taxpayer dollars.

The central mission of DHS is not fighting terror, despite the noble gloss painted by the Bush administration. The department's real job is combating undocumented Mexicans. Secretary Michael Chertoff revealed as much in the wake of the defeat of immigration reform when he announced in August 2007 a new federal offensive aimed at employers in industries like agriculture and food processing who hire illegal aliens. In a stunning turnaround that left many skeptical of their motivation, the Bush administration went from being the immigrants' best hope of reform to their most fearsome enemy. It was almost as if someone in the White House—and with Karl Rove gone, I don't know what White House Machiavelli has assumed the role of bare-knuckled adviser—decided that since Senate Republicans didn't act, they were going to watch their friends in the business community pay the price. We'll show you that populist politics is expensive.

"Our hope is that key elements of the Senate bill will see the

light of day someday. But until Congress chooses to act, we are going to be taking some energetic steps of our own," said Secretary
Chertoff. The steps will "significantly strengthen our hand with
respect to immigration enforcement."

So what work does the Department of Homeland Security carry
out in this climate of immigrant crackdown? In late August 2007,
a contingent of 300 ICE agents descended on the Koch Food plant
in Fairfield, Ohio, arresting 160 people after a purported two-year
investigation. A two-year investigation? It took ICE that long to
figure out that some of the workers at a poultry processing plant
were illegal aliens? Two Boy Scouts could have done the job in half
a day. ICE might as well order pizzas in Manhattan and then arrest
the almost invariably illegal delivery boys. And this is about national
security?

The feds should have watched my NBC *Dateline* "Nueva America" special in 1999, which featured how Hispanic immigrants
working in some of those same Midwestern food processing plants
had totally remade their communities, with Spanish-language
Masses in the churches, bodegas, and burrito shops on every corner
and barbershops featuring *"Aquí Se Habla Español"* signs. It is a phenomenon that existed then and now in bright sunlight.

I am reminded of another question. Why do ICE agents wear
bulletproof vests and full combat gear when they go on these raids?
They are as heavily armed as any SWAT team. Ever since 9/11 they
have worn the aura and costumes of warriors battling terror, but
most of the time they are facing terrified civilian factory workers or
illegal tenement dwellers who know their lives are about to be up-
rooted and are trembling in their pants, holding on to their babies
or looking to run away. Have there been any recorded instances at
all of undocumented workers standing and fighting these armored
knights?

There was a big raid similar to the Koch Food operation the
week before at the Smithfield Foods pork plant in Tar Heel, North

Carolina. That raid at least provoked the United Food and Commercial Workers (UFCW) and the Service Employees International Union (SEIU) to issue statements of condemnation of the administration's actions, characterizing the raids as "political theater" aimed at "pleasing its base." The coalition of unions made a statement the day after the raids:

> We see the cost in families torn apart by armed agents at gunpoint. We see the cost in thousands of innocent U.S. citizens and legal immigrants being rounded up and detained for questioning. We see the cost in lives turned upside down. We see the cost in whole communities coming to fear the knock on the door in the dead of night.

While I suspect that the lives of fewer "innocent U.S. citizens" or "legal immigrants" were "turned upside down," as opposed to illegal immigrants' lives and their families and maybe their bosses, there is no doubt but that these raids are being carried out for political purposes rather than anything having to do with national security. GOP strategists like Ed Rogers admitted as much to the *Washington Post*:

> It's a huge political issue, and a huge chunk of the population and a big part of the Republican Party base is demanding something be done. I hope the point is to establish credibility so maybe the next president has a better opportunity to really fix the problem.

Isn't that what this is really about? It is a political calculation. First of all, there are at least 8 million undocumented workers in this country (the other 4 million or so of the total reckoned at 12 million are the workers' dependents). So what real impact does arresting 716 workers have? That was the number arrested, criminally charged, and deported in 2006, up from just 24 in 1999 before the wave of anti-immigrant loathing covered the nation like a putrid fog. Overall, 183,431 people were deported by ICE in 2006, though never criminally charged.

Republicans and protectionist Democrats, be careful what you wish for in your passionate opposition to reform. If the crackdown continues, business lobbyists predict that hundreds of thousands of workers would lose their jobs, leading to severe labor shortages in some industries and eventually weakening the overall economy. "It's a disaster for us," Craig Silvertooth, a lobbyist for the National Roofing Contractors Association, told the *Austin Business Journal*. Craig Regelbrugge, the government relations director for the American Nursery & Landscape Association, whose workforce is at least two-thirds illegal, told the *Washington Post*'s N. C. Aizenman the impact would be "devastating."

> There is no replacement workforce. This will give people a set of bad choices: Either they terminate their workers, or they take a deep breath and duck and hope the law doesn't catch up with them. For a lot of people, they're just going to make the decision to get out of the business.

"Sadly, the administration's proposal would make our immigration crisis worse," Senator Ted Kennedy told reporters. Mexican president Felipe Calderon in his annual formal address to the nation on September 2, 2007, went further: "In the name of the government of Mexico, I again issue an energetic protest against the unilateral measures taken by the Congress and the United States government that exacerbate the persecution and vexing treatment against undocumented Mexican workers," he said.

Unfortunately, at this stage of the immigration debate anything the president of Mexico says fuels the ire of opponents, who either see a conspiracy to claim or reclaim Mexican sovereign rights in the

United States or just resent a foreigner having anything to say about the way America does business.

Even as it unleashed ICE on sitting-duck targets like workers at food processing plants, the DHS issued regulations designed to make it harder for illegal immigrants to use phony Social Security cards to get work. Under the newly reissued guidelines, when the Social Security Administration issues a letter that says the card filed doesn't match a real person, the employers have ninety days to investigate the discrepancy and, if unresolved, fire the worker or face criminal prosecution. And what are the consequences of employers not acting? "That's going to be awfully hard for them [the employers] to explain to a jury when the time comes for a trial," threatened the Homeland Security secretary who just two months before was extolling the virtues of illegal immigrants and urging the Congress to give them a path toward normalization. At that time, Secretary Chertoff complained, "We don't really have the ability to enforce the law with respect to illegal work in this country in a way that's truly effective," and said that he would "have" to enforce laws even though it would "tear families apart," if immigration reform was defeated.

That is why I hate many politicians. When necessary, they are opportunistic wind vanes. And as of this writing Judge Chertoff is pointing in the direction he thinks the anti-immigration mob wants to see. I preferred him as the crime-fighting prosecutor and then federal appeals court judge he was before his appointment to DHS. Fittingly, the federal courts seem to be standing squarely in the way of his new offensive. By Labor Day 2007, Judge Maxine M. Chesney in San Francisco (God bless federal judges in San Francisco and the rest of the Ninth Circuit) blocked at least temporarily the U.S. government from starting the planned crackdown on employers hiring the un- or falsely documented. Her ruling came in response to a lawsuit filed by the AFL-CIO, several other California-based labor unions, and the American Civil Liberties Union. The suit argued reasonably that the new rules would lead to widespread discrimination against Latino and other immigrant workers as employers panicked about whether the person working for them was provably American.

The second federal court shoe to drop came in October 2007, when another federal judge ordered an indefinite delay in Chertoff's campaign of stepped-up enforcement. Among his many problems with the crackdown, Judge Charles R. Breyer of the Northern District of California said the government could not make a policy change with such "massive ramifications" for employers without giving proper notice. Anyway, what would the real fruits of the employer crackdown be, if all their illegal workers become afraid of paying taxes to phony accounts? They will stop paying taxes! They'll work completely off the books, thereby denying the U.S. Treasury billions of dollars. Doesn't it make more sense to have them all line up, register, get printed, and have background checks, then get a work visa, even if it holds no promise of future citizenship—just the assurance that some SWAT-armored ICE officer isn't going to kick in the door in the dark of night? Why criminalize conduct that is otherwise lawful and contributes to the treasury of the nation?

The first ruling that ordered the Social Security Administration to suspend its mass mailing of 140,000 letters to employers advising them that some of their employees were using mismatched cards was good news not only for the illegal aliens but also for the U.S. Census Bureau. The bureau had asked that ICE stand down for the 2010 Census, as it had done for several months before and after the 2000 Census, so that the bureau could carry out its constitutionally mandated job of counting every U.S. resident, legal or not.

In today's acidic environment the census people were immediately scorned and ridiculed when they requested the ICE standdown. "I don't know what country the Census Bureau is living in," said Representative Candice Miller, a Michigan Republican. "I can tell them the American people have grown sick and tired of their immigration laws not being enforced." But what did ICE say? After initially suggesting that the issue of a cease-fire during the census taking was unresolved, on August 16, 2007, immigration officials cleared up any ambiguity by saying emphatically "No," they will not suspend immigration enforcement to help census takers in 2010. Census accuracy has also fallen victim to anti-immigrant hysteria. Now, if it means we have to suspend enforcement, however temporarily, we don't even want to know how many are here.

As Chertoff's DHS continues to follow through and dramatically escalate the arrests of undocumented workers, Republican business owners are squealing about immigration employment violation enforcement. But that activity, however disruptive, is more in keeping with the department's real job anyway. Claims of terrorism represent a tiny proportion of charges filed in recent years in immigration courts by the U.S. Department of Homeland Security, according to a report issued in May 2007 by the Transactional Records Action Clearinghouse (TRAC), an independent research group affiliated with Syracuse University.

The Transactional Records Action Clearinghouse said that it analyzed millions of previously undisclosed records obtained from the immigration courts under the Freedom of Information Act. In the fiscal years 2004–06, of the 814,073 people charged by the DHS in immigration courts, just 12 faced charges of terrorism: 0.0015 percent—fifteen-ten-thousandths of a percent. The department's status as warriors battling the terrorist bogeyman is the creation of bogus hype. "The DHS claims it is focused on terrorism. Well, that's not true," David Burnham, a TRAC spokesman, told CNN's Scott Bronstein.

TRAC was immediately criticized by DHS for issuing a report that was "ill-conceived" and that "lacked the grasp of the DHS mission." However, nobody in the department denied any of TRAC's conclusions. Furthermore, TRAC is not the first body to point to inflated terrorism claims that have hyped the nation's anxiety and provided fuel for anti-immigrant hysteria. Just look at the controversial performance of a more established department of the federal government. According to a February 2007 Justice Department audit, federal prosecutors counted ordinary immigration violations, including marriage fraud and drug trafficking, among their "antiterror" cases in the four years after 9/11. And they did that even though no evidence linked those acts to real-world terrorist activity. One of the "terrorism" cases they trumpeted turned out to be a marriage broker being paid to arrange six fraudulent marriages between fellow Tunisians and U.S. citizens.

If you need further proof of the DHS's preoccupation with immigration rather than terrorism, consider the fate of Border Patrol sector chief Carlos X. Carrillo. Carrillo addressed a town hall meeting in Laredo, Texas, in August 2007. Asked why his agents weren't strictly enforcing a "zero tolerance" policy that demands the arrest of all illegal immigrants in the Del Rio, Texas, section of the border, the chief explained that his agency's principal mission "is stopping terrorists, not illegal aliens or drug smugglers."

The chief's frankness immediately drew outrage from Representative John Culberson, a Texas Republican, who demanded an apology. To which the chief meekly replied, "It's painfully obvious to me that I could have done a better job of articulating my talking points," and that, "As long as the resources are made available to the people who can make it happen, we will certainly do everything we can to ensure that a zero tolerance policy is brought forward. But to initiate a program like this, without funding, would not be wise." To the enormous satisfaction of the Minuteman Civil Defense Corps, the congressman quickly declared victory: "Chief Carrillo promised me that he will do his very best to implement Del Rio's zero tolerance policy."

The manufactured relationship between terror and immigration is hollow and false. In that regard, the Department of Homeland Security is misnamed. It should be called the Department of

Immigration Enforcement and Disaster Relief. This huge apparatus does have a number of real jobs. They include policing immigrants, like those who overstay a student visa or enter the United States without a health inspection. The DHS also guards the borders (although the Border Patrol and the INS already did that), assists in disaster relief (although FEMA already did that), and carries out a host of other legitimate and necessary, but mundane, tasks.

Just remember that the DHS's lofty status largely depends on the warrior aura it assumed in the post-9/11 era. How many times have you seen Homeland Security secretary Michael Chertoff or his predecessor, Tom Ridge, giving interviews about the terrorist "enemy within"? Yet just a tiny fraction of the agency's enormous resources are being used to stop al-Qaeda.

Most of the rest is being used to stop Mexicans.

Behind the whispered question of race and the more publicly discussed debate about English-language dilution, the issue of terror dominates the discussion of immigration. Does the wave of Hispanic population growth mask a genuine threat to our security? As the United States engages in its global war against Islamo-Fascism, once known as the war on terror, are our foreign enemies infiltrating our nation, hidden among the hundreds of thousands of apricot pickers or meatpacking-plant workers sneaking over the border from Mexico? Is Osama or Abdul disguising himself as Juan or Pedro? Don't they all sort of look alike?

I was among those fueling the paranoia. After I left NBC News to join the Fox News Channel, one of my early assignments soon after the war began was to investigate fears that terrorist operatives were penetrating our borders. It was spring/summer 2002, and with a team of producers and reporters we worked hard to investigate vague allegations that secret radical Muslim agents were residing in Tijuana and similar border towns awaiting the opportunity to sneak across the border to perpetrate savage violence against us.

Chasing tips all along the southwest border, at times accompanying an elite Mexican federal antiterror force, we followed up on leads, however dubious, and even raided several locations. We found nothing save one imprisoned drug dealer of Arab descent who swore he had overheard a group of fellow Muslims in Mexico applauding TV images of 9/11.

There has never been a single verified terrorist penetration of our southern border. On the day the now-failed comprehensive immigration reform bill was formally proposed by a bilateral group of eleven senators, Judge Chertoff told me on live radio that he knew of no case of terrorists breaching our southern frontier, not one. In the interview broadcast on Fox News Radio in June 2007, I asked point-blank if he had ever seen a single verifiable case of terrorists using the Mexican border and he answered unequivocally, "No."

But what about the May 2007 arrests of the Fort Dix Six? Weren't they illegal immigrants and a graphic example of why Mexican border vigilance is key to the antiterror fight?

Pinkerton, Tancredo, and other anti-immigrant activists made much of the fact that of the five alleged terrorists facing the most serious charges, three are brothers believed to have entered the country illegally, perhaps crossing the Rio Grande. During a televised debate on *Good Morning America* between CNN's Glenn Beck and me, the bombastic Beck used this example to link border security to the antiterror fight. What he and they failed to point out is that while four of the men were indeed born in the former Yugoslavia, a fifth in Jordan, and the sixth from Turkey, two had green cards, while a third was a U.S. citizen.

The remaining trio, all brothers of the Duka family, were widely portrayed as sinister illegal aliens who snuck over the all-but-open Mexican border, but they arrived in the United States from Albania when they were small children under the age of five. Perhaps they learned their terrorist ways in a radical Islamic preschool?

Since overstaying its tourist visas, the brothers' family applied several times for legal status, including one claim of asylum and another attempt to obtain a green card in a public lottery. The Duka family's various applications for legal status had been pending for more than a decade at the time the young men were arrested for allegedly preparing to buy automatic weapons to use in the attack on Fort Dix.

Asked if their arrests had any links to al-Qaeda, the then White House spokesman and fair-minded Tony Snow said it appears "there is no direct evidence of a foreign-terrorist tie." The FBI agent in charge of the case, J. P. Weiss, said, "These homegrown terrorists can prove to be as dangerous as any known group, if not more so. They operate under the radar."

The competence, commitment, and bona fides of the Fort Dix Six will be tested at trial. There have been other alleged domestic cells exposed in recent months. First, the Miami-based terror group that in 2007 allegedly plotted to blow up the Sears Tower in Chicago, the members of which would have had enough trouble finding the Sears Department Store in their hometown. Then the aging, bigmouthed Caribbean-based team that wanted to blow the fuel tanks at JFK airport but had no earthly idea how to do it. In the Fort Dix case, the evidence will determine whether two paid FBI informants who infiltrated the group more than a year before the arrests and recorded conversations with the defendants were in fact the alleged conspiracy's driving force and principal protagonists.

In other words, did this hapless crew of American-bred cabdrivers, pizza delivery boys, and bread bakers with no criminal records who worshipped at moderate, pro-American mosques lead the two ex-con informants into this creepy scheme to perpetrate violence on random GIs, or was it the other way around? The government's case against the alleged coconspirators received a boost in late October 2007 when one defendant agreed to plead guilty to supplying the others with weapons. But whether the rest are convicted, since the "Six" had spent virtually their entire lives in the United States, their long-ago refugee status as little children is irrelevant other than shamelessly to aggravate the harsh tone of the immigration debate. And the overwhelmingly innocent and law-abiding group stranded on the short end of that acrimony is the mass of undocumented workers striving to work hard and breathe free.

Ironically, given the fixation with the Mexican border, there have been several attempts to penetrate the Canadian border, including one by the so-called Millennium Bomber. Ahmed Ressam, an Algerian living in Montreal, planned to bomb the Los Angeles Airport on January 1, 2000. Hatched by al-Qaeda, the potentially disastrous plot was thwarted when a sharp-eyed U.S. Customs agent named Mike Chapman noticed Ressam acting suspiciously after arriving in Port Angeles, Washington, on a ferry from Victoria, British Columbia. A search of Ressam's vehicle revealed a cache of nitroglycerin in the trunk and four timers to be used as detonators hidden in the well of the spare tire.

"He came out, kind of put his hands up halfheartedly, and then bolted right across traffic," the vigilant U.S. Customs agent Chapman later told the Canadian Broadcasting Corporation. "We were actually right in the middle of the intersection when I took him down." Turning snitch on his associates in an attempt to get a lighter sentence, Ressam admitted to using a fake Canadian passport to travel to Osama bin Laden's training camps in Afghanistan, where, with the help of the terror mastermind and his lieutenant, Abu Zubaydah, they devised the plot to bomb LAX. Ressam was sentenced to twenty-two years behind bars on July 27, 2005.

"I'm proud to have done my job that day," Chapman told the CBC. "I'm proud that he didn't hurt anybody and he was apprehended."

Under the category of compelling postscript, while in prison Ressam revealed the alleged existence of al-Qaeda sleeper cells within the United States. This seemingly crucial information was later included in the infamous and apparently ignored "Presidential Daily Briefing" issued on August 6, 2001, entitled "Bin Laden Determined to Strike in U.S." More to the point of this book, Ressam never alleged any of the terrorists had arrived in the States through the border with Mexico.

When the hue and cry to tighten the southern border for reasons of national security cooled somewhat in the months following the massive pro-immigration protests of May 2006, the issue was reenergized in the lead-up to the November 2006 election. With unrest over the progress of the war in Iraq deepening, in October of that year there seems to have been a sudden rediscovery of illegal immigration by Republican strategists, who apparently saw it as the wedge issue, the gay marriage/abortion rights/Terri Schiavo of the 2006 election cycle.

Overnight, reformists like John McCain and, during that period at least, even President George W. Bush fell silent on their oft-stated desire for a fair and comprehensive approach to immigration. Rudy Giuliani, by then the leading contender for his party's presidential nomination, suddenly was talking only about strengthening our nation's borders; gone was the public compassion he had displayed as mayor. Their erratic and opportunistic histories on this issue had the foreseeable backlash of costing the GOP crucial Hispanic votes in the 2006 race. But that was not the most unfortunate effect.

Flush with antiterror resources and unable to find many other threats to homeland security, the unlimited force of that now massively bloated agency was turned from terror fighting to terrorizing. I know that sounds harsh and that ICE agents are as patriotic as the next guy. But to dress them up like armored warriors and send them into a civilian factory to snatch men and women whose only offense is that they are here illegally is preposterous overkill. In this chapter I have documented ICE raids on food processing plants. There are more cases.

One of the most grievous examples was the New Bedford,

Massachusetts, raid that will live in immigration infamy. On March 6, 2007, a large, heavily armed team of federal agents swept up 361 workers at the Michael Bianco Inc. leather goods factory. No one can say those otherwise innocent immigrant working people weren't terrorized. As they were being taken away, women pleaded with the ICE agents to be allowed to return to their homes to care for their small children; some said they were nursing mothers. All were initially confined and charged with violating federal immigration law. Most of the men, many of them fathers with wives and children in town, were flown out of the state immediately to immigrant holding centers as far away as Texas. Families were disrupted and fear seeped through the immigrant New Bedford community. Ironically, the workers had been assembling uniforms for the United States military.

In the words of Senator Edward Kennedy, "These men and women had not harmed anyone. They were the victims of exploitation, forced to work under barbaric conditions by an employer who knew that they could not afford to complain. Their children, many of whom are United States citizens, had done nothing wrong at all. None of them had any reason to expect that the Department of Homeland Security would decide to make an example out of them."

In a face-to-face interview in June 2007 inside the Senate Office Building, the old lion of the left seemed pained by the recollection of the tawdry event. Seeing him then reminded me of the first interview I ever did with Teddy Kennedy. It was in July 1973 for a WABC special called *Migrants: Dirt Cheap*, in which the labor leader Cesar Chávez also participated. We were young then, and convinced the country would rise up to fix the inequities in the way migratory farmworkers were treated. Kennedy and I actually did our interview like two grad students sitting under a tree on the lawn outside the Capitol. It was an idealistic and still hopeful time. Now white-haired, slightly hunched, and deflated by the direction the nation has taken on the issue of immigration, the senator told me the New Bedford raid was one of the "worst things he had ever seen" in his long career of public service.

The worst part of this tragedy, as Kennedy said, was that it separated many children from working parents who were whisked away. Ironically, perhaps, President Bush was in Guatemala on a "goodwill" trip through Latin America at the time of the raid. The president tepidly defended the ICE action. "The United States will enforce our law. It's against the law to hire somebody who's in our country illegally." Really? Then why not just make an example of the employer rather than traumatizing young children by denying them their hardworking, otherwise law-abiding parents?

The only good to come out of this extravagant misuse of federal power is that historians may see the revulsion over this event and a similar, even larger immigration crackdown on meatpacking plants in the Midwest as turning points in the debate, waking at least some fair-minded Americans to the bitter turn U.S. immigration policy had taken in the era of the Minutemen, Tancredo, and Dobbs, all in the largely bogus name of fighting terror.

7

Immigrants and Disease

"Burning [down] quarantine [facilities] has for a long time been deemed a pardonable offence by some Staten Island men who hold respectable positions in society—[evidence of] their deep-rooted determination to be rid of their greatest curse."

—THE *New York Times*, SEPTEMBER 1858, FOLLOWING AN ARSON
FIRE SET AT AN IMMIGRANT QUARANTINE STATION ON STATEN ISLAND,
AS QUOTED IN *Coming to America* BY ROBERT BACHAND

The invasion of illegal aliens is threatening the health of many Americans," intoned Lou Dobbs gravely on his April 14, 2005, CNN program, as he led in to a report that made the alarming claim, "There were about nine hundred cases of leprosy for forty years. . . . There have been seven thousand in the past three years." The report's clear and specific intent was to convey the message that sick Mexicans and other aliens, but mostly Mexican migrants, are carrying fearsome diseases that are infecting thousands of innocent and otherwise healthy Americans. And that one result of this distressing phenomenon was a resurgence of this horrible disease that has haunted mankind since the biblical era. The new scourge was leprosy that was said to have been carried into America by aliens.

In May 2007 there was an awkward moment when CBS correspondent Leslie Stahl, in profiling Mr. Dobbs on *60 Minutes*, questioned him about the claim. The awkwardness was due to the fact that unknown to Stahl, the CNN anchor had just gotten a part-time job as a contributor to CBS's own *Early Show*.

Stahl said, "We checked that number and found a report issued by the federal government saying that seven thousand is the number of leprosy cases over the last thirty years, not the past three." Stahl added, "And nobody knows how many of those cases involve illegal immigrants."

"If we reported it, it's a fact," Dobbs answered with his customary arrogance. But it was not a fact, as the Southern Poverty Law Center (SPLC) demonstrated in interviews and in full-page ads in the *New York Times* and *USA Today* demanding a retraction of the inflammatory and false reporting. The fact is, leprosy "is not a public health problem—that's the bottom line," James Krahenbuhl, the director of the National Hansen's Disease Program, told the *New York Times* (Hansens's disease is the medical name for leprosy).

As *Times* reporter David Leonhardt proved, the Dobbs report was a lie, and if it were not for the specious connection to the debate on immigration, the CNN ace would never have reported it. He was wrong and unfair. Dobbs is also "one of the most popular people on the white supremacist Web sites," according to J. Richard Cohen, the CEO of the Southern Poverty Law Center, who told Dobbs to his face on a May 2007 broadcast, "You've got to ask yourself why the Council of Concerned Citizens considers you their favorite pundit." According to Cohen's colleague Mark Potok, "The anti-immigration movement is shot through with bigots, nuts and radicals like the Minutemen's Chris Simcox, who has been quoted as saying he saw elements of the Chinese army mobilizing on the Mexican border! Simcox has been an honored guest on Lou Dobbs's show at least twenty times." The hope at the SPLC is that the ridicule Dobbs received from other reporters, and even from both Jon Stewart and Steven Colbert on Comedy Central, has dulled the CNN commentator's effectiveness. If so, it is long overdue.

As David Leonhardt put it in the *Times*:

> The problem with Mr. Dobbs is that he mixes opinion and untruths. He is the heir to the nativist tradition that has long

used fiction and conspiracy theories as a weapon against the Irish, the Italians, the Chinese, the Jews and now, the Mexicans.

The connection between immigration and disease has long been used to generate distaste toward immigrants that sometimes borders on panic. And often the panic is accompanied by anti-immigrant violence. It is as predictable as the economic cycle of boom and bust. In May 1857, a quarantine facility on Staten Island, New York, designed to care for immigrants with contagious diseases like yellow fever, cholera, and smallpox, was burned to the ground by vigilantes concerned the new arrivals would spread disease to their community and suppress property values.

Another armed gang of thugs, who thankfully removed the patients first, burned a second facility the following September. When authorities could find no witnesses or evidence of responsibility for the arson, the *New York Times* reporter at the time wrote the sentence quoted above about vigilantism directed against immigrants being "deemed a pardonable offence."

To be sure, in the era before effective public health, immigrants were sometimes a source of infectious disease, and they suffered an inevitable backlash when that was the case. In 1892, a cholera epidemic swept through New York, causing a tremendous antipathy toward the German immigrants who brought the disease with them on board a vessel out of Hamburg called the *Monrovia*. As quoted in *Coming to America*, the *New York Times* of all newspapers wrote in an August 29, 1892, front-page article:

These people [immigrants] are offensive at best; under the present circumstances, they are a positive menace to the health of the country. . . . Cholera, it must be remembered, originates in the homes of this human riff-raff.

The whole concept of keeping out the "human riff-raff" became the central theme in America's immigration policy. The passage of the Immigration Act of 1924 capped total immigration at 150,000 a year and specifically set a limit of 2 percent of the population of each race already here. The idea of the racial quotas was to preserve America's ethnic "balance" by keeping out more immigrants from southern European countries, principally Italy, Spain, and Greece, and Slavic Eastern Europeans, who were thought genetically inferior to the nation's then WASP majority. Upon signing the bill into law, President Calvin Coolidge declared, "America must remain America."

And while immigration from the Mediterranean and Slavic peoples was severely curtailed, Africans were not even considered eligible to apply. The anti-immigration forces of the time also hyped fear of diseases like tuberculosis, using it not only to deport Mexican immigrants but also to "repatriate" back to Mexico some migrants who had already become citizens of the United States.

Many believe that it was the anti-immigrant mind-set and the fear of inferior races seeping into our society, as evidenced by the racist Chinese Exclusion Act of 1882 and the National Origins Act of 1924, as much as blatant anti-Semitism, that kept America from offering safe haven to Europe's doomed Jews on the eve of World War II.

In 1939, lobbied fiercely by his own anti-Semitic secretary of state, Cornell Hull, and flat-out threatened by a withdrawal of support in the coming election by southern Democrats, President Franklin D. Roosevelt was not exactly a profile in courage when he turned away the SS *St. Louis*, the infamous ship crammed with almost a thousand Jewish refugees. Their tragic "Voyage of the Damned" ended when the ship returned them to Europe on the eve of the Nazi invasion, where many of the ship's passengers perished.

Commentators of today are playing with the same tried and trusted handbook their predecessors used in the 1930s to justify President Herbert Hoover's policy of repatriation of immigrants, both those thought to have infectious diseases and even those who were healthy, but who it was feared might catch TB and then might need subsidized medical care. Their principal tactic is the generation of irrational fear of the worst kind, fear that close contact with these alien others can cause horrifying disease. The claims have little basis in fact, but the charge, once made, is difficult to rebut. Although leprosy is not the contemporary public health problem the Dobbs report wanted you to believe, a straw poll of Dobbs's viewers would probably indicate otherwise.

It was another bogeyman conjured to make a dishonest point. What will CNN blame the poor Mexicans for next? Venereal disease? Acne? Tooth decay?

Check out this article posted on the Americans for Legal Immigration PAC newsletter:

By Frosty
September 21, 2006
Why? As of Wednesday, 146 citizens in 23 states suffered E. Coli infection and one died. . . . How do you think this disease outbreak occurred? To bring it into sobering focus, please understand that 20 million illegal aliens crossed in to America in the past 20 years without any kind of health screening. They work picking our food, washing our dishes in restaurants and, as is the norm in Third World countries, rarely if ever wash their hands after using the toilet. Additionally, most of them suffer functional illiteracy. They do not practice personal hygiene or health habits most Americans assume as a normal aspect of living.

George Lopez and Carlos Mencia have a long-running feud over who thought up a joke that Frosty wouldn't find very funny. It goes something like: "You know who touches your Taco Bell before you do?" Then the joke gets really gross, detailing how migrant farm laborers can wreak havoc on hygiene to retaliate against societal abuse. It's only funny because it's *not* true. There is not a speck of evidence suggesting that migrant farmworkers are any dirtier than native-born workers. Ever been on a farm, Frosty? Did you bring wipes?

I have a great story about how a clever group of Cuban illegal migrants used the disease paranoia to gain entrance into the United States. In 2005, about forty of them were found at the Gateway International Bridge in Brownsville, Texas, a popular border crossing point. When they were apprehended by U.S. Customs agents, the group's spokesman told the agents they all had tuberculosis. The freaked-out agents then brought them into the United States, where everyone was chest X-rayed by nurses at the Cameron County Health Department. None had TB. Then, because of the unique law regarding Cuban refugees who touch American soil, all were permitted to stay. This is the Trojan Horse of the Cuban refugee saga.

There is one provable and ironic connection between Latino migrants and disease. Some of those who spent time in this country as seasonal workers are reportedly returning home to Mexico infected with HIV/AIDS they contracted in the United States. An eye-opening July 2007 report by Marc Lacey in the *New York Times* revealed an "expanding AIDS crisis among migrants [that] is largely overlooked on both sides of the border. . . . In the United States, it is often assumed that immigrants bring diseases into the country, not take them away." "They think that because it's the United States, [sex] is safer," Dr. Indiana Torres of the Puebla Mexico General Hospital told Lacey. "It's their fantasy and it's not true."

I bet you will never see this HIV/AIDS story reported by Hannity, Dobbs, or Malkin. Stories have to fit their "illegal aliens are bad and bad for you" narrative to be worthy of comment, and their current theme is the imminent destruction of our way of life, famine, war, plague, and pestilence caused by rampant immigration.

8

Immigrants and Crime

"Few stereotypes of immigrants are as enduring, or have been proven so categorically false over literally decades of research, as the notion that immigrants are disproportionately likely to engage in criminal activity."

—"IMMIGRATION AND THE JUSTICE SYSTEM," *Research Perspectives on Migration*, JULY/AUGUST 1997, AS QUOTED BY THE CENTER FOR IMMIGRATION STUDIES

Like the disease paranoia, the specter of an immigrant-driven crime wave is promulgated by the same sloppy and/or intentionally misleading reporting that has helped heap scorn on the community of immigrants and exacerbate the currently hypercharged atmosphere of hate. When, in September in 2007, federal statistics for the year 2006 were released showing a 1.9 percent spike in violent crime nationally, the CNN reporter Kitty Pilgrim, substituting for Lou Dobbs, led the show by solemnly, specifically linking the rise in violence to the rise in illegal immigration—the flood of illegal aliens. I wanted to throw something at the television or phone in, an indignant viewer. Pilgrim made the proclamation without a single source or statistical reference and despite the fact that in making his official announcement of the statistics, FBI director Robert S. Mueller made no mention of illegal immigration.

It is as if CNN has totally abandoned all journalistic rules or ethics when it comes to immigrants, at least when in Dobbs's hour. Just let fly, as long as the allegation paints the wetbacks in a negative light. I wanted to call the station and point out that New York, with over half a million illegal immigrants, saw violent crime drop, while Cleveland, with no appreciable increase in immigration, saw violent crime, especially murder, spike alarmingly.

The early presidential aspirant Republican congressman Duncan Hunter appeared on Bill O'Reilly's show in September 2007 and claimed there were over a quarter million illegal immigrants in local, state, and federal prisons, draining the American taxpayer of billions. I checked the most recently compiled statistics available from the nonpartisan General Accounting Office and found a May 2005 report that states, "We identified a population of 55,322 aliens that . . . had entered the country illegally and were still illegally in the country at the time of their incarceration in the country in federal or state prison or local jail during fiscal year 2003." About half of them were in prison for either drug-related crimes or, more commonly, the offense of being here illegally itself, pending deportation hearings. On average, that group had been arrested eight times each, which is perhaps why Hunter saw five times more than there really are; the same immigrant kept being passed around. At 55,322, the immigrants are less than 3 percent of the total number of prisoners, which now tops out at just over 2 million. Put another way, in 2003, citizens and legal immigrants were 97 percent of our prison population at any given time.

Remember Iowa congressman King's blatantly false or at the very least totally unproven "extrapolated" assertion that illegal immigrants are killing twenty-five native-born Americans every day? The question I have for the congressman is, where can I look up that statistic? Who did that study, the Minutemen? Tom Tancredo? The General Accounting Office or any other reasonably impartial agency certainly did not do it.

The flagging of particularly egregious crimes allegedly committed by illegal aliens, like the summer 2007 Newark triple homicide that so inflamed the anti-immigrant crew, are case studies in how nativists seize on grievous incidents to make a cheap but effective political point, regardless of the facts. Another vivid example of the balls-out propaganda war is the brutal July 2007 kidnapping, rape, and murder of twelve-year-old Zina Linnik in Tacoma, Washington. The child, as I discovered when I interviewed her grief-stricken family, was, ironically, herself a recent immigrant from Eastern Europe. This fact is conveniently left out of all extremist commentary on this case. Zina was snatched as she watched an Independence Day fireworks display near her family's home. Her dad and other horrified eyewitnesses watched as the child was being driven away in a gray van and managed to obtain a partial license plate number, which ultimately led authorities to the perpetrator, Terapon Adhahn, a forty-two-year-old native of Thailand who had a previous conviction for statutory rape.

When it became clear that Zina's alleged abductor was a convicted sex offender and an immigrant, the conservative commentator and frenetic blogger Michelle Malkin and her tribe of fellow thinkers exploded in rage (and joy)! Here was another graphic example with which to make the point, as Malkin did with a July 13, 2007, blog headline, CONSEQUENCES OF OPEN BORDERS: THE KIDNAPPING AND MURDER OF ZINA LINNIK. Malkin went on to decry the actions of "Democrat Washington state governor Christine Gregoire, who is leaving on a trip to lobby for open borders. How politically stupid and insensitive can you be?"

The express point Malkin was making was that the cause-and-effect relationship between lax immigration policy and the death of this poor twelve-year-old was there for all to see. And her blogger mates took the bait, one writing: "It's TIME BUSH to SEAL the borders on BOTH SIDES NOW."

"Blood of the hands of all open borders appeasers! Including our President! This makes me sick. When are we going to take our country away from the elites that prefer a frightened populus!!??" wrote another.

But was there really any connection between so-called open

borders and the rape and murder of Zina Linnik? Terapon Adhahn was indeed born into an impoverished Bangkok, Thailand, family in 1965. His father abandoned his mother, Pennsiri, and her five children, including Terapon. Working as a housekeeper for American families in Bangkok, Pennsiri met and married John Bower, an American soldier serving over there.

In 1977, when Terapon was just twelve years old, the family moved to the United States. Here legally, Terapon later followed in his stepfather's footsteps, obtaining permanent residency and enlisting in the U.S. Army, in which he served two tours of duty, stationed at times at Fort Dix, New Jersey, Fort Lewis, Washington, and a posting overseas in Germany.

Terapon Adhahn married in 1986 and had two children. He and his wife separated when it was revealed he was carrying on an affair with a twelve-year-old who was reportedly his half sister. He was convicted of rape and incest and was classified as a level one (that is, low-risk) sex offender and was required to register. He was later convicted of a second offense involving intimidation with a weapon.

According to Washington State voter registration records obtained by Fox News, Adhahn has been a registered voter since 2002, which means that somewhere along the way he became a naturalized American citizen. Presumably, the government can attempt to have his citizenship revoked, considering the crimes he is convicted and/or suspected of committing. Remember how the U.S. government went after mobsters like Lucky Luciano in the post–World War II era, stripping them of their naturalized citizenship and exiling them back to their native lands? But to attribute this army veteran's crimes to "open borders" is patent nonsense. No, it is worse than that, it is dishonest fearmongering.

On Wednesday, August 22, 2007, Congressman Tancredo appeared on *Hannity & Colmes* to debate me about the Newark triple homicides, the alleged connection to immigration policy, and where responsibility for the triple murder of those youngsters lay. The show started with the producers playing a Romney campaign radio ad talking about how then Massachusetts governor Mitt Romney "acted to make our immigration laws work." To which Tancredo correctly pointed out, "Almost everybody on the stage now that I appear on, Republicans running for president of the United States, that is, all of them now are becoming the strongest anti-immigration advocates in the world, strengthen the borders. They all sound like Tom Tancredo . . ."

He was right and I told him so, saying, "This may be the only chance I get to agree with Congressman Tancredo this evening, so let me just give him props on that one. He is right. He did it first. He did it most ferociously. But now they're all following in lockstep," including Rudy Giuliani, who crafted the policy in New York, the nation's safest big city.

But with the exception of John McCain, the other GOP candidates, including our dear ex-mayor, have drunk the anti-immigration Kool-Aid. "Many do not commit crimes," admitted Congressman Tancredo, setting up the punch line, "but many do. And those are the ones we are concentrating on today, because, of course, the people who are dead today, the three children who are dead in Newark, and the one that's in the hospital, they are in those conditions, they are dead kids and one in the hospital because Newark is a sanctuary city."

I mentioned the congressman's hypocritical interest in these particular homicides as opposed to the sixty others already committed this year in Newark and pointed out that the story was barely mentioned on cable news and indeed, not reported at all by the hard right. I also pointed out the fact that this particular immigrant scumbag/alleged perpetrator came to this country at age eleven; never should have been out on bail in the first place; and that "it had nothing to do with his immigration status. And it's just being used by advocates of this crushing anti-immigration policy to make a cheap political point."

Hannity cut to the chase, correctly summing up the debate.

"The issue here, Geraldo, that you seem to be missing, is this country is angry." Hannity is right. A big hunk of just plain folk are spitting mad about immigrants committing crimes no matter how relatively peaceful these people may be in real life. It is another easy reason to hate the illegal immigrants. That the anger is stoked by inflamed rhetoric, even race baiting, is maddening, but largely irrelevant. Because however inaccurate their position, it incites people already inclined to blame immigrants for everything wrong in their lives, aggravating a perhaps legitimate feeling of loss of control, a dread that the nation is changing, color and otherwise, and that the established order is powerless to stop it.

In the Tancredo debate, I finally tried this: "How many people have enjoyed the benefit of a random act of kindness today from someone who was here illegally? How many children were fed? How many people had their lives improved by an undocumented person today?"

"Three would be alive today," Tancredo replied, ". . . three would be alive."

Because of the emotional resonance of statements like the congressman's, the issue of how to deal with illegal immigrants and the law is vexing communities from coast to coast, and the nation's policy is fragmenting along liberal and conservative lines. Big cities from Seattle to New York, Miami to Los Angeles, still insist that their "don't ask, don't tell" approach is most practical, while smaller communities, less likely to employ immigrants and bothered by issues like loitering day workers waiting to be picked up and transported to jobs in wealthier neighborhoods, are tending more to cooperate with the ICE.

On the afternoon of the Tancredo debate, the New Jersey state attorney general ordered local cops to notify federal immigration officials whenever someone arrested for an indictable offense or drunken driving is an illegal immigrant. Attorney General Anne Milgrim reviewed the state's policy in light of Newark's execution-style killings because "one of the six suspects was an illegal immigrant who had been granted bail on his aggravated assault charges without immigration officials being alerted to his existence."

Whether her order is carried out, and I suspect it will be only in those smaller suburban or rural communities in the Garden State where undocumented immigrants play a smaller role in local society, the irony is I don't really disagree with her stated goal, only her approach, and the fact her motive is suspect. It was a reaction to the populist politics of the day. The state government didn't have the spunk to stand up to Tancredo, who blamed them for the murders. But New Jersey succumbed to the populist mob without fixing the problem.

Here is how the issue could be reconciled. Immigration status should be a factor in the court setting bail for an alleged perpetrator. Bail is supposed to ensure that the accused shows up for trial. If an alleged felon is an illegal alien, it is reasonable to take account of that status when determining the amount of bail, because presumably someone here illegally has more incentive to flee.

And I have no problem with tipping off immigration authorities whenever a prisoner is accused of committing a serious felony. The problem of mandatory notification of the feds of immigration status of all indictable suspects is the new policy's real-life impact. What happens if there is a domestic violence allegation involving a husband and wife here illegally? An abused immigrant wife will now know that if she calls the cops, not only will her husband's status be reported to federal authorities, but so, inevitably, will hers. Is that woman going to call the cops and risk deportation, or is she going to suffer in silence?

"We want people who are undocumented and are victims of crime to report it and not feel that out of fear they can't report crimes," Police Chief Steve Strachan, who runs a department in the community of Kent in Puget Sound, Washington, told the *Seattle Times*.

Because all immigration politics, like all politics, is local, the paper, like others across the country, has been covering the patchwork of different responses by local cops.

In the tiny town of Pacific in southeast King County an estimated 6 percent of residents are illegal, mostly from Mexico. And when they have any contact with law enforcement, even for a routine traffic stop, the feds are notified. "I'm proud of my officers and the job they're doing," Pacific, Washington, police chief John Calkins told the *Seattle Times* as he defended the immigration detention after a traffic stop of a twenty-five-year-old man who is married to an American citizen and was in the process of obtaining legal status. The man was held for eight days and as a result lost his well-paying job as a granite installer, because "the police scared my boss." He was released on bond after presenting his paperwork to an immigration judge. The chief was unapologetic and defended his officers' actions. "I told them if there's a violation, whether federal, state, whatever, they're not to just turn their backs on it."

"There's a lot of confusion about what the appropriate role for state and local law enforcement is, what their actual authority is," Gene Voegtlin, the legislative counsel for the International Association of Chiefs of Police, told the paper.

Remember how my dad agonized over any crime committed by a fellow Puerto Rican? You can imagine my angst in the current charged atmosphere. Any crime committed by a Hispanic, particularly an undocumented migrant, gives me migraines. Aside from feeling compassion for the victims of those crimes, the injuries sustained to the cause of assimilation are, if not as grievous, more broadly felt. The drunk driver in Virginia who mowed down those two teenagers on the cusp of life not only destroyed them, but also cast a pall over the entire Hispanic community, legal and otherwise.

But as I tried to make clear that original volatile night with O'Reilly, statistically speaking, immigrants are no more prone to committing crimes than the native-born. In fact, contrary to what the anti-immigration panicmongers would have you believe, research shows that individuals who are in the country illegally commit relatively *fewer* crimes than the rest of the population. This being the case, it might be said that as illegal immigration goes up, crime, proportionately, goes down.

The nonpartisan Center for Immigration Studies (CIS) compiled research going back more than a century. It uncovered a 1901 federal investigation that found "foreign-born whites were less oriented toward crime than native whites." A decade later, the CIS found, another federal panel by an agency called the Immigration Commission reported that "no satisfactory evidence has yet been produced to show that immigration has resulted in an increase in crime disproportionate to the increase in adult population. . . . In fact, the figures seem to show a contrary result."

According to the CIS, an agency called the National Commission on Law Observance and Enforcement reported in 1931 that their results "seem to disagree radically with the popular belief that a high percentage of crime may be ascribed to the 'alien.'"

More recently, the General Accounting Office, analyzing FBI records, found that foreign-born individuals accounted for about 19 percent of the total arrests in 1985 in six selected major cities. The foreign-born represented 19.6 percent of the aggregate population. In other words, immigrants in these cities committed proportionately no more than and possibly even fewer crimes than the native-born.

And contrary to the frequent moan about alien criminals reoffending at a disproportionately high rate, a five-year INS study of data of criminal aliens from October 1994 to May 1999 shows a lower recidivism rate for immigrants than for the native-born.

Of the 35,318 criminal aliens INS released from custody [but did not deport] during that period there were 11,605 who went on to commit new crimes. This recidivism [repeat offender] rate of 37% was well below the 66% figure for the U.S. criminal population for the comparable period.

And while much is made of the criminal activity of Hispanic gangs like the Salvadoran-based *Mara Salvatrucha* (MS-13), who are a severe and undeniable problem, a study by the Kennedy School of Government of men aged eighteen to forty found that immigrants were approximately one-third less likely to be in correctional institutions than the native-born.

This is as good a time as any to deal with the issue of Hispanic gangs, as unsavory as the topic is for those celebrating assimilation and encouraging others to be optimistic about America's changing demographic profile.

9

Hispanic Gangs

"Make no mistake, this is the largest threat to you and your family in this country, outweighing every terrorist organization's threat, including Al-Qaeda, yet virtually nothing is being done about it."

—MILNET, THE ONLINE MILITARY ENCYCLOPEDIA, 2006

Unless you deal drugs, paint graffiti in East L.A., or are extremely unlucky and get caught in their cross fire, Hispanic gangs are probably not "the largest threat to you and your family." But these are scary dudes who, beginning in East Los Angeles over the last seven or eight decades, have developed a violent subculture that venerates mayhem and feeds off criminal profit, mostly drug dealing, extortion, burglaries, and prostitution, either committing the criminal acts themselves or receiving the equivalent of a neighborhood franchise fee from the actual perpetrators.

According to Rocky Delgadillo, the Los Angeles City attorney, who, like Mayor Villaraigosa, grew up in a gang-infested neighborhood, there are currently thirty-nine thousand gang members in L.A. Speaking at a three-day February 2007 gang summit attended by officials from around the country and from Canada, Mexico, and Central America, Delgadillo claimed good news. "We have seen a thirty-three percent reduction in gang membership in L.A.," down from a high of fifty-seven thousand members a few years ago.

But a heavily armed, hair-trigger, proud, highly motivated and crazy-brave force of thirty-nine thousand is still roughly the size of two U.S. Army divisions, and having covered the story since the 1970s, usually after an innocent kid is killed in a drive-by or cross fire, I believe the city attorney understates an intractable problem that has defied solution since the zoot suit–*Pachuco* days of the Great Depression and World War II. (*Pachuco* was a sharp style of dress among young Hispanics in those days. An argument can be made that Elvis took his unique style from those flamboyant Latinos with peg pants and long, severely tapered jackets.)

Without attempting to rationalize why so many Latino kids gravitate to their ritualized world of gangs and violence (you've heard the reasons: peer pressure, intimidation, isolation, protection, sick tradition, and so forth), let me just say that stripped of whatever romanticism Hollywood has created, gang members represent an established subculture that defines the worst of Hispanic America.

I remember spending one long night with Arizona Maravilla, one of the oldest gang sets, whose East L.A. home turf included several houses on a hill commanding a sweeping view of the big city down and to the west. What is extraordinary is how ordinary the *cholos* (roughly but fondly translated as "lowlifes") see their violent world and *La Vida Loca* ("the crazy life"), where graffiti marks territory, drug dealing pays the bills, and fathers, grandfathers, and even great-grandfathers count themselves as alumni.

It was here before such notorious racist organizations as the Aryan Brotherhood took root or black gangs like the Crips and the Bloods even existed that the homeboys began the stylistic inner-city tradition of emblematic, often body-covering tattoos, secret hand signals, and territory-marking signing. It was here too that pants were first dropped over asses, bandannas over eyes, and the "snitch and die" rule invented.

And over the decades of my experience, the situation has only gotten worse as disorganized street gangs became more organized criminal enterprises. These days, membership in a semi-organized network like MS-13 numbers eight thousand to ten thousand according to the FBI, spread across thirty-three states and Central America. *Mara* (which in this context is said to mean army ant) *Salvatrucha* (slang for a native of El Salvador) began in East L.A. in the 1980s and consisted originally of mostly first-generation illegal migrants from that then war-torn Central American nation.

When targeted by the INS because of widespread criminal activity, the gang members deported back to El Salvador established loosely connected branches back home, recruiting new members, who eventually found their way to Los Angeles and more recently to cities across the United States.

MS-13's most notorious recent claim to infamy was the assassination of a pregnant seventeen-year-old, Brenda Paz, who was killed and whose body was dumped along the banks of the Shenandoah River in Virginia to prevent her testimony in federal court about MS-13's expanding criminal enterprises.

Comparing them to the Mob, here is how the FBI described MS-13's methods in July 2005:

> They've severed the fingers of their rivals with machetes . . . brutally murdered suspected informants, including a 17-year-old pregnant federal witness . . . attacked and threatened law enforcement officers . . . committed a string of rapes, assaults, break-ins, auto thefts, extortion, and frauds across the U.S. . . . gotten involved in everything from drug trafficking to prostitution and money laundering . . . and are sowing violence and discord not just here in the United States, but around the world.

In December 2004, the FBI launched a multiagency MS-13 National Gang Task Force, even reaching out to law enforcement in El Salvador, Honduras, and Guatemala. But despite the arrest of hundreds of members, the organization and others like it, including the long-established 18th Street Gang (which is probably the biggest of the bunch, dating back to the 1940s), and the deadly, prison-based Mexican Mafia, continue to thrive, helping tear communities apart, disrupting schools, spreading intimidation and fear while perpetrating a wide variety of crimes, including racketeering, murder, narcotics trafficking, and the new favorite, money laundering.

Making the situation even more egregious in Los Angeles is the fact that in recent years some Hispanic gang members have been engaged in a kind of ethnic cleansing directed at African-American residents of changing neighborhoods like Watts, Highland Park, South L.A., Harbor Gateway, and others where Hispanics are becoming the majority.

When in December 2006 members of the Hispanic 204th Street Gang intentionally murdered a black fourteen-year-old named Cheryl Green, the U.S. Attorney's office officially called it "ethnic cleansing." Mayor Villaraigosa cited a 14 percent increase in gang-related crime over the past year, even as the overall crime picture dramatically improved, and vowed that gang violence would be his number-one priority in 2007.

Of all aspects of modern Hispanic life in the United States, this area is the most frustrating, disappointing, and embarrassing. Over the years, usually after a widely publicized crime like poor Cheryl Green's murder, I have watched countless politicians vow to clean up the gang problem. President Bush even got in the act in his 2005 State of the Union speech when he announced the appointment of First Lady Laura Bush to head up a new $150 million program to curtail gang violence through faith-based initiatives and other community programs, saying,

> Now we need to focus on giving young people, especially young men in our cities, better options than apathy, or gangs, or jail. Tonight I propose a three-year initiative to help organizations keep young people out of gangs, and show young men an ideal of manhood that respects women and rejects

violence. [Applause.] Taking on gang life will be one part of a broader outreach to at-risk youth, which involves parents and pastors, coaches and community leaders, in programs ranging from literacy to sports.

As if.

I have walked up and down the mean streets of East L.A. with four generations of parents, priests, preachers, ministers, teachers, coaches, community leaders, reformed bad guys, and social workers who were all courageous, committed, earnest, eager, and ultimately unsuccessful in altering substantively a weird lifestyle that for all its bluster is ultimately a destructive and self-defeating combination of everything bad in Latino-American culture.

Not incidentally, no one in Los Angeles, including Bruce Riordan, the senior supervising attorney for Anti-Gang Activities, has seen any of the promised federal antigang money.

"I remember that speech," Riordan, who at the time was still in the U.S. Attorney's Anti-Gang office, told streetgangs.com reporter Annette Stark. "I was the gang coordinator for all Los Angeles, so I was excited to hear it. I never heard another word about it except when someone asks, 'What happened to that?' I know the program existed, I heard about it in the State of the Union and I never heard about it again." Other than the certainty that gangbangers make up just a tiny percentage of the Hispanic population—in the case of Los Angeles just thirty-nine thousand among a Latino population of 2 million—my only genuine comfort is the Kennedy School study cited above, showing that immigrants between eighteen and forty are one-third less likely to be in prison than the American population as a whole.

I would be lying if I told you I wasn't defensive, deflated, and discouraged by the enduring problem of Latino gangs. I also have no patience for those who extol the mythical virtues and supposed mystique of gang life in songs like WC's "The Streets" or films like *Boyz*

N the Hood, *Menace II Society*, or *Blood In Blood Out*. If you want a taste of what the life is really like, watch Edward James Olmos's *American Me*. It is a graphic and compelling look at the Mexican Mafia and its victims. And after making it, Eddie was on the receiving end of several death threats from associates of the prison-based killing mob offended by his spot-on portrayal of them and their criminal enterprise. Those who wax fondly on the virtues of today's gangsters remind me of the 1970s New York intellectuals who styled themselves hip fans of graffiti. Most of them lived nowhere near the scribbled scrawling nor understood the antisocial impact of gang graffiti's almost unfailingly disruptive and anarchistic message.

These gangsters are nothing like the Young Lords, the radical activist group based in New York that played so large a part in my own evolution in the 1960s, or even the original Black Panthers. The Panthers and the Lords were similarly defiant and even militant, but whatever they became under duress or changed circumstance, they stood first for something selfless: social equity for what used to be called the underprivileged.

Frustrated authorities have sometimes turned to desperate measures, determining that the only way to eliminate gangs is to eliminate the neighborhoods in which they fester, which has happened from central Brooklyn to Cabrini-Green in Chicago to the worst sections of East L.A. In 1971, I won my first Columbia-Dupont award for a searing portrayal of the gangbanging heroin addicts who had twisted East 100th Street between First and Second avenues into "the worst street in America." That piece was so powerful because it was the first time ever that junkies were shown full face on camera, shooting up, nodding out, puking, then going out to hustle and rob to get the dough they needed to feed their insatiable habits, destroying any chance of a normal life for the other residents of that hapless, horrible place. It shook people up, and politicians, too.

A few years after "Drug Crisis in East Harlem" aired, New York City condemned the entire block on 100th Street and knocked it down. Now it is another gentrified continuation of the Upper East Side of Manhattan. Chicago's Cabrini-Green suffered a similar fate. The housing project was an example of an irretrievable, physically run-down sinkhole of gang violence and inner-city despair for its twenty thousand residents. And knocking it down was the best option, as I determined after numerous visits to its gloomy towers, including one memorable attempt accompanied by football great Jim Brown to engage the worst of the gangbangers.

But these are extreme examples. Neighborhood demolition and resident dislocation is way too high a price to pay for the disruption of neighborhood gangster life. And many of the Los Angeles neighborhoods most affected by gang violence are outwardly suburban-looking and deceptively pleasant, some consisting of well-maintained single-family homes fronted by lawns and even palm trees. There are stores and restaurants with schoolchildren playing outside. Absent the overwhelming police presence that follows a specific act of violence, a kind of rough quiet prevails. Until a perceived trespass or slight, the only outward manifestation of the gang virus is that ominous graffiti. And given the multinational character and increased criminal competence of organizations like MS-13, the 18th Street Gang, and the Mexican Mafia, even the obliteration of the neighborhoods in which they thrive will not be a deterrent.

Although many civilians are cowed to silence, these criminal organizations get little sympathy from the Hispanic community. They should legitimately and lawfully be targeted as the Mafia was targeted, using racketeering statutes, lawsuits, heightened surveillance, and real, rather than symbolic, assistance from the feds. Instead of hunting down those hardworking, law-abiding textile workers in New Bedford or raiding the homes and workplaces of the meatpackers and meat processors in the Midwest, here is a tough, dangerous area of law enforcement where Homeland Security can help real cops bust outlaws and keep the peace. And perhaps help justify the department's so-far lackluster existence.

10

Do Hispanics and Other Immigrants Steal Our Jobs?

"Demand Illegal Aliens Be Deported. The Job You Save May Be Your Own"

—Billboard on the California-Arizona border, 2007

"The welfare queens are one of the most despicable varieties of immigrant because they come here and hang outside strip clubs so they can get knocked up. Once they squirt out a few dozen kids, Uncle Sam starts sending them checks to reward them for being sluts. Things are pretty easy when you have regular welfare checks and don't have to work. These immigrants have so much time on their hands that they literally spend their entire afternoons hiding in parking lots so they can steal some hardworking American's job."

—Center for Rational Debate, 2007

"Immigrants contribute mightily to the economy, by paying billions in annual taxes, by filling low-wage jobs that keep domestic industry competitive, and by spurring investment and job creation, revitalizing once-decaying communities. Many social scientists conclude that the newcomers, rather than drain government treasuries, contribute overall far more than they utilize in services."

—L.A. Times ANALYSIS, JANUARY 1992

Because so much of the suspicion and acrimony directed at America's burgeoning Hispanic population has to do with the perceived negative economic impact of illegal immigration, this question deserves closer inspection, although I suspect that like most Americans, you have already made up your mind on the issue.

By mid-2007, the scars left by the cutting congressional debate left the nation ideologically polarized. Most social conservatives (as opposed to the pro-business wing of the GOP) tend to agree with the substance of the quotes above about protecting jobs and migrant welfare "sluts" hanging outside strip clubs looking to get pregnant, while liberals would agree with the latter quote about migrants' "mighty contributions." On the assumption that facts still count, here is one no one can deny. Historically, there has been an inverse relationship between prosperity and resentment. Today's debate is profoundly different precisely because times are relatively good and yet anti-immigrant sentiment is so bitter and coarse. I pray that the fall 2007 downturn in the housing sector caused by the crisis in sub-prime mortgages doesn't lead America into a recession, because if history is any indicator, if you think the anti-immigrant sentiments are tough now, they are going to get really ugly.

Thankfully, the nation is still at near-full employment, which means the economy has absorbed the 12 million or more here illegally, while the citizen workforce remains almost fully employed. If you parked a bus in downtown L.A. or Chicago or Seattle or Dallas or Miami or New York, which carried a sign that read "Citizens Only—Come Get a Job Paying Minimum Wage for Child Care, Roofing, Factory Work, Dish Washing, or Grass Cutting," would any citizens get on board? How about those savory jobs slaughtering chickens or beef? It's never easy to cut off a cow's head, especially in the summer in Iowa.

And that's assuming those employers looking for citizen workers were also looking to pay the new federal minimum wage. If they were forced by the marketplace and immigration enforcement to pay more for those jobs, how much would they be worth? How much is a nanny or dishwasher or seamstress worth when virtually every citizen already has a job?—$50,000 a year, $60,000? How much would you be willing to pay for a watermelon or an avocado? Twenty bucks each? Thirty?

"When I went in 2007 to the immigration marches, I got outright hostility from blacks," Reverend Al Sharpton told me when I asked directly if blacks felt Hispanics were "stealing" their jobs. "Blacks would call my radio talk show saying, 'How could you be out there fighting for them? They're taking our jobs. How could you be out there demonstrating for them? I've been with you for years, you're wrong on this one.' It made me realize how we have been divided, by those that are adversarial to both, and how the media has played this wedge game. And we're falling for it in the African-American and Latino communities." Sharpton continued:

> I went to speak at the national conference of La Raza [the important Hispanic civil rights and advocacy organization] this year. And what I said to them was, "Why do crabs in a barrel pull each other down? Because they're all in a cornered place. If the crabs ever got together and lifted the lid off the barrel, there'd be enough room for all the crabs. Now, we're crawling on each other's backs." So, we are saying the immigrants are taking jobs that we never had. First of all black unemployment has been double to whites before anyone ever came here from Mexico or anywhere else. So, it's absurd.
>
> Second of all, the immigration battle, when you fight for archaic and draconian, reactionary immigration rules, that also covers Haiti and Jamaica and you're all brothers and sisters. So, are we being so blinded by people? Do you think they want to protect the borders to protect us? Protect us from whom? I mean the people that are trying to protect the borders from this great evil coming across the borders of Mexico are the same people that won't employ us. They won't give us health care and education. Funny they don't

want to build a fence from Canada. It's only one border they're concerned about. And we can't be that stupid. When you look at the data, it's really not competition for the same work. It is a false competitiveness.

Yet, despite the hollowness of the job-stealing argument, the formidable and intensely aggressive, grassroots, anti-immigration movement continues to gain in strength and virulence. And the tenor of the antireform attack agenda anticipates the coming sound and fury Republican politicians will unleash as their last, best chance to keep Democrats from taking back the White House in November 2008.

The Republican Revolt

Of all the nation's political leaders, President Bush has perhaps ironically been the most passionately in favor of immigration reform. He hasn't been afraid to take off the gloves and directly challenge his opponents. It is a stance that caused a bizarre confrontation with the people who had helped bring Bush the presidency. It ended with Rush Limbaugh and his "Dittoheads" threatening to withdraw their support for the president's Iraq war policy. The anti-Bush talk-radio–fueled Republican revolt followed a May 2007 speech in which the president seemed to question the patriotism of opponents to immigration reform.

"If you want to kill the bill," the president, speaking before an audience of cops at the Federal Law Enforcement Training Center, plunged right in, "if you don't want to do what's right for America, you can pick one little aspect out of it, you can use it to frighten people. Or you can show leadership and solve this problem once and for all, so the people who wear the uniform in this crowd can do the job we expect them to do."

"Don't want to do what's right for America"? Ouch.

Feeling smeared as unpatriotic by the embattled party leader they had stood behind despite plunging poll numbers and a bloody war, social conservatives from Limbaugh to Peggy Noonan essentially told the commander in chief to go scratch. He was rolled over along with the rest of the reformers by the anti-immigration freight train, which, most vociferously, consists of angry and/or worried, white, monolingual, non–passport-carrying Reagan Democrats, most at or near retirement age. I suspect that is the demographic also responsible for 90 percent of my ugly e-mails, bringing to mind Thomas Paine's elegant and compassionate remark on nativism: "We surmount the force of local prejudices as we enlarge our acquaintance with the world."

In fairness, it must be added that protectionist North Dakota Democratic senator Byron L. Dorgan, and several other old-line, reflexively pro-union Dems, also deserted their party in its time of need. Dorgan, the chairman of the Democratic Policy Committee, accelerated the unraveling of the fragile compromise the bill represented by inserting an amendment that after five years would have ended the guest worker program. The senator insisted without objective evidence that he was doing it because immigration was causing a decline in jobs and standard of living for American citizens. But the net effect was to dishearten Republican moderate supporters of the legislation and essentially doom it to failure. The author of a book called *Take This Job and Ship It: How Corporate Greed and Brain-Dead Politics Are Selling Out America*, Senator Dorgan, like many Republicans, is staunchly anti-globalization and apparently saw this issue in that context. Of course, Democrats might not have really wanted to bear the cross of passing immigration reform into the next national election cycle in the face of the bitter uprising against it; maybe they calculated secretly that it was better to let the legislation fail and blame that failure on the GOP.

One of the fierce organizations bombarding Congress with anti-immigration faxes during the 2007 debate was a group called

Numbers USA. The executive director, Roy Beck, at least conceded that illegals:

> Don't intend us harm. But they are wage thieves nonetheless. They break the law to steal jobs to which they are not entitled and in the process depress wages of millions of other American workers. They steal wages from American workers and steal taxes from the American taxpayers who must subsidize the social and physical infrastructure for these mostly low-wage workers.

Do immigrants really "steal" jobs, wages, and taxes? The opinion expressed by Mr. Beck is certainly widely held (again, like the myth of Saddam Hussein's involvement in the 9/11 attacks).

The 2006 General Social Survey published by the National Opinion Research Center found that 73 percent of Americans felt immigrants were likely to cause crime and 60 percent felt they were likely to cost native jobs. And that was taken before 2007's acrimonious debate turned really nasty.

Neither premise is true, but that didn't stop the creation of a sympathetic database. The most inflammatory rhetoric used in the not-so-great debate over job stealing came in April 2007 from the staunchly conservative, but not usually intellectually dishonest, Heritage Foundation. Authored by senior research fellow Robert Rector and widely promoted on cable news channels like my own, the report argued that low-skilled immigrant households cost American taxpayers $89 billion more each year than they pay in taxes.

Rector also claimed much more dramatically that it would take ". . . three hundred years of subsequent earnings to make up for the first and second generation" of immigrants. Three hundred years to pay off the public debt created by just two generations of immigrants? It makes a great sound bite, but how would he know?

Rector found an eager ear in dependable nativist Lou Dobbs,

telling him outrageously in June 2006 that "if you're bringing in high school dropouts who aren't married and have children out of wedlock, what are they going to do? They're going to be on welfare. It's going to cost at least seventy billion dollars a year!" Putting aside the fact that "welfare" programs have been famously curtailed since the first Clinton administration and that noncitizens in any case are not eligible (both points were omitted from Rector's report), let us assume for the moment they get public assistance in some form, food stamps, say, or Aid to Dependent (citizen) Children. In this case, how much would the tab be?

That dark prince among anti-immigration crusaders in the House, the Iowa Republican Steve King, says he knows. By "extrapolating" the various results, the man who absurdly accused illegal aliens of causing the deaths of twenty-five native-born a day also claimed preposterously on various sympathetic talk-radio programs that each low-skill immigrant household was going to cost the American taxpayer a million dollars!

Now that's what I call welfare. Where can I sign up?

Most nonaffiliated, nonpartisan economists disagree strongly with Rector's Heritage Foundation report. The Southern Poverty Law Center, which has led the charge on this issue, cites many economists as it continues its lonely fight for what is right and proper. One major survey on the net economic effects of immigration, published in 2006 in the *New York Times Magazine*, lists only one economist, George Borjas of Harvard, claiming a net negative economic effect of immigration. All the rest disputed Borjas, including U.C. Berkeley professor David Card, who told the magazine what I believe is at the real heart of this matter: "If Mexicans were taller and whiter it would probably be a lot easier for the public to accept the majority view of economists that the net effects of immigration, which is predominantly Latino, are positive."

Oh, if only they were taller and whiter! It is no accident that all the hateful, anti-immigrant cartoons portray some overweight, mustachioed clown of a Latino peasant, usually popping his buttons or pouring sweat as his pants get stuck jumping the fence. Or that the only image shown during discussions of the illegal alien situation are of wetbacks scurrying across the Rio Grande or through gaping holes in the border fence near Tijuana.

Why don't they ever show an illegal Irishman tending bar in Boston? Or a comely Northern European au pair who never goes home? Or the Asians gradually spreading through the digital economy on the high end or doing laundry or driving cabs on the low? Have the Minutemen checked out Chinatown recently? How about those Sicilian pizza places? Or the West African vendors selling fake Gucci bags on the streets of cities up and down the East Coast? How about the flood of folks from our new best friends from Eastern Europe and Russia? Mexican immigration is exceptional, but it is not an isolated phenomenon.

And what does immigration really cost the American taxpayer? In June 2007, the White House issued a report prepared by the President's Council of Economic Advisers (CEA) reviewing the best available economic research. The report concluded that foreign-born workers have accounted for half of the labor force growth in the past decade, fueling overall economic output, creating jobs, and increasing earnings for native-born workers by as much as $80 billion a year. Those lower-paid foreign workers have also contributed mightily to suppressing inflation. The CEA report also claims that immigrants and their children, those first and second generations Rector complained about so publicly, actually had a "modest positive influence" on government spending, contributing about $80,000 more per person in tax dollars over the long run than they claim in government benefits and services.

Without belaboring the point, and working again on the risky assumption that facts still count in this debate, "Dollars without Sense," a brief from the Immigration Policy Center (IPC) of the American Immigration Law Foundation, admittedly a pro-immigrant group, excoriates the Rector report's questionable accounting. "Children whose education is counted in the Heritage report as 'costs' attributable to their parents grow up to become taxpaying adults who often earn higher incomes than their parents," the IPC report says.

> Creative accounting aside, the simplistic "fiscal distribution analysis" on which the Heritage report is based does not come close to accurately gauging the impact of any group on the U.S. economy as a whole. . . . Nor does it account for the upward economic mobility that many low-income families experience from generation to generation, particularly immigrant families.

Immigrant families like mine. The Immigration Policy Center report also cites the tremendous growth and enormous contributions to the U.S. economy of Hispanic buying power and Hispanic-owned businesses. A walk through almost any town in the USA will provide evidence of Hispanic ambition and immigrant energy and vitality in businesses large and small. And despite the real problems in public schools from coast to coast, the Latino community is getting better educated. According to the IPC report:

> Far from being the fiscal freeloaders portrayed in the Rector [Heritage] report, second and third generation Hispanic men have made great strides in closing their economic gaps with native whites. The reason is simple: each successive generation has been able to close the schooling gap with native whites, which then has been translated into generational progress in incomes.

A 2003 RAND Corporation report adds that Hispanics are also becoming more competitive with the mainstream. "Each new

Latino generation not only has had higher incomes than their forefathers, but their economic status converged toward the white men with whom they competed."

"Mexican Americans and the American Dream," a 2006 report by the scholar Richard Alba, states, ". . . Each generation of Mexican-origin individuals born in the United States improved upon their parents' educational attainment by roughly 2.5 years worth of school." So the children of immigrants are becoming better educated than their parents, but what about the pesky job stealing?

A pre-9/11 U.S. Department of Labor study prepared in 2001 for the Bush administration called the perception those immigrants are stealing American jobs "the most persistent fallacy about immigration in popular thought."

Again, you see how that monumental terror attack destroyed what Bush was crafting as a faster track for immigration change. The president was busy, vigorously setting the country up for a big reform that would have been passed before the ink was dry, until the planes smashed into our buildings and the world changed.

But the facts haven't. A 2006 Pew Hispanic Center study, "Growth in the Foreign-Born Workforce and Employment of the Native Born," found no evidence that the large increases in immigration since 1990 have led to higher unemployment among American citizens.

The opposite is probably true. According to a recent study by my alma mater, the University of Arizona, cited by the American Immigration Law Foundation, if all undocumented workers were removed from Arizona's workforce, economic output would drop annually by at least $29 billion, or 8.2 percent. In Arizona alone, noncitizen immigrants are in high demand, adding $6.56 billion in construction output, $3.77 billion in manufacturing, $2.48 billion in service sectors, and $600.9 million in agriculture. Specifically addressing the concern that immigrants are taking jobs from our most vulnerable citizens, the Pew report added that there was "no apparent relationship between the growth of foreign workers with less education and the employment outcome of native workers with the same level of education."

But the bottom line is vividly clear. Look around. Able citizen workers are just not going to get on that "Jobs-R-Us" bus for immigrant kind of money. Would you? If you want to throw out all those millions of honest, otherwise law-abiding, hardworking undocumented immigrants, then you have to pay for it in more ways than money.

"The big message here is there is no job loss from immigration," the University of California economist Giovanni Peri, who extensively studied the employment situation in the Golden State, told the SPLC.

It is true that immigrant labor lowers the price of low-end jobs, principally in agriculture, construction, and domestic services. But enormous savings are also created. That strengthens the overall economy and creates more jobs than any that might be lost. Let's say that a contractor hires illegal immigrants to do his roofing, even as native-born workers do the higher-skilled, higher-paid jobs of plumbing and electrical work. The contractor is going to save money, so he can charge less; the home owner is going to save money, and they're both going to spend some of that saved money, which will create demand for more goods and services. That is the way free enterprise works.

Remember that America is getting older. As the relatively large baby boomer generation ages and our children have fewer children than we did, our country is also getting darker. Non-white immigration is certainly a big part of that browning process, but an equal role is played by relative birth rates among homegrown racial/ethnic groups. White people aren't having as many babies as they used to and Spanish people are taking up the slack. The average age of a white American is now about forty years. The dynamic Hispanic population now averages approximately twenty-seven years, and about one of every two people added to the nation's population last year was Hispanic. And you better root for their success because they are the people who will be supporting the elderly of the future with their Social Security payments.

And there has been demonstrable economic progress shown by the Hispanic population. According to the Census Bureau, poverty rates were statistically unchanged for whites, blacks, and Asians, but decreased to 20.6 percent from 21.8 percent among Latinos. The poverty rate among Hispanics is lower today than the poverty rate among blacks (24.3 percent). The per capita income also increased across the board. Whites were up by 1.8 percent, blacks by 2.7 percent, and Asians by 8 percent, while Hispanic incomes rose by 3.1 percent. (Don't Asian Americans kick butt? I want to bottle the essence of their drive and put it in our rice and beans.)

Still, too much of the Hispanic community remains impoverished, with one in five living below the federal poverty guidelines; about 33 percent have no health insurance, and our performance in the area of education continues to be relatively woeful. In my Puerto Rican community, just 63 percent have high school diplomas; for Mexicans it's worse at 49 percent, compared to 84 percent of whites and Asians and 74 percent of blacks graduating high school. "Puerto Ricans and other Hispanics are not taking advantage of the education resources available to them," the former congressman, borough president, and chairman of the board of trustees of the City University, Herman Badillo, told me. He continued:

In New York in the summer of 2007 public school chancellor Joel Klein reported that only 40 percent of Hispanic students were graduating high school within four years. That means 60 percent are not. This is a true tragedy. Puerto Ricans are in the fourth and fifth generations in the States, and we're acting like we're still in Puerto Rico. What we have to do is change the culture of our community. We have to make education a priority like the Asians. They're 4 percent of the population and they make up 20 percent of the student bodies at the Ivy League colleges and elite high schools. You go to a graduation at Bronx High School of Science and you look at the audience and the Asian parents are there. The mother may be dressed in shabby clothing that looks like she works in a Chinese laundry or the dad in a Chinese food restaurant, but their kids are becoming scientists and engineers. On the other hand, we've been on a five-hundred-year siesta in terms of education. Some Latin American nations don't even have mandatory public education much past sixth grade. Some, none at all. That's a self-defeating tradition we have to get rid of.

However harsh Badillo's assessment of Latino sentiments toward education may be, and as I said, many in the community chastise him for airing them publicly, there is no way to sugarcoat or discount the grim reality. Well into the twenty-first century we continue to be plagued by astronomical dropout rates and all the accompanying social ills: illegitimacy, drug use, gang violence, and so forth. There are obvious societal costs associated with these negative aspects of our community's lives, but it's impossible to determine exactly what percentage of the gross national product these costs represent, or even whether the costs were incurred by someone here legally or illegally, regardless of what the Heritage Foundation or any other ideologically motivated think tank might tell you.

Remember that while Hispanics are near the bottom of the socioeconomic ladder, we are climbing up just as previous immigrant groups have done. During the period between 1995 and 2005, according to a September 2007 Pew Hispanic Center report written by Rakesh Kochhar,

Many foreign-born Latinos stepped out of the low-wage workforce and headed toward the middle of the wage distribution. Some conservatives assert that the U.S. is importing impoverished immigrants from Mexico who are destined to remain that way. These fears are misplaced. The data show that over time Latinos can and do climb the economic ladder, much as previous immigrant groups have done. . . . We hate to spoil the morose political mood with such contrary optimism, but we have to follow the facts where they lead.

In December 2006, I received the Distinguished Media Entrepreneur and Lifetime Charter Member Award from the Minority Business Roundtable at a luncheon and congressional briefing in Washington, D.C. The keynote speaker was Carlos Gutierrez, the Cuban-born former chairman of the board of the Kellogg Company who since 2004 has been President Bush's secretary of commerce. I explained to the audience of businesspeople how I formed my own company, Maravilla Productions, early in my career and that most of my savings come from the twelve years I owned my talk show. Both the secretary and I extolled the virtue of working for yourself. I never have been and never will be Oprah, but following in the footsteps of Desi Arnaz, who in the 1950s founded Desilu Productions with Lucille Ball, it didn't take this *Boricua* too long in public life to understand the opportunities that are available within a free-enterprise system.

I was motivated by my dad's melancholy experience to try to achieve business and financial independence early in life. After working in the cafeteria concession of the defense plant for twenty years, he was fired when the concessionaire sold out to a national chain. The new owners said he was both too old and too highly paid to keep on board. My dad was both heartbroken and nearly broke. He lamented the cruel fate that allowed him to be set adrift after so many years of loyal service, and he ultimately did go bankrupt. I vowed never to allow anyone to have that kind of control over me, and started my own business as soon as I was able. And I'm not alone. There are about seventy-eight thousand Hispanic chief executives in the United States. True, many of them are owners of bodegas (those one-stop shopping, grocery, department, hardware, quickie loan stores located mostly in the barrios), taco stands, or Laundromats, but among them are many professionals and some captains of industry.

As my friend Tony Bonilla of Texas says, there is not nearly enough Hispanic representation on the boards of Fortune 500 companies, but we are moving up. And even among those still struggling—and there are too many for sure—the public costs associated specifically with undocumented immigrants are grossly overstated. They are not the ones draining government entitlement programs, as the Heritage report alleges. The simple fact is they are ineligible for public benefits like welfare. In fact, the reverse is probably true. Instead of draining public programs, those here illegally are subsidizing the rest of us, paying into programs with no hope of being paid back.

"Illegal immigrants are pumping the Social Security system with as much as $7 billion a year and contributing to Medicare in payroll taxes, yet they are unable to collect on the benefits," according to the *New York Times*. The *Times* makes the obvious point that a person working with a false Social Security number or paying taxes because they or their bosses don't want to be guilty of tax evasion is never going to get a tax refund or redeem their old-age benefits. The *Times* reports:

> Starting in the late 1980s, the Social Security Administration received a flood of W-2 earnings reports with fake Social Security numbers. It stashed them in what it calls the "earnings suspense file" in the hope that someday it would figure out whom they belonged to. $189 billion worth of wages ended up recorded in the suspense file over the 1990s.

The Immigration Policy Center puts it this way: "Unlike most Americans, who will receive some form of a public pension in retirement and will be eligible for Medicare as soon as they turn sixty-five, illegal immigrants are not entitled to benefits."

There are obviously public costs associated with illegal immigrants, principally in emergency medical care and public education. In New York and several other states, there is a fight going on right now with the federal government over whether chemotherapy is "emergency" medical care. If it is not, then the states will not receive federal reimbursement for treating illegal immigrants for cancer. New York has said it will treat them nevertheless; other states are not as compassionate. But let me throw a few more comforting statistics at you. Among Hispanic Americans, there are forty-nine thousand physicians and surgeons, fifty-eight thousand postsecondary teachers, and thirty-three hundred news analysts, reporters, and news correspondents, including this one.

I talked with New York senator Chuck Schumer at another sidewalk interview during the 2007 Puerto Rican Day Parade. "New York needs immigrants," he told me. "We all have to look at this thing and make proper arrangements. We can't have families torn apart. And we can't kid ourselves into thinking the twelve to twenty million people are going to be moved out of the country. So let's get realistic. Let's live with reality. Maybe we've made mistakes. I think we have. But it's time to pick up the pieces."

As I have tried to demonstrate in this chapter, the nonpartisan, nonideological, scientific data proves that immigrants contribute greatly to the American economy. They are a net positive without whom future economic progress could be compromised. Senator Schumer put it to me very succinctly that day at the parade: "America needs immigrants."

II

Saint Cesar and the Immigrants

"Cesar Chávez, Minuteman: The UFW leader was no friend to illegal immigration—until he became an ethnic figure-head."

— *The American Conservative*, FEBRUARY 2006

"Viva la causa. Sí, se puede." ("Long live the cause. Yes, it can be done.")

—CESAR CHÁVEZ

Had he lived, the farmworker, labor leader, and civil rights activ-ist Cesar Chávez would have turned eighty on March 31, 2007, just in time to watch immigration reform go down to defeat. Though he died in 1993, Chávez, an undisputed hero to millions, especially His-panic Americans, was still caught up in the debate on the fourteenth anniversary of his death. A proposed Senate resolution to honor the great man's birthday was shot down because of the insistence by Ken-tucky Republican Mitch McConnell that to be approved, it had to mention that Chávez was opposed to illegal immigration. The Demo-crats refused to accept the condition and his eightieth birthday went unnoted in official Washington. But could it be true? Did Saint Cesar oppose illegal immigration? Let me explain.

At the beginning of the twentieth century and including the period around the First World War, Japanese and Chinese laborers were specifically prohibited by the "exclusion acts" from entering the country. At the same time, Mexican nationals were informally invited to work our dynamic nation's expanding network of farms and the railroads that serviced them. Then came the Great Depression and the first great bait and switch. Driven by the cyclical fear of job stealing and severely aggravated by the worst economic conditions in the nation's modern history, the federal government, acting with broad support and flush with the belief they were evicting an inferior, resource-grubbing people, began the mass deportation of Mexicans from the country. The "Mexican Repatriation" in the 1930s was a historical embarrassment that scars our nation's history. Authorized by President Herbert Hoover, at least 500,000 Mexicans and Mexican Americans—60 percent of them children—were forced across the border during those hard times.

Contemporary accounts graphically describe how even American citizens of Mexican descent "repatriated" voluntarily in those awful years between 1931 and 1934, rather than face the raw animosity on the Anglo side of the border. Others were conned into leaving by social workers who spoke of the better life back in old Mexico, where conditions were actually so bad that in one reported instance, twenty recently repatriated souls living in an open corral died of exposure and disease.

As egregious as the later internment of Japanese Americans during World War II, this episode has likewise commanded latter-day regrets. In 2005, the state of California passed the Apology Act, recognizing the "unconstitutional removal and coerced emigration of United States citizens and legal residents of Mexican descent," and apologizing "for the fundamental violations of their basic civil liberties and constitutional rights."

World War II changed everything again for Hispanic immigrants. American industry and agriculture were humming and there was an insatiable need for able-bodied workers to do the jobs of GIs drafted to fight in the global struggle against fascism. In 1942, the first formal *"Bracero"* program invited hundreds of thousands of Mexicans across the Rio Grande to work in the factories and on the farms of the country. (*Bracero* is a Spanish word for an unskilled worker.)

When the war ended and GIs began coming home, pressure mounted again to get the Mexicans out. The same hands that had proven so vital during the war were now just stealing jobs from Americans. Citing a *New York Times* report that exposed the fact that 1 million unauthorized immigrants were crossing the border annually, in 1954, President Dwight D. Eisenhower mounted Operation Wetback, mobilizing the Border Patrol, which conducted broad sweeps of Hispanic neighborhoods, including random stops and identity checks of "Mexican-looking" people, ultimately evicting between 500,000 and 700,000, many of them citizen children, some carried away by refugee ships as far south as Veracruz, the major port southeast of Mexico City, to prevent their sneaking back into the States. It was only when cries of police brutality and racism swelled from Hispanic leaders discovering their civic voices that the aggressive effort was finally dulled.

The *Bracero* program officially ended in 1964, ironically after it came under pressure from the same groups that today are the most pro-immigration. U.S. labor unions, including the AFL–CIO, the Kennedy and later Johnson administration, and Democratic leadership in Congress all worked hard to close the guest worker program down and bring deportations up.

But even as immigration officials swept back that tide of workers, what they could never stop was the demand for cheap labor. In the *Bracero* years, relationships were established between employer and employee. With an annual official ceiling on all Western Hemisphere visas during the period set at an impossibly low 120,000, an unwritten, underground protocol replaced the structured program, an acknowledgment that "if you get here, I'll put you and yours to work." Driven by the continuing need for hands throughout the 1960s, businesses like the American Farm Bureau Federation and the National Beet Growers, and ranchers exerted enormous

Saint Cesar and the Immigrants

pressure on all levels of government to go easy on the "wetbacks" and offer just token border enforcement.

Then came the intersection of Cesar Chávez and illegal immigration. Hailed as the Latino community's most important labor and civil rights leader in the mold of Reverend Martin Luther King Jr., Chávez has been widely and rightfully honored with parks, schools, libraries, scholarships, and streets now bearing his name for the epic role he played on behalf of exploited U.S. farmworkers, and, by extension, downtrodden people everywhere. Raised in a dirt-poor adobe home near Yuma, Arizona, he went to work in the fields, dropping out of school after the eighth grade so he could help support his mother. After service in the U.S. Navy during World War II, inspired by Gandhi's philosophy of nonviolence, Chávez was drawn to community service, voter registration, and workers' rights. In 1962, Chávez and the dauntless Dolores Huerta cofounded what became the United Farm Workers of America (UFW) union, leading a strike by California grape pickers, and at Easter 1966 marching the 250 miles from their headquarters in Delano to Sacramento, demanding recognition.

Forty years later, I still remember meeting Dolores, who had come to New York in 1968–69 to organize the historic grape boycott this incredible duo had conceived to pressure growers into paying workers a living wage. She is a woman of amazing strength, resilience, and character, and a wonderful role model for generations of young women, including today's. In many ways, she seemed the practical navigator of the UFW, complementing Cesar's more philosophical, inspirational leadership. I was a newly minted activist lawyer swelling with ethnic pride and the desire to do something meaningful. Her message of worker oppression and the need to fight back resonated so deeply I still feel an aversion to table grapes. No matter what else you did in your life in this period, you boycotted grapes.

I met and interviewed the great man himself several times over

173

the years as he forged his coalition of unions, churches, students, and minorities, and even, ultimately, the consumers. The first time was when the new dean of the Episcopal Cathedral of St. John the Divine, the Very Reverend James P. Morton, and his boss, the new bishop of New York, the Right Reverend Paul Moore (both wonderful men and social activists), hosted Chávez and Coretta Scott King in February 1973. In those days the huge cathedral, which stands proudly between Columbia University and the then almost entirely Puerto Rican Upper West Side, was the center of the activist, pro–civil rights, anti–Vietnam War, anti–President Nixon universe.

So many years later, it is hard to precisely distill my fresh feelings at that moment from all the encounters in between. But let me attempt to describe the awesome impression of him that I will always carry, of a man so humble and deeply spiritual, hardened by struggle, frail and weakened by his frequent hunger strikes. There was no swagger, no bravado. But he radiated power. Chávez seemed to be, literally, a saint. As a Latino, I was profoundly proud of him, totally committed to his cause, and worried that a crazy person would kill him the way they killed Martin Luther King and Bobby Kennedy, each of whom also loved him.

So how did this heroically compassionate person become an anti-immigration activist? And what is the relevance of his stance to today's debate? First the facts. Even before the five-year grape boycott, 1965–1970 (iceberg lettuce came later), Cesar and Dolores opposed the *Bracero* program, believing that it undermined domestic workers by putting them at a disadvantage to Mexican nationals who would cross the border to work for less.

In 1968, Chávez enlisted the support of Senator Robert F. Kennedy, who once called him "one of the heroic figures of our time." Cesar urged the former attorney general and, in those months before his assassination in Los Angeles, presidential candidate, to pressure federal officials "to remove Wetbacks who are being recruited to break our strike." Kennedy's death stunned Chávez, but did not stop his mobilization of Senate liberals, whose anti-immigrant sentiments only continued to harden during the emotionally and physically draining times.

As anti-immigration activists are quick to point out, Chávez in 1969 did lead a march through the agricultural heartland of California, the Coachella and Imperial Valleys, to the Mexican border to protest the use of illegal aliens as strikebreakers. Accompanying him for part of that march was the successor to Reverend King, the Reverend Ralph Abernathy, and senator and later vice president Walter Mondale, who took up the flag of the farmworkers in the congressional assault on illegal immigration. At Senate hearings, Mondale warned that if the federal government did not "stop the hemorrhaging along the Texas border and along the California border," it would be impossible to protect domestic agricultural workers from abuse and substandard pay.

Part King, part Gandhi, Cesar Chávez was also a tough labor leader following the playbook established by other foundational movement leaders before him, men like John Lewis of the United Mine Workers and Walter Reuther of the United Auto Workers. He knew that his union had no chance of taking root as long as growers had an unlimited supply of, dare I say it, "scab" workers to replace his labor for less.

Driven by pro-union liberals, the government worked overtime to rid the market of the illegal workers. In the decade between 1961 and 1970, a total of 1,608,356 unauthorized migrants had been arrested and deported, according to the INS Statistical Yearbook, an average of 161,000 a year. But between 1971 and 1980, the number of deportees exploded to 11,883,328, more than seven times as many as the previous decade. To give you an idea of how vast that number is, in 1980 there were only about 36 million people between the ages of fifteen and sixty-four in the entire nation of Mexico. While many of those deported returned to the United States only to be deported again, the number of illegal immigrants into the

United States, as a proportion of the entire working population of Mexico, was gigantic.

As the suppression of illegal immigration gathered momentum, Chávez broadened his union's reach, declaring a strike and calling for a boycott of iceberg lettuce. "Greetings, fellow lettuce boycotters!" Senator Ted Kennedy exclaimed, opening his speech to the Democratic National Convention in September 1972. But this effort never enjoyed the success of the original grape campaign. It ultimately foundered in a sea of court battles, confusion over what type of lettuce was acceptable and which was not, confrontations with other unions, like the Teamsters, and legislation in states like Arizona, Kansas, and Idaho, among others, that prohibited boycotts, required farm-union elections before strikes could be called, and restricted strikes during harvest season.

On July 27, 1973, Cesar Chávez was my first guest on my first-ever national television show, *Good Night America,* on the ABC network. I just screened that ancient tape and once again I was deeply moved by that noble man who worked for subsistence pay of no more than $5,000 a year. Even then, it was clear that in some ways the best days of the struggle were over. After the UFW's initial success in winning contracts for the farmworkers, the circumstances by then had become dire. The historic three-year deals the union made with the California grape growers had expired in April 1973, and the Teamsters had made an end run around them, negotiating what Chávez called "sweetheart" deals with the growers, shutting out the UFW. By the time he appeared on my debut show, widespread and sometimes violent confrontations had broken out between members of the UFW and men Cesar called "paid goons." He said:

> The Teamsters have imported paid goons to beat our people up. They couldn't discourage us in any other way. So in order to try and get us to abandon our work of social change, social

justice, the picket lines and the boycotts, they imported men who are experts at beating people up.

"We're in a very difficult position. One hundred eighty-two contracts have been taken away from us and given to the Teamsters. It's an awful thing," he told me that night, his voice tinged with melancholy, "that we cannot use this valuable time to bring our movement to the fields of Florida, the Carolinas, and Texas. But if it means we have to do it all over again, we'll do it again. We'll do whatever it takes, as long as it is moral, legal, and nonviolent."

The very success of the UFW's ongoing iceberg lettuce boycott also turned problematic. With polls showing an estimated 17 million Americans honoring the boycott, demand dropped precipitously. Concentrated in California's Salinas Valley, growers reported shipping only 300,000 cartons a day, instead of the usual 400,000. But consumers who liked lettuce in their salads and sandwiches had a difficult time finding UFW-sanctioned lettuce, rather than lettuce harvested under the auspices of the Teamsters or no union at all. Despairing of political correctness, many just gave up on lettuce completely until the boycott ran out of steam. This was a period, coinciding with the end of the Vietnam War and the resignation of President Nixon, in which activist passions in the country as a whole were somewhat dulled.

After countless court battles and union-to-union confrontations, and under pressure from growers to end the renewed grape, lettuce, and Gallo wine boycotts, in 1975 the activist governor Jerry Brown guided California into enacting the Agricultural Labor Relations Act. The law gave farmworkers the right to organize and hold free union elections, and required employers to bargain with the union representative elected by the workers. As a result elections were held throughout the Golden State, by far the nation's most important supplier of fresh fruit and produce.

By then, the business of agriculture itself had changed, becoming more centralized and corporate, making unionization easier than it had been in the earlier era of the family farm. Now, management was a well-organized business, which could factor decent wages and benefits into the cost of its product. As a result, at its peak, tens of thousands of farmworkers were gathering under the UFW's black eagle banner, and in so doing receiving higher pay, family health coverage, pensions, and other benefits. But what about the illegal workers? In 1979, Cesar was still bitter about the cynical use of undocumented workers by certain farm owners bent on disrupting and undermining his union. He said so before Congress:

> When the farmworkers strike and their strike is successful, the employers go to Mexico and have unlimited, unrestricted use of illegal alien strikebreakers to break the strike. And, for over thirty years, the Immigration and Naturalization Service has looked the other way and assisted in the strikebreaking. I do not remember one single instance in thirty years where the Immigration Service has removed strikebreakers. The employers use professional smugglers to recruit and transport human contraband across the Mexican border for the specific act of strikebreaking.

The UFW continued to oppose illegal immigration and temporary guest worker programs through the early 1980s, claiming they represented an obstacle to unionization. The union even supported the use of employer sanctions to reduce competition for jobs. That philosophy began changing only during the Reagan years, when the union evolved and fell in line with the more progressive, pro–civil rights agendas of organizations like the National Council of *La Raza* and MALDEF, the Mexican American Legal Defense and Education Fund, opposing employer sanctions on the grounds that they exacerbated discrimination against all Hispanic workers. Unlike most of the rest of the AFL-CIO, the union also backed President Bill Clinton's NAFTA treaty with Canada and Mexico, developed an innovative cooperative health insurance program in cooperation with the Mexican government, and campaigned aggressively against the use of toxic pesticides that were adversely affecting the health of all agricultural workers.

In one of his last grand gestures, in 1988 the sixty-one-year-old Chávez, his frail body badly weakened by decades of tireless activism and self-inflicted abstinence, used another hunger strike, the thirty-six-day "Fast for Life," to protest the harmful effects of pesticides on farmworkers and their children. I visited with him then, at the modest headquarters of the UFW in La Paz, California, outside Bakersfield. Surviving just on water, he insisted that the two of us play handball. He loved handball. He was good at it and the new focus of workplace health had reenergized the prematurely aged crusader. It was a trip, both of us stripped to the waist, sweating in the late-afternoon California sun. I was thinking, *Here I am playing handball with Cesar Chávez!* Chávez was a living icon. But his playful nature during the game didn't fool me; it was clear that the fight against indiscriminate pesticide use had become his passion. He wrote at the time:

> During the past few years I have been studying the plague of pesticides on our land and our food. The evil is far greater than even I had thought it to be, it threatens to choke out the life of our people and also the life system that supports us all. The solution to this deadly crisis will not be found in the arrogance of the powerful, but in solidarity with the weak and helpless. I pray to God that this fast will be a preparation for a multitude of simple deeds for justice. Carried out by men and women whose hearts are focused on the suffering of the poor and who yearn, with us, for a better world. Together, all things are possible.

It was recognized that Chávez's opposition to illegal immigration was a product of the times and part of a process to do the most good for the most people. In this spirit, in 1991 the Republic of Mexico awarded Chávez the Aztec Eagle (*Aquila Azteca*), its highest civilian award to people of Mexican heritage who have made major social contributions outside Mexico. The next year, shortly before Christmas, I interviewed him for the last time for an episode of my old daytime show called "Deadly Poison." On the show he debated a guy named Warren Stickle, the president of the Chemical Producers and Distributors Association, and lamented the fact that there had been "almost no movement at all" in the regulation of pesticides.

Chávez made a push for organic farming, and called for a third boycott of table grapes, concluding that most pesticides should be banned as they had been in Germany and Scandinavia, saying, "It's been banned in a number of places. It should have never been used here, and it should be banned." The audience applauded.

Four months later, on April 23, 1993, Cesar Chávez died in his sleep near Yuma, Arizona, not far from the small family farm in the Gila River Valley where he was born. Chávez was buried back at the UFW's La Paz headquarters in a rose garden at the foot of a hill he had often climbed to watch the sunrise. More than forty thousand people attended his funeral. He was sixty-six years old.

The following year, he was posthumously awarded the Presidential Medal of Freedom by President Clinton, the highest civilian honor in the United States. In 2003, Chávez was additionally honored with a new U.S. postage stamp, commemorating "a common man with an uncommon vision" of nonviolent social change and service to others. The postmaster general, John Potter, issued a statement describing him as someone who "understood the hardships of working people and fought hard to bring justice and quality of life for them and their families." His son Paul said at the time, "His example and values continue to resonate with people of goodwill, just as they did during the forty-odd years that he marched, fasted, and stood with the less fortunate."

It is a sad irony that Cesar's stance on illegal immigrants during the 1960s, viewed through the lens of today's bitter debate, has allowed organizations like the Minutemen to use his memory to support their own reactionary agenda. He has been further marginalized by contemporary accounts that describe his union and its more recent history in less than flattering terms. Having known and admired him, I understand the context of the obvious contradictions, and still believe Chávez was a great man who sacrificed his health to help others. He died broke and, perhaps, bitter. The attacks on his noble soul remind me of the similar revisionist assaults on the memory of Martin Luther King Jr. And as with Dr. King, history will look past the wrinkles in Cesar's life and see the quality of man he was.

Unions to the Rescue

Most of American organized labor finally changed its institutional attitude toward illegal immigrants seven years after Cesar's passing. At that time union officials in California, including those of the UFW, urged the movement to help protect illegal workers facing low wages and lives of misery because of the way immigration rules enable unscrupulous employers to exploit them. In February 2000, at their annual meeting in New Orleans, the executive council of the AFL-CIO adopted a call for blanket amnesty for all illegal aliens in the country, contending that federal immigration policy too often enabled employers to exploit undocumented workers.

"The present system doesn't work and is used as a weapon against workers," John Wilhelm, the chairman of the federation's Committee on Immigration Policy and president of the Hotel Employees and Restaurant Employees Union, told the Associated Press. "The only reason a lot of employers want to hire a large number of illegal aliens is so they can exploit them."

"I think the AFL-CIO's decision is going to be a shot heard 'round Washington," Frank Sharry, the executive director of the National Immigration Forum, an immigrants' advocacy group, told the AP. "You have a variety of employer groups saying, 'We need more immigrant workers and we want our workers to be legal.' And you have the AFL-CIO saying, 'We want more immigrant workers to be legal and we're willing to talk to employers about their legitimate needs.' You have the makings of a business-labor compact that could draw new immigration policies for the next decade."

In 2005, the AFL-CIO helped establish what the nation's largest labor organization called the Change to Win, a coalition of unions representing about 15 million public and private workers, or about 12.7 percent of the total U.S. labor force. One of the group's primary platforms was the mutually beneficial objective of bringing undocumented workers into the union fold. "There is no good reason why any immigrant who comes to this country prepared to work, to pay taxes, and to abide by our laws and rules should be denied what has been offered to immigrants throughout our country's history—a path to legal citizenship," Ana Avendano, assistant general counsel for the AFL-CIO, which represents fifty-three unions nationwide, told the AP.

John Keely, a spokesman for the anti-immigration Center for Immigration Studies, responded to the Associated Press reporter that it was "a cynical and desperate plea to get new customers." When Keely said, "It's the ultimate reversal of policy," he was right. This move would have been unthinkable in the past. But as union membership has plummeted, union attitudes toward immigrants have shifted dramatically. They need new members and the biggest pool of new workers is immigrants, without regard to status. In 2004, private-sector unions represented just 7.9 percent of the private workforce. At their peak in 1955, they represented 33.2 percent, according to federal statistics. Whether the shift in attitude toward immigrants is "cynical" or "desperate," it is certainly the "ultimate reversal of policy." The shift is real, and now the nation's largest coalition of unions, which includes Cesar Chávez's UFW, backs amnesty for all undocumented workers.

The sea change in union attitudes became clear in December 2006 when more than a thousand federal agents swarmed Swift & Company meatpacking plants in six states, arresting 1,282 illegal aliens. The United Food & Commercial Workers Union, which represents most of the employees at five of the six plants, responded immediately with outrage. "Essentially, the agents stormed the plants, many of them in riot gear, in an effort designed to terrorize the workforce," said UFCW food division director Mark Lauritsen in a prepared statement.

The union that filed five separate federal lawsuits to prevent the ICE from deporting the arrested workers is largely made up of those undocumented workers; its fate is inextricably linked to theirs. In a statement announcing its September 2007 convention in Chicago, Change to Win made clear its opposition to the federal crackdown that followed the defeat of immigration reform in the Senate. The union decried the kinds of raids we described in the chapter on the war on terror, saying in its release:

> In the aftermath of the failure of comprehensive immigration reform, the Bush administration has launched a harsh, enforcement-only policy that seems more focused on terrorizing immigrant workers than sorting out who's undocumented and who isn't. Immigration and Customs Enforcement (ICE) agents are using military-style tactics in raids across the country—donning combat boots, full riot gear and automatic weapons—and the workplace is their front line.

Cesar Chávez would have been proud.

12

Anchor Babies

"All persons born or naturalized in the United States, and subject to the jurisdiction thereof, are citizens of the United States
and of the State wherein they reside."

—Fourteenth Amendment of
the United States Constitution,
Section One (ratified July 28, 1868)

"It was never meant to actually allow people who are here illegally to achieve legal status for their children by having them
born here."

—Tom Tancredo, Colorado Republican
congressman and candidate for the 2008
Republican presidential nomination

"They come to stay and they stay to multiply."

—Edward Abbey, *One Life at a Time, Please*

In the emotional anti-immigration debate, nothing stirs our xenophobic ire like the citizenship clause: section one, sentence one of the
Fourteenth Amendment as quoted above. It is a counterintuitive quirk
in America's charter that riles protectionists and infuriates neo–Know-
Nothings. Ratified in the wake of the Civil War to ensure that the
children of former slaves would have full and unalienable citizenship,
the sentence has consistently been construed to mean that practically
any child born within the United States is a citizen of the United
States, regardless of the citizenship or legal status of his or her parents.

Kids born to illegal immigrants are often described as "anchor babies" because they supposedly convey some advantage to their parents' quest for citizenship. In other words, it allows them to drop anchor in this country. But it's not true that an anchor baby who is a citizen guarantees that Mom and Dad will also have citizenship bestowed. Once the infant grows up and turns twenty-one, he or she can petition for the family to start the citizenship process. But anchor babies are not a guarantee of family members following in their footsteps, nor does their status entitle their parents to benefits, like health care.

The law wasn't always even this generous. When the Fourteenth Amendment was passed, Native-American children were deemed to be citizens only of their respective, sovereign tribes (although off the reservation they should have been granted the same rights awarded the child born of every other "visitor"). In any case, all aboriginal people, including Eskimos, were specifically granted American citizenship in the Indian Citizenship Act of 1924. By the twenty-first century, the lone remaining exceptions to birthright citizenship are children born to foreign diplomats assigned here and children born to enemy soldiers occupying our territory during war, which is a purely theoretical distinction because I don't think it has ever happened.

Most anti-immigration activists argue that this interpretation of the amendment is overly generous and destructively broad. They contend that the Supreme Court has never definitively stated that a child born to a parent here illegally was "subject to the jurisdiction" of the United States, as the citizenship clause requires.

That is incorrect.

In several cases spanning a hundred years, most recently *Plyler v. Doe* (1982), in which a Texas law denying funding for education of the children of illegal immigrants was declared unconstitutional, the Court has addressed the issue. In *Plyler* it said specifically, "No plausible distinction with respect to Fourteenth Amendment 'jurisdiction' can be drawn between resident aliens whose entry into the United States was lawful, and resident aliens whose entry was unlawful."

The obvious problem, legal and logical, with claiming illegal aliens are not subject to the jurisdiction of the United States is that they would be immune to all criminal and civil prosecutions and would not be subject to any of our laws.

By hook or by crook, anti-immigration advocates work to deny rights that are ingrained in our Constitution. The late Madeleine Cosman, the "medical" lawyer whose bogus research allowed Lou Dobbs to claim falsely that leprosy was on the rise because of illegal aliens, harshly made a case in the *Journal of American Physicians and Surgeons*, in spring 2005:

> Rescind the citizenship of anchor babies. We must overturn the misinterpretation of the Fourteenth Amendment to the U.S. Constitution. . . . We must be vigilant against congressmen voting to extend the list of those born here to include illegal aliens or other lawbreakers, conferring American citizenship and its generous social and medical benefits on babies born to criminals. It is irrelevant that some lawbreakers are hard-working women willing to do hard jobs for low pay, or that they are wives, daughters, cousins, lovers, or concubines of men willing to do America's hard work. Gravid wombs should not guarantee free medical care and instant infant citizenship in America.

Gravid wombs? There is not a law student in this country that favors law over ideology who believes Ms. Cosman's potboiling rant would stand up in any federal court in the land. Unless the Supreme Court decides to unravel over a century of precedent (which is unlikely, even given the ideological makeup of the current court), attempts by Congress to legislate a narrower definition of citizenship are inherently doomed. Bills like H.R. 1940, introduced in April 2007 by Nathan Deal, Republican of Georgia, are patently unconstitutional. Congress cannot pass a law altering the Constitution. No law passed by a simple majority vote of Congress can change the founding document. The architects of our democracy, aware of the power momentary passions have on elected officials, insured that changing the original contract with America would be difficult. Amendments to the Constitution cannot even be proposed other than by two-thirds votes in each house of Congress or by two-thirds of the state legislatures. Then, any amendment must be ratified by three-quarters of the states. If there is any doubt how hard it is to get an amendment passed, just think back to the failed Equal Rights Amendment that was going to eliminate discrimination based on gender.

The established law is clear. Whether a child is born to an immigrant who is here illegally or to someone here on a work, student, tourist, or other visa, or if someone somehow stumbles onto American soil or falls to the earth here and spurts out a baby, then that child is an American citizen. You may not like it, but absent a constitutional amendment proposed by two-thirds of the Congress or the states and ratified by three-quarters of the states, it is going to stay that way. In America birthright confers citizenship, period.

The United States and some of our neighbors in Latin America are almost alone in granting birthright citizenship (it doesn't exist in Europe, Asia, or the Middle East). There are several important issues contributing to the animus directed at the citizenship clause besides the fact that so few nations confer this right.

First, there is the reasonable distaste over the fact that women are coming to the United States specifically to have their children born here. But let's be real—rich or poor, who wouldn't want their baby to be an American citizen? Is there a better passport to hold than the one that bestows so many potential benefits from the world's most generous and caring government? There may be passports that open up more of the world, given the realities of twenty-first-century politics, but none offer unfettered access to the home of the free and the land of the brave.

Then there is the question of numbers. Conservative commentators often use the statistic that between 200,000 and 300,000 babies a year are born here to noncitizens, some of whom are here illegally. The U.S. Census Bureau estimates the population of the nation increased by 2,891,423 between July 2005 and July 2006. Of that total, immigration accounted for 1,204,167, or 42 percent, of the total. The problem is determining how many of this number were legal or illegal, adults or anchor babies. Clearly, the number of babies is not inconsequential.

Because no government agency keeps track of anchor births, the estimates on the total number taking place each year tend to be inflated or understated depending on which side of the argument is presenting the statistic. Needless to say, this makes the stats unreliable. The *Los Angeles Times*, which is smack in the middle of the immigration cauldron, has struggled to provide reliable statistics, usually saying that "as many as seventy thousand illegal immigrants a year use state-funded prenatal services" in Los Angeles County, and that "two-thirds of all births in the county are to foreign-born mothers." But then the paper falters, finding it difficult to determine what percentage of those foreign moms giving birth in L.A. are there illegally, because the question is neither asked by hospitals nor by most local officials.

The late Madeleine Cosman, Lou Dobbs's favorite medical lawyer, was willing to quote a number:

> American hospitals welcome "anchor babies." Illegal alien women come to the hospital in labor and drop their little anchors, each of whom pulls its illegal alien mother, father, siblings into permanent residency simply by being born within our borders. Anchor babies are citizens and instantly qualify for public welfare aid. Between 300,000 and 350,000 anchor babies annually become citizens because of the Fourteenth Amendment to the U.S. Constitution.

Aside from the demonstrated falsity of Ms. Cosman's contention that birthright kids automatically make citizens of their parents, while tens of thousands of immigrant babies are being born in the United States each year, they are not all born to the stereotypical pregnant Mexican migrant who came stealing across the desert with her belly full to throw down her anchor.

In the *Denver Post*, Craig Nelsen, the director of Friends of Immigration Law Enforcement, is quoted as claiming the existence of a "huge and growing industry in Asia that arranges tourist visas for pregnant women so they can fly to the United States and give birth to an American baby." This has long been a favorite trick of some members of the jet set and other high-end immigrant or visiting mothers who are obviously able and eager to provide for their own medical expenses once they get here. A pair of well-to-do newlyweds I know, he a naturalized citizen from Pakistan, she a citizen of Belgium, stayed in a ritzy Las Vegas hotel during the late stages of her recent pregnancy, giving birth to their healthy American baby in a private hospital room with a view of the Strip. Soon after the citizen baby was born, the happy family returned to their seaside villa in Monaco. Who needs the hassle of citizenship ambiguity for your children?

Still, many illegal parents do use public taxpayer-supported emergency medical facilities. Moreover, thanks to *Plyler v. Doe*, even noncitizen immigrant children are entitled to a public school education, K through 12. But the extent of their use of subsidized care is overblown, even according to the anti-immigration think tank the Center for Immigration Studies, which said in 2004:

> In terms of welfare use, receipt of cash assistance programs tends to be very low, while Medicaid use, though significant, is still less than for other households. Only use of food assistance programs is significantly higher than that of the rest of the population.

In addition to the offense they take from the mere existence of the Fourteenth Amendment, section one, opponents of birthright citizenship fear the multiplier effect, the fact that the babies will be able, when they reach the age of twenty-one, to sponsor their own parents and extended families for citizenship. But I believe that given the crushing anti-immigration hysteria currently gripping the nation, the odds are long and getting longer that those children will be able to affect the immigration status of their parents going forward. A baby girl born to an illegal immigrant in 2008 will have to wait until 2029 until she can start to petition to change the status of her mother. If that mother is a Mexican illegal, no matter how much she contributes to the economy, in the current climate I would have no confidence that she will benefit from the law.

Until 2029, the mother of the so-called anchor baby would be in a very vulnerable position. Under current law, an illegal immigrant parent seeking residence or a move toward U.S. citizenship cannot use the fact that their child is a citizen, unless the minor would suffer extreme, exceptional, and unusual hardship if the parent were deported. Mere separation of parent and child or deportation of both parent and child does not constitute "extreme, exceptional, or unusual hardship," unless, for example, the mother was nursing a baby or a child needed particular medical care available only in the United States.

It is very easy to discuss the law in the abstract, but anchor babies and their parents are real people, each with a unique story. I recently interviewed a Haitian immigrant already served an order of deportation because of a prior, drug-related arrest in the early 1990s, who is married to an American citizen, and together they have four anchoring children. The man owns a store that he inherited from his deceased father, who had become a naturalized citizen. The father was a pillar of the West Indian community and his store was a fixture in his Brooklyn neighborhood. I once interviewed the elder man for a story on traditional medicines, which were his specialty. Is it realistic that the son should uproot his entire family and go back to chaotic Haiti? I think not. Happily, the deeply compassionate clergy at Judson Memorial Church in New

York's Greenwich Village, whose pastor I interviewed, agree, and they've granted the family sanctuary until the man's situation can be resolved.

In August 2006 and again in March and June 2007, I spent time in Chicago with Elvira Arellano, the woman at the center of the nation's best-known case involving an anchor child. Elvira had sought shelter inside a modest inner-city Methodist church, only to be arrested and deported in August 2007. Before she decided to become an advocate for immigration reform, Elvira's story was fairly typical. A native of Mexico, at the age of twenty-one she entered the United States illegally, only to be soon apprehended and deported. Returning within days, she made her way to Oregon, where her son, Saul, was born an American citizen in 1999.

Quiet, proud, and hardworking, Elvira brought Saul to Chicago after hearing about available jobs cleaning airplane toilets at O'Hare Airport. It was unpleasant work and not popular with the native-born. When in 2002 the airport got tough on employee screening in the aftermath of the 9/11 attacks, Elvira was caught again and convicted in immigration court of using a fake Social Security card. Ordered deported on August 15, 2006, Elvira instead sought refuge the same day in the little church in the heavily Hispanic Humboldt Park section of Chicago.

Elvira had been in the church only a few days when I arrived with my camera team for the first of several stories on her plight. On a chill, rainy Chicago afternoon, the dark storefront church was packed with neighborhood supporters. Elvira was living in a tiny apartment above the church with her son. Everyone was nervous that the ICE, the Immigration and Customs Enforcement people, were about to storm in and forcibly remove the two of them. The feeling that the church was under siege by the feds reminded me of the church in East Harlem the Young Lords had occupied in 1970, when the world was different and I was a much younger, more idealistic man. Then, as now, the occupants feared the doors were about to be smashed in by the Man. But the Man had decided then, as now, that an assault wasn't worth the bad press it would surely bring.

Waiting for the mother and child to come downstairs, I spoke with the Reverend Walter Coleman, the lanky, deceptively easygoing pastor of Adalberto United Methodist. I say "deceptively" because his casual demeanor masks a fiery commitment to using the church to gain justice for Elvira and Saul and for broader immigration reform. Surrounded by community activists and parishioners, Reverend Coleman told me then how unfair it was to deport this mother when her citizen son needed the special education he was receiving in the Chicago school system. He predicted Elvira's story would become a rallying point for advocates of remedial change.

When the mother and her then seven-year-old son walked hesitantly into the sanctuary, they looked frightened. Each was so small—how could they not be enormously sympathetic figures? They appeared to tremble in the soft light. They certainly did not seem like a pair of fugitives who had commanded so much attention over the course of their long fight to avoid deportation, which reached from Chicago to Washington, D.C. Elvira told me how Saul couldn't leave the States and how she couldn't leave her son. "My boy is an American citizen. He has the right to stay in his own country. I'm his mother, I have the right to stay and take care of him."

Saul told me how scared he was and asked me in a plaintive voice, if his mother was deported, "Who will take me to school?" It really was heartbreaking, and the idea of deporting her seemed cruel, gratuitous, unnecessary, and deeply unfair. Over time, Elvira became a national symbol for illegal immigrant parents as she continued to defy her deportation order and spoke out from her sanctuary for immigration reform. Undoubtedly sensing the public's revulsion if they broke into the church to arrest Elvira, immigration officials continued to leave her alone. But with the subsequent stunning defeat of President Bush's proposed legislation, a sense of frustration and malaise fell over even the activists inside Adalberto United Methodist.

Once-shy Elvira had by that time become president of *La Familia Latina Unida* (United Latin Family), a lobbying group for families like hers that could be split by deportation. Elvira decided to leave the safety of the church and take her act on the road. Elvira left Chicago and on August 19, 2007, soon after a soulful speech to families gathered at Our Lady Queen of Angels Church in downtown Los Angeles, federal authorities arrested Elvira. Some Chicagoans were overjoyed.

"Hooray to Immigration and Customs Enforcement officials for removing Elvira Arellano from our great country."

—Dave Hoffman of Hometown, Illinois,
to the *Chicago Sun-Times*

"I'm disgusted with the press given to this criminal. That is exactly what she is: a criminal. . . . All I have to say to her is 'Good riddance.' . . . I just hope that next time, we don't wait as long to ship her 'home.' "

—Lincoln C. Glab, Hoffman Estates, to the *Chicago Sun-Times*

Elvira was immediately deported over the border to Tijuana, Mexico. She decided that Saul would remain in the States with his godmother, Emma Lozano, a well-regarded community activist I've met and interviewed several times in Chicago. Emma drove Saul down from L.A. to visit his mom in Tijuana and told the *Sun-Times*, "We've all been living together. He knows his mom is okay. He's going to be sad sometimes," and noted that Saul was about to begin third grade back in the Windy City. She also held out the possibility that the boy, who has already testified before the Mexican Congress, would tour the United States lobbying for reform.

"They were in a hurry to deport me because they saw that I was threatening to mobilize and organize the people to fight for legalization," Elvira told the paper. "I have a fighting spirit and I'm going to continue fighting."

"The manner of the arrest and deportation in this case raises concerns in our community," said L.A. mayor Antonio Villaraigosa. "As mayor of a city that is over forty percent foreign-born, I can tell you, when families are torn apart, our communities are torn apart."

The immigration authorities were unimpressed. "We don't think she's a martyr," Jim Hayes, the director of ICE in Los Angeles, told the *Chicago Sun-Times*. "She was a criminal fugitive who is in violation of the law."

Let me ask you readers whether Elvira Arellano is the image that comes to your mind when a respected lawman uses the expression "criminal fugitive." The L.A. ICE director is technically correct, because Elvira was convicted in the immigration court of using false ID to get her job cleaning airplane toilets. But come on, folks, is she the threat to national security that you had in mind when you cheered on the creation of the Department of Homeland Security? Is America safer now that this mother is separated from her son? She was cleaning toilets, working hard to raise her boy, and paying Social Security into an account from which she will never redeem a dime. And now this fugitive is living thousands of miles from her son.

As I write this, Elvira is in Mexico and her son is attending third grade in public school in Chicago. He has become America's youngest immigration activist, visiting Washington, advocating on behalf of his mom and other families similarly situated. As you separate the rhetoric of fear from the human tragedies that are its consequence, do you believe our national security has been strengthened by Elvira Arellano's ouster?

Anchors aweigh.

13

Immigrants and the Church

"For us, sanctuary is an act of radical hospitality, the welcoming of the stranger who is like ourselves, the stranger in our midst, our neighbors, our friends."
—RABBI MICHAEL FEINBERG OF THE GREATER
NEW YORK LABOR-RELIGION COALITION TO THE AP, MAY 2007

"Our golden rule has always been to serve people in need— not to verify beforehand their immigration status."
—HIS EMINENCE, CARDINAL ROGER M. MAHONY, ARCHBISHOP OF LOS
ANGELES, IN A DECEMBER 2005 LETTER TO PRESIDENT BUSH CONDEMNING
AN ATTEMPT TO REQUIRE CHURCHES AND PUBLIC SERVICES TO VERIFY THE
STATUS OF PARISHIONERS AND ONLY SERVE THOSE LEGALLY IN THE USA

"Tonight, the effort to secure this nation's borders has a new opponent. It is the Catholic Church."
—LOU DOBBS ON CNN's *Lou Dobbs Tonight*

Elvira Arellano knew when she left the sanctuary of the little church in Chicago that it was inevitable she would be arrested. Her motive in leaving the relative safety of Adalberto United Methodist was to bring attention to failed immigration reform, and specifically the predicament that parents of so-called anchor or citizen children like her son, Saul, can find themselves in. But by virtue of her heart-wrenching family story, the focus also fell on the church that granted her sanctuary and on the role of organized religion in the current debate.

The New Sanctuary Movement, as it is called, began in earnest on Ash Wednesday, March 1, 2006, when Cardinal Roger Mahony called upon American Catholics to defy attempts to criminalize illegal immigrants and those who help them. In placing himself squarely at the center of the nation's immigration debate, the cardinal bluntly criticized the House bill that would have turned most people and institutions aiding illegal immigrants into felons. Calling the proposed legislation "blameful and vicious," he vowed a campaign of civil disobedience in the archdiocese's 288 parishes in the majority Hispanic Los Angeles Catholic archdiocese. Scores of other religious institutions representing all the major faiths across the land ultimately signed on, including Jews and Muslims, who at least symbolically offered their own institutions as sanctuaries to protect illegal immigrants from deportation.

In the words of the Immigration and Customs Enforcement spokeswoman Virginia Kice, agents have "the authority to arrest those who are in violation of our immigration laws anywhere in the United States." But the assumption, which has so far proven true, thank God, is that federal authorities do not invade a holy place to bust a nonviolent immigrant. This is not a universally applauded stance. Ira Mehlman, the spokesman for the Federation for American Immigration Reform, a staunchly anti-immigrant lobby group, argues, "Churches have been actively involved in aiding people who are breaking the law. Churches should not expect to be exempt when they're disobeying the law." Mehlman also suggests that many Catholics oppose the concept of "sanctuary." "I'm not sure the Catholic population necessarily goes along with everything that comes down from on high. Look at the debate over abortion and birth control."

The central idea of the movement is not literally to offer a place to live for the more than 600,000 families nationwide facing orders of deportation—this is, of course, a logistical impossibility. Rather, with a relatively small number of cases like Saul and Elvira's, they wish to highlight the church's opposition to current government immigration policy.

The Hollywood-born Cardinal Mahony recalled an incident in his youth that helped shape his feeling toward illegal immigrants for John Pomfret of the *Washington Post*. The cardinal was about twelve years old and working in his father's poultry processing plant in the San Fernando Valley when law enforcement agents searching for illegal aliens raided the facility. "I will never forget them bursting through those doors. I was terrified by it. And I thought, 'These poor people; they're here making a living supporting their families.' It had a very deep impact on me throughout the years." One of the future cardinal's father's workers was taken away, reported Pomfret.

The New Sanctuary Movement promises "to protect immigrant workers and families from unjust deportation." Remarkably, it includes even some evangelical Christians, remarkable only given their historic political conservatism. The Reverend Samuel Rodríguez, president of the National Hispanic Christian Leadership Conference, which claims to serve 15 million evangelical–born again Christians, said in an interview in *Sojourners* magazine in the fall of 2007:

It's not typical for evangelical churches to be engaged in political activities that have historically been interpreted as walking the fine line between the violation of law and the application of our biblical narrative. However, with the egregious damage caused to the families that are being separated now, we find the church to be the only sanctuary that can accommodate the needs of our people. The immigration issue affects the Latino community more than any other community, so to us it is not just a matter of political expediency, it's a matter of survivability. . . . At the end of the day, the church is the last safe haven. We respect the law; however, our congregations are filled with undocumented members. And if our churches need to protect and offer safety to those members, they will do it.

In September 2007, the *Los Angeles Times* reported that the movement includes "representatives from 18 cities, including Los Angeles; 12 religious traditions; and seven denominational and interdenominational organizations. . . . More than 50 churches, synagogues and temples have joined the coalition, at least 35 of them in southern California." The paper listed some of the prominent churches involved, including Immanuel Presbyterian, St. Luke's Episcopal, Our Lady Queen of Angels (where Elvira Arellano was busted), Echo Park United Methodist, and Angelica Lutheran.

Predictably, Representative Tom Tancredo blamed the church's stance on "left-leaning religious activists." Representative Peter King of Long Island, New York, the ranking member of the House Homeland Security Committee and another staunch opponent of illegal immigration, told Bill O'Reilly that he blamed the church's position on "political correctness." "This has become the politically correct tune," King said. "Too many people in the Catholic church have signed onto this. It's fashionable."

I did a half-hour radio interview with the congressman in July 2007. After referring to the usually cordial nature of our relationship, I strongly criticized King's stance on illegal immigration. King joked that my criticism paled in comparison to what his fellow Irishmen were saying about him. There is an entire underground Irish immigrant lobby in this country with several dedicated Web sites, including Voice of the Undocumented Irish and The Blanket, a Journal of Protest and Dissent, serving the twenty-five to fifty thousand Irish here illegally. Here is what one blogger on the Blanket said about Congressman King in September 2006:

The numbers speak for themselves, out of 1.4 million visas given out by the US last year, the Irish got 2,000! We the "undocumented" know we

came here and stayed without visas, but what are our chances . . . less
than half a percent. The US immigration system is broken, but instead
of trying to fix it, the likes of Peter King would rather lock everyone up
and anyone who helps them. YES, Peter King turned his back on the
Irish, they got him elected and like Judas, he took his "gold" from the
higher powers that be.

Typically, Lou Dobbs was harshly bottom-line on the issue of sanctuary, accusing the church of looking south of the border just "to add a few folks to those pews." His insufferable cynicism aside, there is no doubt that the Catholic church, by far the nation's largest with 69 million members, has been reenergized by its aggressive stance on immigration. "We are relearning what it means to be an immigrant church," Mark Franken, the head of migration and refugee services for the U.S. Conference of Catholic Bishops, told Paulette Chu Miniter of the Phillips Foundation in *USA Today*. Miniter goes on to trace the theological underpinnings of the church's position:

For the church, the migrant's plight is a universal one tracing back to the Holy Family. Pope Pius XII, in 1952, declared the Holy Family of Jesus, Mary and Joseph to be the archetype of every refugee family. He based this on their flight into Egypt, calling them "the models and protectors of every migrant, alien and refugee of whatever kind who, whether compelled by fear of persecution or by want, is forced to leave his native land, his beloved parents and relatives, his close friends, and to seek a foreign soil."

The bishops' call for "just and humane" immigration reform is no different from what the church's leaders have advocated: from Pope John XXIII, who said, "Every human being has the right to freedom of movement," to Pope John Paul II, who in an annual message for World Migration Day in 1995 said, "The illegal migrant comes before us like that 'stranger' in whom Jesus asks to be recognized," and Catholics must help these strangers whatever their legal status with regard to state law.

Today's sanctuary movement draws its inspiration from a similar move by churches in the 1980s, to harbor Central American refugees fleeing civil wars in their home countries. Having covered that bloody anarchy for ABC News, the graphic images of violence and dislocation are still seared in my memory, like the breathtaking instant in June 1979 when my colleague Bill Stewart was told to get on his knees and was then executed at point-blank range by an officer in Nicaraguan dictator Anastasio Somoza's National Guard, even as Bill's cameraman secretly kept filming. But because U.S. troops were not directly involved in the shattering conflicts, few Americans recollect their barbaric nature. In El Salvador, Guatemala, and Nicaragua, as in the South American nation of Colombia today, the wrong political affiliation can mean torture, exploitation, exile, or death. In the 1980s, tens of thousands of war refugees fleeing the violence sought safe harbor here, only to be turned away.

The refugees' last best hope was the faith-based community and antiwar activists who saw sanctuary as a protest to Reagan-era policies, like the clandestine support for the Contra rebels in Nicaragua. Then, as now, many individuals were motivated by what they saw as the contradictory and discriminatory federal policy concerning asylum seekers fighting deportation. If the refugee was fleeing an ideologically friendly nation like El Salvador, however dysfunctional or dangerous life there might be, they were turned away. But if they were running from Communist Cuba, regardless of their own personal plight, essentially everyone was welcome.

The sanctuary movement was a spontaneous, grassroots response to the politics and policies of the day and it enjoyed impressive success. By 1987, four hundred churches and schools, even some entire cities, had declared themselves sanctuaries to refugee immigrants, cities including Detroit; Fairbanks, Alaska; Denver; New Haven, Connecticut; Chicago; Cambridge, Massachusetts; Los Angeles and Santa Cruz, and most other California cities; Washington, D.C.; Oklahoma City; Seattle; Salt Lake City; Madison, Wisconsin; Charlotte, North Carolina; and Austin, Texas, to name a few. The actions of those civic and church leaders were not without personal cost. While a handful of pastors and lay leaders were prosecuted, their sanctuary movement is credited with having helped create the climate for the Immigration Reform and Control Act of 1986, which granted amnesty for most of those who had crossed over illegally during the war years.

I believe that as with abortion rights, immigration enforcement will continue to be strictly local—that is, some cities will agree to enforce the federal regulations, and others will continue to defy it, some more flamboyantly than others. Even a specific declaration from the Supreme Court of the United States mandating compulsory local participation in immigration enforcement will not be enough to make a meaningful difference in the short term.

As Ms. Miniter made clear in her excellent essay quoted above, the right of sanctuary is an ancient custom recognized for more than a millennium in English common law. "We want to put a human face to very complex immigration laws and awaken the consciousness of the human spirit," Father Richard Estrada of Our Lady Queen of Angels Catholic Church in Los Angeles told the Associated Press.

Liliana, whose last name is withheld by the church that shelters her, presents another human face to this issue. If anything, Liliana's story is even more upsetting than Elvira and Saul Arellano's, because her deportation order is based on an even more strained interpretation of existing law. According to a widely circulated article by the reporter Greg Mellen of the *Long Beach Press Telegram*, Liliana's parents and seven brothers and sisters emigrated from Michoacan, Mexico, aided in their migration by Liliana's older brother, who was already established in the United States. A teenager, she wanted to stay behind to finish high school in Mexico before joining the rest of her family in the United States. Liliana claims that when the time came nearly a decade ago to apply for a visa, she was turned down; so she crossed illegally after purchasing a fake birth certificate from a smuggler. That was her first attempt to enter. Stopped at the border, she was convicted by an immigration judge of posing as an American citizen and sent back.

Technically a felon, and as a result ineligible for either permanent resident status or citizenship, Liliana was understandably desperate to reunite with the rest of her family. She dared the border again two months later, this time succeeding. She later met and married her husband, Gerardo, a legal resident at the time who subsequently earned his American citizenship in 2003, according to Greg Mellen, who takes up the story:

> When Gerardo later petitioned for legal status for Liliana, her conviction came to light and Liliana was given an order for voluntary departure. Liliana, who by that time had two children, Gerardo Jr., now 7, and Susi, who was a toddler, ignored the order. Three years later, on May 6, 2007, immigration officers arrived at her home to take Liliana into custody. "I knew they were there for me," Liliana said through an interpreter. "I didn't want to be separated from my children."

How could I not root for a woman who has the same name as my two-year-old daughter; a woman married to a hardworking, taxpaying man whose name is a variation of my own? By the time the ICE came knocking, Liliana had another American citizen child, six-month-old Pablo. She sought sanctuary at Long Beach's St. Luke's Episcopal Church on June 8, 2007. "Liliana will be here as long as necessary," Julie Wakelee-Lynch, the assistant rector at St. Luke's, told the *Press Telegram*.

Barbara Coe, the chairwoman for the California Coalition for Immigration Reform, an anti-immigrant group, told the paper that she resents the idea of the church granting sanctuary for illegal immigrants, saying, "They are aiding, abetting and harboring illegal aliens, criminals, and they should be prosecuted." But just take a deep breath and take stock of this absurd situation. Here you have a woman whose entire family, including her parents, seven brothers and sisters, her husband, and their three children are all citizens or permanent legal residents of the United States. What good does kicking Liliana out of the country do? As of this writing, she remains in the sanctuary church. But if she is to be tossed out, who is better off, whose life is enhanced as a result?

"The movement as a whole is responding to families being broken by a broken immigration system," Alexia Salvatierra of Clergy and Laity United for Economic Justice, which helps organize sanctuary cases, told the *Press Telegram*. "There's a moral and spiritual circle that's created [around churches] that the government has decided not to cross."

In all my acrimonious debates with those opposed to immigration reform, and as I'm acutely aware of the racially based motivations of so many of the opposition, the fact that holy places are still considered sacrosanct in this country gives me hope that a middle ground will be found. Perhaps we still have an unwritten code of humane and rational conduct, which might be unique among nations, that no momentary emotion, however inflamed by talk media, can trump.

14

Heroes and Deportees

"I am proud to be a U.S. Marine. And to defend and protect the freedom and Constitution of America. . . . If anything happens to me just remember I already lived my life to the fullest and I am happy with what I lived. . . . Don't feel sad. Don't feel lonely."

—Excerpt from the last letter Marine Sergeant Rafael Peralta sent from Iraq to his kid brother Ricardo; killed in action, the sergeant was a former illegal alien from Mexico

I was in Iraq for the eighth time in February 2007. My team and I accompanied a unit of the Stryker Brigade on a sweep of the Dora market and east Baghdad. The "surge" of additional U.S. combat forces was on and my assignment for Fox News was to gauge its preliminary impact. My frequent war buddies from the First Cavalry were now in charge in the war-ravaged capital city, "Living the Legend," as their division motto proclaims, and taking the fight to the enemy in sections of town that had been ceded to them up until that point.

After a sweep of the notorious market, the mission of our six-strong Stryker column was to support the demolition of a reinforced concrete structure. It overlooked the main ring road around eastern Baghdad. As it was in easy rifle range it was frequently used as an enemy sniper site to disrupt allied traffic. After a convoy had come under fire that morning, February 16, the decision was made finally to take the building out, not merely suppress the fire and move on. That was presurge thinking. The imperative now was to take and hold, or as in the case of this sniper villa, render it useless to the enemy.

The rock-solid building bordered a large palm grove also frequently used by the enemy. The structure was situated in a walled compound made of concrete blocks rather than the usual flimsy adobe or mud construction. It appeared to be the prewar home of a Hussein-era big shot, perhaps an officer or Baath party operative. On the concrete roof, spent shell casings were everywhere, hundreds of them, evidence of its recent usefulness to enemy sharpshooters.

As our sappers began wiring the place for demolition, I walked out front and passed the open hatch of one of the surrounding Strykers. Over the course of the long war, my opinion of these strange-looking armored vehicles had changed from skepticism to admiration after watching them in action. They are formidable offensive vehicles and are surprisingly resilient to enemy attack. As I looked in the window, the driver's expansively smiling face looked back. It was a Chicano kid with some shiny metal caps on his teeth. Recognizing a fellow Latino traveler, I said, *"Hombre, qué tal?"* (Hey man, what's happening?), to which he replied in East L.A.–gangster-accented English, "I'm from the hood, Inglewood, and I'm up to no good!"

Then he laughed, making it sound like a good-natured yet defiant and pointed theme song. Inglewood is one of those L.A. communities where Latinos have been moving in and traditional African–American residents are moving out. Located just a few miles from LAX, the town has fallen on relatively hard times. Never an upscale community to begin with, there was a thirty-year stretch of relative prosperity when the "Fabulous" L.A. Forum hosted the unbeatable basketball Lakers of Kareem and Magic Johnson and the hockey Kings of the Great Gretzky, and the prices of the modest homes ticked upward. Now that the teams are gone to the Staples Center in downtown, the no-longer-fabulous Forum is owned by the Faithful Central Bible Church, one of those black megachurches that holds Sunday services and still rents the place out for second-tier rock concerts.

HISPANIC

But black flight from Inglewood is the reality. Hispanics are moving in, and the community is already split about fifty-fifty between the two groups. Latino street gang activity is on the upswing in an increasingly bleak neighborhood that I always thought seemed sun-baked and down on its luck even when the Lakers were there.

The kid in the Stryker would be indistinguishable now from a thousand others cruising or hanging out on Manchester Boulevard. I thought about him as we pulled back about a half mile to the ring road and watched the engineers demolish the sniper nest building with a thunderous blast.

This cheerful kid had obviously been plucked from the inner city by army recruiters using the current *Yo Soy el Army* campaign that saturates Univision, Telemundo, and Spanish radio and represents a big push to bring up Latino enlistment. He reminded me of all the Hispanic soldiers and marines I have seen on battlefields from Afghanistan to Iraq since 9/11. They are everywhere, and more often than not serving in disproportionate numbers as frontline troops in either the army or the Marine Corps. Targeting Los Angeles, the rest of Southern California, Phoenix, and Sacramento, the Pentagon has publicly stated that it wants to double Latino enlistment, which currently lags in proportion to the eighteen-to-twenty-four-year-old U.S. Hispanic population. "Even recruits who score out of the infantry choose it anyway," marine recruiter Gunnery Sergeant Jorge Montes told *U.S. News & World Report* from his office in an East L.A. strip mall, where the corps recruits heavily in nearby high schools. He laid on the warrior's appeal. "There is a certain pride in being in the front lines at the tip of the spear."

Latinos have served honorably and bravely in all U.S. wars since the nation's founding, including some who fought against the Mexicans in Texas and California. Puerto Ricans became American citizens in 1917, just in time for 18,000 of them to serve in World War I. By the Second World War II, the number of Puerto Ricans serving jumped to more than 65,000, including my dad, one of 400,000 Latinos in the U.S. armed forces.

In the annals of courage, the segregated 141st Regiment of the 36th Texas Infantry Division stands out. Made up entirely of Spanish speakers, in 361 straight days of combat in Italy and France during 1944–45, the regiment suffered 1,126 killed, 5,000 wounded, and more than 500 missing in action. For their service and sacrifice the 141st was awarded 31 Distinguished Service Crosses, 12 Legions of Merit, 492 Silver Stars, 1,685 Bronze Stars, and many other decorations and commendations.

In the Korean War, part of the Fighting Sixty-fifth Infantry, the Regimental Combat Team from Puerto Rico, "the *Borinqueneers*" (*Boriken* is the pre-Spanish name for our island), slugged through nine brutal campaigns, earning the following praise from their commanding general, William Harris:

> No ethnic group has greater pride in itself and its heritage than the Puerto Rican people. Nor have I encountered any that can be more dedicated and zealous in its support of the democratic principles for which the United States stands. Many Puerto Ricans have fought to the death to uphold them.
>
> —(In *Puerto Rico's Fighting 65th U.S. Infantry: From San Juan to Chorwan*)

Hispanics were involved in the widespread opposition to the war in Vietnam. At the 1970 National Chicano Moratorium, thousands marched in East Los Angeles, clashing with police in rioting that left three dead, including the *Los Angeles Times* reporter Ruben Salazar. Still, the Hispanic tradition of service continued, with approximately eighty thousand Hispanic Americans serving in Vietnam. More than twenty thousand participated in Operations Desert Shield and Desert Storm in the first Iraq War.

Over the past decade, the number of Hispanic service members has increased by 30 percent, faster than any other group. Now, about ninety thousand Hispanic Americans are on active duty, most of them in frontline army combat units like the First Cavalry or the Stryker Brigade or in the elite marines, where 11 percent of the corps is now Hispanic. My cousin Eddie Rivera, my uncle Ramon's son, was a U.S. Marine. He is older than me, and in the 1950s I was always thrilled when he came home from North Carolina's Camp Lejeune in his dress blue uniform.

I also remember the pride I felt interviewing Lieutenant General Ricardo Sanchez, commander of all coalition ground forces in Iraq in 2004. The highest-ranking Hispanic in U.S. Army history, his personal story is inspirational. Born into a dirt-poor Chicano family in Rio Grande, Texas, Sanchez worked his way up all through the ranks. We met at Saddam's former palace inside the sprawling U.S. base known as Camp Victory. Behind his thick glasses, the quiet man seemed almost professorial, with none of the swagger I've come to expect from these hard-core veterans. In those days before the insurrection hit its deadly stride, he seemed confident, his future unbounded, propelled by the killing of the dictator's sons, Uday and Qusay Hussein, and the recent capture of Saddam himself by the Fourth Infantry up near Tikrit.

Then the Abu Ghraib prison scandal exploded on his watch, and as the top gun, General Sanchez took the fall. He retired in November 2006, in many ways a scapegoat for the architects of this improvised war.

The Hispanic American Legion of Valor includes somewhere between thirty-nine and forty-two winners of the Medal of Honor, which is especially remarkable considering that segregation in the armed services was the rule until Vietnam. These were men who won the medal despite often being relegated to less-than-elite units. The precise number of Medal of Honor winners is hard to determine because some of the honorees have Anglo surnames and some recommendations have yet to be formally approved by Congress.

And those heroes prevailed despite the armed services' notorious record of racial segregation. One graphic example of the prevalence of discrimination came with the return of the remains of army Private Felix Longoria following the Second World War. Killed in action during a daring volunteer mission during the last days of the war in the Philippines, Longoria's body was returned to his hometown of Three Rivers, Texas. Located halfway between San Antonio and Corpus Christi, the community was then and still remains sharply divided between Churchill Acres, the rich, white neighborhood, and the Barrio, which is overwhelmingly Latino and downmarket. The town cemetery was also sharply divided into "Mexican" and "Anglo" in 1948, the sections separated by barbed wire.

When the town's only funeral home refused to allow the Longoria family to use its chapel, because "the whites would not like it," the family appealed to Dr. Hector Garcia, a returning veteran and the founder of one of the first Hispanic civil rights groups, the enduring American GI Forum. Dr. Garcia turned to then Texas senator Lyndon Johnson, who arranged for the fallen hero to be buried with full honors at Arlington National Cemetery.

With segregation gone, one big problem now in recruitment is the level of recruits' education. High school dropouts aren't ineligible to serve, but neither are they encouraged to enlist, and they tend to do badly on the standardized examinations. Even when they are educationally competitive, the other great problem is citizenship. Many of the youngsters who are ripe for recruitment are not citizens of the United States. They are fit, young, gung-ho and macho, and their families can certainly use the increasingly generous enlistment bonuses being offered by the manpower-deprived military. But until recently, only citizens could enlist.

In a move that some criticized as recruiting mercenaries, but which I applauded as being practical and only fair, shortly before the

Iraq war began in 2003, President Bush signed an executive order allowing noncitizen permanent residents to serve in the military, and once in the military to apply for citizenship on a fast-track basis, sidestepping the usual three-year waiting period. The federal government currently encourages legal immigrants to enlist by streamlining their application process, eliminating fees, and making it easy to file paperwork while serving overseas. And if they manage to enlist even if they are not legal residents, the Immigration and Customs Enforcement (ICE) postpones deportation proceedings until after discharge, making it improbable in most cases, at least for the serviceman himself, that he will ever be deported once having served.

Over the last four and a half years about 35,000 mostly Latino noncitizens have served in the military, and as of November 2006, 22,500 service members have become naturalized citizens as a result. The president's order also allows noncitizen soldiers who are killed in action to be granted citizenship posthumously. That may sound like a hollow gesture, but it has had real legal consequences in terms of benefits for widows and surviving children. Distressingly, while it is only just and proper that GIs are granted citizenship in the country they have sworn to protect, to serve, and sometimes to die for, the order did nothing to ensure that the families of those soldiers and marines were taken into account. And that has led to some heartless situations. Families of soldiers and marines who are risking, and in some cases giving, their lives overseas are finding themselves under threat from government agencies back in the United States.

Remember the stories of illegal immigrant crime in Newark, Virginia, and elsewhere? Remember how anti-immigrant forces fixate on these incidents as though they represent the sum total of what immigrants do when they get to this country? There are other stories. I want to present some that you will never hear from Lou Dobbs or Michelle Malkin.

Fallujah. The name of the war-ravaged city in the bloody al-Anbar province is synonymous with Iraq at its worst. In late 2004, following a Sunni insurgent raid that killed at least two dozen Iraqis from both sides, my brother Craig, producer Greg Hart, and I arrived early enough to see the bodies of the Iraqi defenders piled one on another like wood stacked beside a fireplace. In a shattered nation that was by then already the world's most perilous for an American, no place was more dangerous or unnerving than the bleak, brutal town of Fallujah.

In one of a depressing series of violent offensives and humiliating withdrawals that characterized too much of this discouraging war, in November 2004, the high command sent the First Battalion, Third Marine Regiment in to retake the city. This time they called it Operation Phantom Fury. "A" Company led the charge.

It was a long week after the first cataclysm of battle, and twenty-five-year-old Sergeant Rafael Peralta was leading his platoon in the hair-raising job of clearing the enemy. Going house by house, room by room, the marines doggedly did the dirty and dangerous job, kicking in doors and, while covering one another, looking for the highly motivated enemy, who accepts death in battle as martyrdom and asks only to kill as they are being killed.

Burly and rugged, Peralta led the way into one house, kicking down doors and finding the first two rooms empty. The third room proved his undoing. As he entered, the sergeant was immediately hit by small-arms fire. Wounded in the face and chest, Peralta fell, remaining barely conscious enough to roll out of the way so that his comrades could fire on the enemy within. At that moment, one of the three Iraqis inside the room tossed a fragmentation grenade toward the advancing marines. They attempted to scatter, but there was no escape. In the fraction of a second before the fuse detonated the lethal device, Peralta grabbed the grenade and cradled it to his body, absorbing most of the blast.

"He saved half my fire team," Corporal Brannon Dyer told the *Army Times*.

"I was in that house on that day, and I was with the bravest men in the world. It was an honor to be among them, and to carry our fallen brother, Sgt. Peralta, from the battle. I will carry him, and our other fallen brothers in my heart forever. . . . Semper Fi, Sgt. Peralta," Corporal Dyer wrote on Peralta's page on fallenheroesmemorial.com.

During his noble but failed attempt to get the Senate to pass his immigration reform, President Bush asked Hispanics in his administration to do their best to rally support for the cause. In a prepared speech before the U.S. Hispanic Chamber of Commerce, Attorney General Alberto Gonzalez talked about the sacrifice of Latinos in the armed forces, saying:

> One such hero was Rafael Peralta. An immigrant from Mexico, he enlisted in the Marine Corps shortly after the U.S.-led invasion of Iraq. Just before the battle of Fallujah, he wrote his fourteen-year-old brother, quote, "We are going to defeat the insurgents. Be proud of me, I'm going to make history and do something that I always wanted to do." A few days later, Sergeant Peralta gave his life to save his fellow marines. Although most immigrants are not called upon to sacrifice their lives for our country, many make sacrifices that improve and protect the lives of all Americans.

Indeed Peralta was an "immigrant from Mexico," as the attorney general described. And a "Mexican American," as the conservative columnist Rich Lowry wrote in an article in the *National Review* extolling Peralta's virtue and courage and advising Americans, "Everyone should know his name." But what neither man admitted was that Sergeant Rafael Peralta had come to this country as an illegal alien. The son of a truck mechanic and a washerwoman, Rafael was born in Mexico City and raised in the border town of Tijuana. After he was beaten there by gang members, his parents sent him across the border to live illegally in the United States, where he stayed with relatives and attended high school in San Diego.

After graduation, Peralta went to work for the state, seeking to earn permanent residency and, after getting his green card, join the U.S. Marines. After that goal was accomplished, he wanted to become a U.S. citizen. "Ginger" of San Diego wrote on Sergeant Peralta's memorial blog:

> *I did the paperwork to hire Rafael into the California Conservation Corps when he was 19 years old. I watched him develop from a fine young man into a finer young man. I watched as he was promoted to crewleader within 6 months. He had an impact on all who knew him and I liked him very much. The last time that I saw him was when he came to our office in his dress blues and looking so handsome & proud. He was about to be deployed.*

"Thank you, from my family, for your sacrifice. May God bless you and your family, and keep you always!" wrote Brooke Tarvin of Hamilton, Ohio, echoing the feeling of dozens who felt the urge to praise this fine young man who started life in the United States so humbly and ended so bravely.

In December 2004, Congressman Bob Filner, Democrat of California, introduced legislation to award the fallen hero the Medal of Honor. In April 2006, the police chief of San Diego posthumously awarded Sergeant Peralta the honorary title of San Diego Police Officer. In May 2007, the History Channel produced a documentary about his life entitled *Act of Honor*, which was also presented in Spanish as *El Honor De Un Sacrificio*.

Rafael isn't the only hero.

Orphaned before he was four years old, Jose Gutierrez lost both his parents to the health problems that afflicted his impoverished barrio in Guatemala City. Living off the mean streets of the capital city plagued by high crime and a long-festering civil war, Joselito finally found his way to Casa Alianza, a charitable shelter for Guatemala's tribe of homeless street urchins. He was eight years old at the time and so alone "he would inhale a toxic shoe glue to escape from the hunger and loneliness," Bruce Harris, Alianza's director, told CNN.

At the age of fourteen, following the well-trod path of 700,000 of his countrymen, young Joselito began his trek to the United States alone, hopping freight trains and hitchhiking the dangerous two thousand miles through rough and tough Mexico. Without papers, money, or friends and living by his wits and through the kindness of strangers, it took the teenager a month and fourteen different trains to make it to the U.S. border near Tijuana. Detained there by U.S. immigration authorities, Jose benefited from the informal rule that existed at the time that the United States does not deport Guatemalan minors who arrive without adult family members. Jose was placed in a series of group homes and foster families. Despite obvious challenges, under the tutelage of legal resident Marcelo Mosquera, a machinist from Ecuador, and his wife, Nora, the lanky teenager learned English and managed to finish high school in suburban Lomita, California.

According to Fernando Castillo, Guatemala's consul general in Los Angeles, at the age of eighteen Jose was rewarded with permanent U.S. residency. His foster parents say he wanted to become an architect and dreamed of earning enough money to bring his sole surviving sibling, his sister Engracia, here from Guatemala. But in 2002, he put his college plans on hold to join the U.S. Marine Corps. There was a war on. "He wanted to give the United States what the United States gave to him. He came with nothing. This country gave him everything," his foster sister said.

Lance Corporal Jose Antonio Gutierrez, the former illegal alien, was one of the first U.S. soldiers killed in combat in Iraq. He was killed in a firefight on the third day of the war in the assault on Umm Qasr, the important Persian Gulf naval base. His sister Engracia arrived in the United States in time to meet his flag-draped coffin and attend a standing-room-only Mass at St. Margaret Mary Catholic Church in Lomita in April of 2003. There Gutierrez was honored in a Mass presided over by L.A.'s Cardinal Roger Mahony, who called the corporal "a great man."

Engracia told reporters, "I do feel proud, because not just anyone gives up their life for another country. But at the same time it makes me sad because he fought for something that wasn't his."

It became his. Lance Corporal Jose Gutierrez was posthumously awarded U.S. citizenship. His sister now hopes to be allowed to live here. In a poem he called a "Letter to God," which was read at his funeral, Jose wrote, "Thank you for permitting me to live another year, thank you for what I have, for the type of person I am, for my dreams that don't die. May the firearms be silent and the teachings of love flourish."

Of the first fifty-eight Americans killed in Iraq, four were Latino marines from the Los Angeles area. "If you can wait just a little, we'll see each other in the summer, God willing," wrote marine Corporal Jorge A. González to his parents on March 10, 2003. Jorge joined the marines right out of high school, looking for a future brighter than his tough El Monte neighborhood provided most Hispanic youngsters. An entry on fallenheroesmemorial.com tells the awful story of how Corporal González's parents learned of their son's death not long after he had written them:

> *Two weeks later, as they watched a newscast on the Spanish-language network Telemundo, they saw footage from Al-Jazeera of four Marines who had been killed in the fighting outside An Nasiriya. An Iraqi soldier lifted one of the bodies for the camera, and the parents recognized their son. Left behind was his wife, Jasty, and a 3-week-old son he never saw.*

The parents of PFC Francisco A. Martinez-Flores were presented a framed certificate of naturalization a month after their twenty-one-year-old was killed during convoy operations when the bridge his tank was traveling over collapsed into the Euphrates

River in the big push to Baghdad. Born in Mexico, his family had crossed into this country illegally from Guadalajara when Francisco was only three. He joined the corps to get money for a college education because his ambition was to eventually be a stockbroker or a police detective. Francisco's mother said her greatest regret was not being able to say good-bye to her son, because she was back in Mexico when he was shipped out, attending the funeral of her own father.

Twenty-one-year-old marine Corporal Jose Angel Garibay was an infant carried into this country in the arms of his mother, an undocumented woman who worked her way across the line in search of a better life, settling in the Costa Mesa area after traveling the thousand miles from Jalisco, Mexico. A hardworking hospital housekeeper who is now legally documented, Angel's mother, Simona, told the *Orange County Register*, "I just sat down and cried" when three men in uniform knocked on her door, walking past the U.S. and Mexican flags proudly planted in her front lawn. "It was so sad. He's my son. I love him," she told the paper as she sat near a shrine to her son. "He was very proud to be Mexican," his uncle Urbano Garibay told the *Register*. "He always spoke Spanish to us. But look at the American flags around the house. He was a typical Latino. He worked hard, wanted to buy a house for his mother. He wanted to come home after the war and be a police officer." Jose Angel Garibay posthumously became a naturalized citizen in April 2003. "He grew up here," his sister Crystal told the *Arizona Republic*. "And he said this country had given him everything."

"Young Latinos have been among the first killed and the first captured," Roberto Suro of the Pew Hispanic Center told *U.S. News & World Report* at the time. "And it has brought them to people's attention, with an element of surprise."

Surprise and sometimes outrage. As young Hispanic noncitizens flock to the armed services to get on the fast track toward becoming Americans, their families are left out in the cold. That is because citizenship for the soldier does not mean citizenship for the soldier's family. In May 2007, army Specialist Alex Jimenez, twenty-five, of Lawrence, Massachusetts, and several of his fellow GIs went missing when their Tenth Mountain Division unit was ambushed south of Baghdad. The nation's attention was riveted when, after the soldiers' ID cards were found in a terrorist safe house, a group linked to al-Qaeda claimed on the Internet that it had killed them. A massive search was fruitless and veteran observers of the brutal conflict conjured up graphic images of the horrors the captured soldiers must have been enduring.

In the meantime, Jimenez's wife was an illegal immigrant facing deportation, even as she awaited news of her husband's fate. This infuriated senators like Ted Kennedy, John Kerry, and Colorado's Ken Salazar. As he was advocating immigration reform Salazar told me, "I cannot imagine what it must be like for a wife to be sitting in jail knowing that her husband has probably been killed in Iraq defending her country. And the fact that she is sitting in jail in our America, because we have a system of disorder and lawlessness, ought to be of concern to all Americans, Democrats and Republicans alike."

Alex and Yaderlin met in the Dominican Republic, where they were high school sweethearts. He later joined his father, Andy Jimenez, a naturalized citizen living in Lawrence, Massachusetts. In 2001, she paid a smuggler $500 to bring her in through Mexico, and walked four days until she crossed the border into the United States. She joined Alex at Fort Drum in upstate New York, where the couple married in June 2004.

Of all places, the happy newlyweds ran afoul of immigration authorities when attempting to enter Canada to honeymoon at Niagara Falls. With his new bride facing deportation, Jimenez, who had been wounded and awarded a Purple Heart following his first tour of duty in Iraq, petitioned for his wife to receive a green card and attain legal residency as he shipped off for a second tour in Iraq. Appearing in dress uniform before the immigration judge, Jimenez managed to win a postponement until he could return from the war. Then he went missing, and Yaderlin faced deportation if her husband did not come back.

Yaderlin's case came to a full boil even as the Congress was in the act of torpedoing the president's immigration reform bill. Under assault from Massachusetts's two powerful senators, Ted Kennedy and John Kerry, DHS Secretary Chertoff announced that Mrs. Jimenez could apply for legal, permanent resident status without first being deported to her native Dominican Republic and waiting the requisite ten years to apply. "The sacrifices made by our soldiers and their families deserve our greatest respect, and we will ensure that her immigration case is given every possible consideration," Chertoff said.

In July 2007, Yaderlin Hiraldo Jimenez became a legal resident. "I am happy," the missing soldier's father told his Lawrence hometown newspaper, the *Eagle-Tribune*. "She's my son's wife, and it's good that she's going to be here when he returns."

Realistically, the odds of Specialist Jimenez ever returning alive are the longest of long shots. And while his wife Yaderlin's immigration plight was resolved, the ad hoc nature of the decision does nothing to help the growing number of military families in similar straits, with no powerful congressmen lobbying on their behalf. "Every [military] base has immigration problems," Margaret Stock, an army reservist and immigration attorney teaching at West Point, told the AP. "The government they're fighting for is the same government that's trying to deport their families."

The unfairness of these cases is best articulated by U.S. Navy Petty Officer Second Class Eduardo González, a citizen whose wife entered the country illegally from Guatemala when she was five years old and is now in deportation proceedings. As Eduardo González told Juliana Barbassa of the Associated Press, "If I'm willing to die for the United States, why can't I just be allowed to be with my family?"

Isn't Petty Officer Eduardo González right? With our enormously stressed armed forces eager for new recruits, and given the president's executive order encouraging legal noncitizens to enlist as a fast track to citizenship, isn't it only fair and logical that we eliminate this obvious contradiction? Stories abound about serving GIs having their families evicted from military bases because as illegal aliens those foreign civilians have no legal business even being in this country, much less on government property. Assuming Congress is incapable of passing any legislation that alleviates the misery of undocumented service families, the president can do it with an amended executive order that grants the same conditional rights to the immediate families of serving GIs as it does the soldiers themselves.

Why should we turn our backs on the youngsters here without proper documentation who are eager to serve, if only to have a track toward citizenship, but who can't because they are here illegally? How many white and black kids join the service so they can fund their college education or learn a trade? Face it, absent national emergencies like the Trade Center attacks, when the aura of patriotism is red-hot, or when service is a family tradition, relatively few kids sign up because they feel it is their national duty to do so. Iraq is not Nazi Germany.

Hooray for idealism and its selfless sacrifice, but the fact is most individuals join the service these days for pragmatic reasons. Recruiters know this and their advertising agencies design their slick campaigns to make the uniform services competitive with other career choices. Remember "Be All You Can Be!" and "Join the Navy and See the World"? That is not a bad thing. This is practical patriotism and it serves to fill the ranks with smart, sharp, able-bodied youngsters who will fight like hell for their adopted country, even as they learn skills and earn credentials that will make them better men and women, better Americans.

I know they will because I have seen them do it. Remember Jesus Apodaca, the undocumented Denver honor student who sought in-state tuition at a Colorado university? Federal legislation known as the Dream Act, the Development Relief and Education for Alien Minors Act, would provide routes by which "provisional" legal residency could be granted to undocumented immigrants who entered the U.S. before age sixteen, which after six years would become permanent legal residency. Those include earning a college degree, or completing two years in college working toward that degree, or two years' honorable service in the United States military. In testifying on behalf of the bill, Under Secretary of Defense David Chu said:

> According to an April 2006 study from the National Immigration Law Center, there are an estimated fifty thousand to sixty-five thousand undocumented alien young adults who entered the U.S. at an early age and graduate from high school each year, many of whom are bright, energetic and potentially interested in military service. Provisions of S. 2611, the Dream Act, would provide these young people the opportunity of serving the United States in uniform.

Given the current political climate, the Dream Act has no chance of passage, as the Senate demonstrated in a late September 2007 test vote. How could it succeed with one typical right-wing blogger calling it the "Treason Lobby's Dream Act," and claiming it envisioned an "illegal alien legion"? Despite heart-wrenching stories of courage and commitment like those presented here, even some sober anti-immigration activists worry publicly about the ultimate loyalty of these noncitizen soldiers, many of whom retain citizenship in their country of origin, particularly Mexico.

Ironically, even some pro-immigration groups, like the Association of Raza Educators, also oppose the Dream Act; they fear that because so many undocumented young people are struggling with education, the act would constitute "a de facto military draft for our undocumented youth." That opposition is born of the fact that according to early reports from Iraq, those immigrant youth faced combat more often, relative to their numbers in the military, than soldiers of other ethnicities. "I'm totally against joining the military as a way out," Carlos Montes, the director of Latinos Against the War With Iraq, told the *Arizona Republic.* "I say go to college and get a good job."

I agree and I disagree. Mr. Montes correctly reflects Latino opposition to the war in Iraq, which closely tracks how other Americans feel about the conflict. In fall 2007, almost two-thirds of both the Latino community and Americans as a whole wanted us out of there. But if you can, put aside for a moment specific opposition to the war in Iraq. The armed forces are bigger than that one conflict, however horrific or misconceived. Having spent so much time with the military, particularly in the last decade, I've come to appreciate that the armed forces contain some of the finest, smartest, most able and honorable young men and women I have ever met. That is why I applauded the decision of my own nineteen-year-old son, Cruz, to join his college ROTC. Every kid should get as much education as they can. College is the best ticket out of poverty, and it is the best indicator of future success, even for kids like my son who are relatively privileged. But the military is another way out, and for some, the best way. And if it can earn an undocumented kid whose family is living in fear of deportation an opportunity to realize the American Dream, so much the better for the kid and for the country.

15

The Other Side of History

"The cavalries charged, the Indians died, oh the country was young, with God on its side."

—BOB DYLAN, "WITH GOD ON OUR SIDE"

One of the most important conclusions I reached in the course of researching and writing this book is that for the first time in modern U.S. history, Hispanic and Latino Americans are forging an identity, a community of interests that links a disparate conglomerate of races and gives it a kind of overarching, almost corporate existence. We are following in the footsteps of African-Americans in that regard. Rather than just being defined by the majority culture, we are becoming self-defining. Over the centuries, that external definition, from the Anglo majority, has not been kind.

I began this book saying that the panic over Hispanics could not exist but for the issue of race. The anxiety stems from the more general tension between Anglos and all others, but since we are the biggest and certainly most visible "other" in the United States at the moment, most of the current angst is directed at us. Since the Spanish were cultural rivals and political enemies for so long, it appears almost instinctive in Anglo culture to regard Hispanic culture with scorn, suspicion, and a lack of esteem. "Mexicans are untrustworthy. Puerto Ricans are noisy. Cubans are slick." It is easy to overlook the fact that what is happening now is nothing new. It has been happening for all of the five hundred years Anglo and Hispanic societies have clashed.

The image of Spanish people as cruel, loose, greedy, and greasy dates back to the era of the great race to discover and colonize the New World from the late fifteenth through the nineteenth centuries. Since pioneering historian Julián Juderís in 1914, Latino writers have used the term "The Black Legend" (*La Leyenda Negra*) to describe the negative view of Hispanics created by anti-Spanish writers. Spain was the enemy and the English justified every act from conquest to piracy because they were the superior race. Of course, Spain did nothing to help its own image when it expelled the Jews and Muslims from the Iberian Peninsula, started the Inquisition, suppressed the Protestants in its New World colonies, and defied the rise of imperial England everywhere. The contemporary Latino historian Nicolas Kanellos quotes Phillip Wayne Powell's *Tree of Hate: Propaganda and Prejudices Affecting United States Relations with the Hispanic World*:

> Our (English) ancestors established themselves in America during the seventeenth century and this colonization process was nourished by their hatred of Spain and their desire to break the Spanish New World monopoly.

Spain and its progeny take a major bad rap on cruelty to native peoples, some justified. But history also records that the English had more than their own share of sadists, crooks, pirates, and profiteers, not to mention generations of slave snatchers, holders, traders, and plantation owners. And while the English made a habit of spreading their seed in any native female they fancied, they regarded the Spanish as inferior because under pressure from the church, Catholic Latinos frequently legitimized the status of native women, often through marriage.

History is relevant here because the stereotypical dark, arrogant, and invariably cruel Spanish conquistador as described by the English Enlightenment is the direct ancestor of the grotesque image attached to many Latino immigrants today. If you need proof of how deeply engrained "the Black Legend" is in American cultural history, I got this e-mail in September 2007:

> Gerald, you need to take a serious look at your Heart, before it is to late. You have a hatred of White European Men, and it is shown by the way you "take up" for the Hispanics and Blacks, when there is conflict between the Races. Many Blacks and American Hispanics have a deep down hatred, of the Europeans. They try to keep it hidden, but sometimes it will come out. I believe it is cause by Jealousy, of the success of the Europeans throughout History.
>
> The Liberal Politicians may give everything to certain groups of people, but the day is soon coming, that the evil ones will no longer exist.
>
> Warren, Tennessee

The "evil ones will no longer exist"? What does Warren have in mind?

Nicolas Kanellos has written about "the Spanish Black Legend [that] provided the ugly image of the Hispanic enemy that would fuel hateful speeches in Congress, yellow journalism, and popular culture to justify the expansion of the United States westward and southward." Not to mention frontier clashes and ultimate Anglo conquest from Florida to Louisiana and Texas, Mexico to the Philippines, Guam, Puerto Rico, Panama to Cuba.

Kanellos writes about the mind-set that the Protestant United States inherited from its English forebears that would allow the nation to regard the lowly Spanish as ripe for replacement: "The early Americans soon found an ideology that would allow them to replace the 'iniquitous Spanish' and their bastard progeny, at least in North America: Manifest Destiny."

First, the Spanish colonies in the south and southeast were taken: Baton Rouge in 1794, Mobile in 1811, and Pensacola in 1814. Soon after, successful independence movements swept Argentina, Chile, Colombia, Mexico, and Santo Domingo, humbling the Spanish Empire. The loss of Santo Domingo was particularly galling to the Spanish since its island of Hispaniola was the first of the discoveries of Christopher Columbus to be colonized. The nail in the coffin of the empire came in 1822, when President James Monroe recognized the independence of the former Spanish colonies and then boldly declared the entire Western Hemisphere off-limits to further European colonization. With the Monroe Doctrine in place, what was Spain's would become America's or hers to control.

Texas went first. When on April 21, 1836, the Lone Star Republic won its independence from Mexico after defeating the hapless general Antonio Lopez de Santa Anna, it was widely regarded as a foreordained conclusion. The victorious Sam Houston soon revealed both the racial aspects of his victory and his vision of a much larger Texas when he declared, "The Texian standard of the single star, borne by the Anglo-Saxon race, shall display its bright folds in Liberty's triumph, on the isthmus of Darien."

It took the U.S. another sixty-odd years, but our flag ultimately flew over the isthmus of Darien, a nation we carved from neighboring Colombia, christened Panama and used to link our coasts with the breathtaking and long-imagined Panama Canal. By then Puerto Rico and the Philippines had fallen to the conquering Americans. And as American hegemony spread throughout the New World, at home, Anglo-Americans consolidated their control over what was once Mexico. In his book *Thirty Million Strong: Reclaiming the Hispanic Image in American Culture*, Kanellos has written,

In the period of the Texas Republic and during statehood, Mexicans lost many of their [old Spanish] land grants, quite often through illicit means, to the rapidly growing, land-hungry Anglo population. Quite often the justification for the land grabs was racial, and racially motivated policy in education and labor and other areas would come to characterize the life of Mexican Americans in Texas thereafter.

Because we believe our nation to be essentially good and just, stories of land grabs and race-based social attitudes are difficult to credit from the distant perspective of the twenty-first century. But like the history of Anglo and African-Americans, and Anglo and Native Americans, the historic record of the relations between the Anglo and Hispanic Americans cannot seriously be disputed.

Flash forward to the massive May 2006 marches across the country in favor of immigration reform, which shocked everyone by their size and spontaneity. Cumulatively millions took to the streets of New York, Chicago, Denver, Los Angeles, San Francisco, Dallas, Houston, and other cities, many waving Mexican or Central American flags. Conservative radio hosts and other commentators reacted with horror and scorn. How dare they? They want to come here and enjoy the fruits of life in America and yet they're waving those wretched foreign flags?

What the grassroots demonstrations revealed was that for many residents of this country, legal and illegal, there is an alternative reality, a different historical script, a feeling that they didn't move over the border, the border moved over them.

On May 11, 1846, at the request of President James K. Polk, citing a fake border clash, the Congress of the United States declared war on Mexico. This episode has echoes in the Gulf of Tonkin Incident, the alleged provocation used to justify the Vietnam War more than a hundred years later. In 1846, the Mexican

nation was just twenty-five years old and still in shambles following its long, costly war of independence from Spain and its humiliating, eviscerating defeat in Texas. Before this impossible
conflict with the mighty United States was over, another vast slice
would be cut from the heart of the Republic of Mexico, including
land that became the states of California, Nevada, Arizona, New
Mexico, and Utah.

> Mexico was poor, distracted, in anarchy, and almost in
> ruins—what could she do to stay the hand of our power, to
> impede the march of our greatness? We are Anglo-Saxon
> Americans; it was our "destiny" to possess and to rule this
> Continent—we were bound to it! We were a chosen people,
> and this our allotted inheritance, and we must drive out all
> other nations before us.
> —(*The American Whig Review*, July 4, 1846)

These nineteenth-century conflicts between lowly Mexicans
and triumphal "Anglo-Saxon Americans" remain relevant in the
discussion of illegal immigration because the land principally being
trespassed on by the horde of undocumented immigrants from
Mexico once belonged to their great- or great-great-grandfathers.
Although the Treaty of Guadalupe-Hidalgo, which ended the Mexican War, guaranteed to protect the property rights of the indigenous people, those guarantees, like the early treaties with Native
Americans, were almost universally disregarded, and the land trans-
ferred to Anglos by one means or another.

And like the American conquest of the Indians, the invasion of
Mexico would not have been possible but for the attitude that
Anglo-English Protestant culture was superior to Mexican-Spanish
Catholic and that as we fulfilled our "Manifest Destiny," we were
also doing the racially and socially inferior Mexicans the favor of

exposing them to a modern, essentially secular, enlightened society. The irony is that many noted political figures of the time, including young Abraham Lincoln, former president John Quincy Adams, the poet Ralph Waldo Emerson, and the writer Henry David Thoreau, opposed the Mexican War, viewing it as an arrogant war of conquest. Adams said he feared that the United States was becoming a "conquering and warlike nation." Emerson predicted the nation would devour more territory, "as the man swallows arsenic, which brings him down in turn," while Thoreau refused to pay "war taxes," went to jail as a result, and there wrote his famous essay on "Civil Disobedience."

There was an added concern in that era before our own Civil War, especially given the tensions growing menacingly between America's North and South. After the earlier revolt of Texas and its admission to the Union as a slave state, Anglo liberals like Lincoln feared that Negro slavery, an odious institution that for a generation had already been illegal in "savage" Mexico, would likewise spread throughout the Southwest. Indeed, slavery was introduced into Texas only after it was taken by the United States from Mexico in 1836.

The United States rounded out its conquest of Mexico in 1853 when we forced then President Santa Anna to sell us the vast, 29-million-acre Mesilla Valley, which runs along the entire southern borders of Arizona and New Mexico. We needed the long stretch of land for our planned transcontinental railroad. Fearful of another widescale American military intervention, the spineless Santa Anna sold the land for $10 million, again displacing Mexicans who had moved to the valley from the territories already yielded to the United States following the end of the war. One of history's biggest losers, Santa Anna is still remembered as *"Vende Patria,"* the Seller of the Nation. Kanellos quotes a nineteenth-century Mexican ballad, *"Corrido de los Americanos"*:

People, be careful
Of the American race . . .
They're coming to throw us out of our country
And to take our land.

To many contemporary Mexicans, the monumental land grab is America's original sin. As with the French and Germans, the French and English, the Israelis and Palestinians, Poles and Russians, Turks and Armenians, Chinese and Tibetans, English and Irish, and all the other historic national catastrophes centered on culture clash, the fact that the entire Southwest once belonged to Mexico/Spain/Hispanics is remembered on one side as if it happened yesterday.

Is this really so extraordinary? Jews didn't forget Jerusalem after two thousand years. Neo-Confederates, sometimes in uniform, still refight Pickett's Charge at Gettysburg like it was that bright summer day in July 1863 when the South was still in the ascendant. Similarly, it should not be surprising that some of the seminal events from that (to Mexicans) epochal period are seen through a different lens than ours. Most famously, the Alamo is remembered more ambiguously than it is in films highlighting the doomed exploits of Davy Crockett, Jim Bowie, William Barret Travis, and the other Texas Spartans.

Since reading *Blood and Thunder,* Hampton Sides's wonderful book chronicling the "Epic Story of Kit Carson and the Conquest of the American West," I've been eager to present the other side of the story. Like how September 13 is celebrated in Mexico as *El Día de Los Niños Héroes de Chapultepec* (the Young Heroes of Chapultepec Day), in honor of the teenage cadets from their military academy, some as young as thirteen, who left their classrooms to march out and die on that date in 1847 facing the invading American army.

Closer to home in the San Pasqual Valley on the outskirts of San Diego, Sides vividly portrays in the terrific *Blood and Thunder* the Battle of San Pasqual, the high-water mark of Mexican resistance to the American invasion. After surrendering a vast swath of the Southwest from Santa Fe to the outskirts of San Diego, the Mexicans finally made a stand.

The invading American army, until then gloriously commanded by General Stephen W. Kearny, had been badly weakened and was dangerously scattered after crossing the parched, scorching Arizona desert. Now comprised of just 139 soldiers and marines, including friendly Indian scouts, Negro slaves, drovers, and the dauntless Indian-fighter Kit Carson, they were nevertheless in hot pursuit of an untested unit of Mexican lancers led by General Don Andres Pico. Pico was a consummate politician who managed to survive the war with his fortune and reputation intact; Pico Boulevard in Los Angeles is named in honor of his accomplished family. His adobe home on Sepulveda Boulevard, now a park, is the oldest in the San Fernando Valley, built in 1834.

Early on the dark, damp, cold, fog-shrouded morning of December 6, 1846, while still nearly a mile away, the scattered, mule-mounted Americans charged Pico's encampment. Mounted on fresh horses, the Mexicans easily outdistanced their pursuers, killing one of Kearny's key officers, Captain Abraham R. Johnson, in the first skirmish. Not to be denied, the brave Americans regrouped. Now led by Captain Benjamin D. Moore, the Americans charged again after Pico's lancers. Handicapped by wet powder that made their firearms unusable, the Americans were forced to use their swords. Sensing that his pursuers were vulnerable, Pico wheeled his lancers. Jose F. Palomares, one of Pico's men at the battle, recalled:

> With our lances and swords we attacked the enemy forces, who could make good use of neither their firearms nor of their swords. . . . We did not fire a single shot, the combat

was more favorable to us with our sidearm [lances]. Quickly
the battle became so bloody that we became intermingled
one with the other and barely were able to distinguish one
from the other by voice and by the dim light which began
to break.

—(*The Journal of San Diego History*, "The U.S.-Mexican
War in San Diego, 1846–1847: Loyalty and Resistance")

Moore fell, his sword impotent against the bitter points of the
longer lances. Fort Moore in Los Angeles is named for him. According to Dr. John S. Griffin, Kearny's surgeon, the Americans lost
a total of seventeen dead and eighteen wounded out of the fifty men
who actually took part in the fight; thirty-five casualties out of fifty,
including brave Kearny himself, gravely wounded. Pico's group suffered just two killed and eighteen wounded.

It was America's worst defeat in the Mexican War, but the effect
would be temporary. Looking for reinforcements, Kearny sent the
incomparable Kit Carson on a daring midnight foray to Commo-
dore Robert F. Stockton (yes, the Stockton the city is now named
for), headquartered in San Diego. Pico retreated to Los Angeles, and
his Lancers Charge, which would have been as legendary as Bunker
Hill if the Mexicans had turned the tide and won the war, instead
became a forgotten footnote in history. Still, if you are in the Escondido
area near San Diego, the San Pasqual Battlefield State Historic Park
is worth a visit.

And then there are the *San Patricios*. Widely reviled as traitors by
Americans of the period, the St. Patrick's Battalion was composed
of between three hundred and eight hundred deserters from the
U.S. Army who fought for Mexico in the war. Made up almost
entirely of Catholic immigrants, mostly from Ireland, but with substantial contingents from Germany and Scotland, they came to the
United States harboring deep resentments against the British. De-
ployed or settled in the American Southwest, these religious and

economic refugees from Europe's famines and discrimination found they identified more with their fellow oppressed Catholics, the Mexicans, than they did with their Anglo-American officers.

The turncoats were motivated perhaps by idealism, discontent, revenge, and/or the promise of property and citizenship in Mexico. They were first combined with other foreign volunteers and mustered into Mexico's Foreign Legion (*Legion de Extranjeros*). By September 1846 they had been formed into an elite artillery unit called the St. Patrick's Battalion and they fought bravely in several major engagements. Under the command of Captain John Riley, a daring and competent Irish-born British army veteran, and officers like Santiago O'Leary and Patrick Dalton, their stand at the battle of Monterrey is legendary in Mexico and Ireland. Fighting under their banner of green silk, the Irishmen also fought courageously at bloody Buena Vista, losing a third of their force in repelling the Americans.

The end for many of them came shortly after the Battle of Churubusco in August 1847, where the renamed *Legion Extranjeros Patricios* barricaded themselves inside the town's stout convent. Fighting with the ferocity of men who knew their lives were forfeit if captured, they were nevertheless overrun by the indomitable Americans after running out of ammunition and following brutal hand-to-hand combat.

A month later, outside the gates of the citadel city of Chapultepec, where the Mexicans had mounted a desperate defense in the face of a determined American assault personally led by commanding general Winfield Scott, a grisly and seldom mentioned chapter in American military history unfolded. Following the destruction of the battalion of teenagers whose hopeless charge is remembered in Mexican lore, Scott took his revenge on the *Patricios* captured in Churubusco.

Following several earlier executions of captured Irishmen, and soon after the capitulation of the last defenders after days of savage fighting, thirty *San Patricios* were hanged outside the gate of the citadel of Chapultepec. What made the scene so bizarre is General Scott's choreography of the executions. He ordered the Irishmen hung in full view of both the Mexican and American armies, but only at the precise moment of victory in the battle for the city. So the doomed prisoners were held bound and ready to drop for hours until the Mexican flag was finally hauled down and the U.S. flag floated from the citadel. Among the condemned men hung that day was Francis O'Connor. What made his execution particularly gruesome is that both his legs had been amputated the day before following a grievous battlefield injury.

The battalion is remembered with commemorations in Mexico on the recognized anniversary of the executions, September 12, and on St. Patrick's Day, March 17. Ireland also remembers the hopeless yet noble sacrifice of these Wild Geese, as they are called at home, these Irish mercenaries serving in the armies of Catholic countries or causes around the world, even as their own impoverished and oppressed homeland continued living under English rule. In honor of Captain John Riley, the Mexican flag flies daily from the town square in Clifden, County Galway, where he was born. I have to point it out to my colleagues Bill O'Reilly and Sean Hannity if we ever take a company field trip to Ireland.

After the war ended and through the rest of the nineteenth century, Anglo-Americans consolidated their control. Mexicans and Mexican Americans yielded ownership of ranches and mines and found themselves on the wrong side of restrictive legislation known as Greaser Laws, and other widespread anti-vagrancy acts and attitudes that helped cement their status as the region's underclass. The attitude of the Indiana congressman William Wick, speaking in 1846, was widely held: "I do not want any mixed races in our union, nor men of any color except white, unless they be slaves. Certainly not as voters or legislators. . . ."

The peerless Kanellos points to the different paths to statehood followed by California and New Mexico as one easy-to-understand example of the genuine loathing that many Anglo-Americans of the moment felt toward Hispanics. Although both became territories of the United States following the conquest of Mexico, only California was quickly admitted as a state of the Union, in 1850. There, the discovery of gold, vibrant seaborne trade, fear of Russian expansionism, and the planned transcontinental railroad quickly made Anglos the dominant class. The importance of California's treasures and strategic location helped overcome the fears of contemporary politicians like the Florida senator James D. Westcott, who did not want to be "compelled to receive not merely the white citizens of California and New Mexico, but the peons, Negroes, and Indians of all sorts, the wild tribe of Comanches, the bug-and-lizard-eating 'Diggers,' and other half-monkey savages in those countries, as equal citizens of the United States."

"Half-monkey savages," yikes! But you know what I find really scary? How many contemporary anti-immigration activists still believe deep in their hearts, as Westcott, Wicks, and General Kearny believed, that whites are inherently, fundamentally, irrevocably superior to Hispanics.

In 1912, sixty-two years after California, New Mexico and neighboring Arizona were finally admitted into the union. By then, slavery was no longer an issue and Anglo culture had firmly taken control from the bug and lizard eaters.

Reconquista

> "I believe that what we are fighting here is not just a small group of people . . . but it is a civilization bent on destroying ours."
>
> —CONGRESSMAN TOM TANCREDO

Under the terms of the Treaty of Guadalupe-Hidalgo that ended the Mexican War, all residents of territories ceded by Mexico to the

United States became American citizens, but the new national border cut through their farms and grazing ground, and divided families. The Encarta Encyclopedia and other sources estimate that 10 percent of today's Mexican-American population can directly "trace their roots to 17th and 18th Century colonists who settled in Mexican territories that are now part of the United States."

By 1868, the Citizenship Clause of the Fourteenth Amendment confirmed the citizenship of everyone who remained within the expanded United States (including those who were subsequently run out during the Great Depression). But while the new national frontier separated transborder families, as often as not it has been honored in the breach, treated as a tide, ebbing and flowing depending on the mood of the North, with generations of Mexican nationals allowed back into their former territory whenever we needed their sweat and toil.

Anti-immigrant propagandists now use the strong historic claims of Mexicans to their former national territory against them. Various commentators, politicians like Tom Tancredo, and groups like the Minutemen want to doubly punish the successors, playing a kind of Losers Weepers, Finders Keepers when it comes to the inestimable fruits of that adventurous Mexican War. They also want to exploit the understandable longing for the not-so-distant past as a reason to fear Hispanics.

But there is not and has never been a substantive threat by today's Mexican Americans to take their land back. There have been occasional wild-eyed mystics, like Reies Tijerina, labeled "Don Quixote" by the contemporary press. His civil rights–era quest to restore rights to descendents of the original Mexican and Spanish property owners culminated in a lunatic raid on a New Mexican courthouse. Before he flamed out in 1967, the group he created, called Alianza, boasted twenty thousand members.

On June 3, 1967, scores of activists assembled in the dusty New Mexican village of Coyote. Their mission was to free several of their members arrested earlier at a property rights rally by cops who feared they were communists. In Tijerina's raid on the Rio Arriba County Courthouse, a prison guard and a sheriff's deputy were shot and two hostages were taken as the fugitives fled to the rugged mountains of New Mexico. After the largest manhunt in state history, Tijerina surrendered to authorities in Albuquerque. Charged with fifty-four counts, including kidnapping and assault, he was tried and acquitted on all state charges, but was later convicted by a federal court and sentenced to two years.

Like the Japanese soldiers holed up on lonely Pacific islands who didn't hear that World War II was over until years later, Tijerina really was the last of the separatist Mohicans. And the context was 1967, when the rest of the nation was reeling from assassinations, urban rioting, an already unpopular Vietnam War, and rapidly spreading social upheaval. There are claims by the most extreme anti-immigration activists that meaningful contemporary Hispanic groups secretly plot the creation in the Southwest of "Aztlan" (the mythic homeland of the Aztec Indians), or "Mexifornia" (as in Mexican California), or the *"reconquista"* (recapture) of territories lost by Mexico a century and a half ago to the United States. But there is no serious succession movement.

As the Anti-Defamation League and other pro-immigrant groups now frequently suggest, the notion of *reconquista* primarily exists in the "fever dreams of white supremacists." Those individuals, like the snarly shock jock Michael Savage, who allege that groups like the National Council of La Raza (NCLR) is either racist or separatist are smoking too much peyote, metaphorically speaking. With its work in areas like voting rights, criminal and juvenile justice, and tax and education reform, NCLR is a civil rights and advocacy group as mainstream as the NAACP, which Savage probably doesn't like either.

That is not to suggest that there aren't a handful of radical Hispanics, mostly college campus activists, who proclaim nonsense. For example, there is apparently an underground splinter group called the Nation of Aztlan. According to the Anti-Defamation League, "The group's nationalist message is blurred by frequent appeals to anti-Semitism, anti-Zionism, homophobia and other expressions of hatred." The ADL cites a lone incident back in 1998, when "a group of ten people wearing masks, including Juan 'Ralphy' Avila, a spokesman for the Nation of Aztlan at the time, burned a U.S. flag in front of city hall in Fresno, California." As far as I know, that incident was the last of its kind by this particular organization.

To suggest as Michelle Malkin did in March 2006 on *The O'Reilly Factor* that "the intellectual underpinnings of *reconquista* are embraced by the vast majority of mainstream Hispanic politicians" is sheer slander. Politicians like whom? Senators Salazar and Martinez? Representatives Serrano, Ros-Lehtinen, or the Diaz-Balart brothers? Herman Badillo? Mayor Villaraigosa? The NCLR? Me?

When contemporary commentators deride pro-immigration demonstrators for brandishing the Mexican or other Latin American flag, are they similarly distressed by the marchers proudly waving Irish, Italian, or Israeli flags at their various national celebrations? I am not fond of immigration activists waving the Mexican flag or reciting the Pledge of Allegiance in Spanish precisely because it is fodder for the radical nativists. But for God's sake, however history happened, all but the lunatic fringe agrees that modern boundaries are now firmly and forever established. Every reasonable commentator understands that. Where history should be relevant is when it comes to how we treat these so-called trespassers from Mexico.

At least Native Americans have experienced some belated justice in recent decades. It didn't come to the Indians without a fight. The mainstream public's attitude toward them is a product of decades of activism. Contemporary society forgets the significance of the occupation of Alcatraz Island between 1969 and 1971, and more important, the American Indian Movement (AIM) occupation of Wounded Knee in 1973, which put the Indian experience in perspective for millions of Americans like me who had been raised on cowboy and Indian movies.

Only after those controversial public actions was a climate created in which the wrongs done to the original inhabitants of the New World were compensated by court rulings and remedial legislation defining rights. Among more noble aspects, the rulings also permit gambling and other commercial activity, like Connecticut's lavish Foxwoods Resort and Casino on sovereign reservations.

There were no casinos or oil leases for the Mexicans excluded from their historic lands along with the Apache, Navajo, Comanche, Sioux, and Seminole. Like the occasionally voiced claims by African-Americans for reparations for four hundred years of slavery, that request would generate widespread ridicule and rejection. The era of in-your-face activism that worked for Native Americans in the day is over, ended for sure when the world changed on September 11, 2001. In any case, no Mexican American I know is asking for anything back.

But no one can deny that the surprisingly vast and spontaneous turnout at the various immigration rights rallies around the nation in 2006 helped quash the loathsome Sensenbrenner legislation that would have made felons of landlords, priests, and social workers. And isn't it reasonable in today's debate that there be some small recognition of the shared history between Anglo and Hispanic America; some recollection of the long decades of peonage and benignly neglected transborder life; some small advantage given, particularly to Mexicans, when it comes to immigration?

16

The Threat to
the Two-Party System

"The reason Cubans continue to come here—and let's face it,
the Cubans are not nearly so desperate as the Haitians—is because they know that if they make it to the beach, chances are
that they'll be allowed to stay."
—Wayne Smith, Senior Fellow, Center for International Policy
and former head of U.S. Interests Section in Havana, quoted in
Fort Lauderdale *Sun-Sentinel*, September 21, 2000

"Any Latino who votes for a Republican is an Uncle Tom."
—Legendary music performer Carlos Santana
to the author, Washington, D.C., June 1999

I'm a veteran high-seas sailor, and there is nothing as terrifying to
me as a shark feeding frenzy. Having stood on the deck of my sail-
boat in the South Pacific and the Bahamas and watched the killing
machines tearing apart man-sized tuna, I shudder to imagine the
hellish scene before dawn one Friday morning in May 2007 when a
rickety, twenty-five-foot boat was struck by a sudden squall near the
Turks and Caicos Islands. The vessel was grossly overloaded, jammed
with 150 Haitian migrants. As passengers panicked by the choppy
seas started pushing and shoving each other, the vessel capsized in
shark-infested waters.

In the terror that followed, it was every man for himself, with
the strong surviving the frenzy by kicking, clawing, and clinging to
wreckage at the expense of the weak. In the frenzied two hours it

took the Coast Guard and other rescuers to arrive, half of the migrants were killed, including scores of women and little children, some found half eaten, with arms and legs missing. Others were plucked from the grisly soup, some bloody and injured, but extremely lucky to be alive. Sixty-nine of the seventy-eight survivors were men. Just nine females made it safely ashore and almost none of the survivors were children.

The worst Haitian refugee disaster in years, this horrible accident reminded me of the vast disparity that exists between the treatment received by illegal refugees from Haiti and neighboring Cuba. It is as vast as the geographic distance between the neighboring Caribbean island nations is small. Haiti and Cuba are separated by only the fifty miles of the Windward Passage. But like the Negro slavery that accompanied the Anglo conquest of Texas in 1836 and is barely mentioned in the "Remember the Alamo" legend, the fundamentally discriminatory character of our immigration policy toward these island neighbors is not much talked about in either Miami or Washington. It is undeniable that all refugees are not created equal.

A Cuban who touches America's shores has a reasonable expectation of remaining in the United States. Haitians and all other "boat people" are routinely detained and their removal back to Haiti or other country of origin expedited. And even though then presidential candidate Bill Clinton condemned the first Bush administration for a "cruel policy of returning Haitian refugees to a brutal dictatorship," neither he nor his successor, George W. Bush, lifted a finger to change the policy. Clinton's lame explanation was that he didn't want to start a stampede of refugees from Haiti by seeming to encourage them to rush willy-nilly to America.

After his administration played the central role in having Elián González sent home, Clinton was probably also afraid to anger the Cuban community any more than he already had. He probably made the calculation that whatever segment of the Haitian-American community was eligible to vote was going to vote Democrat whether he really helped them out or not. President Bush at least has been blunt and public about directing the Immigration and Naturalization Service not to allow Haitians even to be released from detention pending the outcome of their removal hearings—that is, no bail.

Which brings me back to my Cuban cousins, most of whom have been here only since the Castro convulsion of 1959, but who nevertheless in the election of 2000 proved to be among America's most cohesive, motivated, and united voting blocs. Given the crucial role Florida's electoral votes played in Bush versus Gore, the Cuban Americans almost single-handedly gave George Bush the state and, by extension, the presidency.

Why do you think the majority of at least those Cuban Americans living in the Sunshine State, alone among U.S. Latinos, has been solidly Republican, while the majority of every other Hispanic group is heavily Democratic? Like Dominicans, Puerto Ricans, Mexicans, Venezuelans, and every other subdivision within the Latino community, Cubans tend to be more socially conservative than Anglos on issues of faith, like abortion and gay marriage. By the same token, Hispanics all tend to be similarly hardworking, churchgoing, and traditional as opposed to secular and progressive. Nor can social class or economic status explain the phenomenon. While the initial wave of Cuban immigrants was made up of the cream of island society and was presumably more inclined to be attracted to the pro-business party, by the time of the 1980 Mariel boatlift, the refugees no longer fit the GOP stereotype.

Isn't it reasonable to assume, then, that the relatively gracious way Cubans are treated when they enter this country without proper documentation, as opposed to how their immigrant cousins from other nations are treated, is one factor in their subsequent choice of political affiliation? Or perhaps is it the converse, that they are treated more leniently because once they get to Florida they tend to rally behind elected officials and a largely Republican political establishment?

Of course, America's unique and continuingly bitter mini–Cold War with Castro and communist Cuba affects all policy toward the community, immigrant and otherwise. Some of the enduring loyalty to the GOP, particularly among the older Cuban exiles, still dates back to Ronald Reagan's landmark 1983 visit to Miami's Little Havana when the Great Communicator thrilled particularly the old-timers by crying, *"Cuba sí, Castro no!"* (Campaigning in Miami in March 2007, presidential candidate Mitt Romney tried to borrow a page from the Gipper's handbook, but he screwed up the Spanish and ended up quoting Castro instead of condemning him.)

The fact that the only Hispanic group treated humanely on the issue of immigration is also the only Hispanic group that favors the Republicans is not insignificant. And even here, the glow from long-ago Reagan may not be enough to salvage the GOP, even in South Florida. At the time of the Romney gaffe, the Associated Press opined that drinking "café con leche and shouting *'Viva Cuba libre!'* may no longer guarantee votes in a community that has moved from the margins of society to the professional and political mainstream."

No political party can prevail nationally on Anglo votes alone, so the long-term danger to Republicans is that their party is sending a message to Latinos that it doesn't want us. "There has been too much of an anti-immigration tone," Representative Lincoln Diaz-Balart, one of the three South Florida Republican congressmen, told *USA Today.* "When people start to perceive that immigrants are being put in the same category as a threat to national security, it's hard to get your message across."

Which brings me to the GOP's stinging defeat in the 2006 midterm elections and the prospect for 2008 for the party that deserted its own president's immigration reform legislation and is now attempting to whip its base into a frenzy on the backs of illegal aliens. Two June 2007 polls showed an overwhelming number of Hispanics now identify themselves as Democrats—58 percent according to a *USA Today*/Gallup poll and 51 percent according to one conducted by NBC News and the *Wall Street Journal*. The same polls showed Hispanics identifying as Republican at 20 percent and 21 percent, respectively.

The Republicans have by their actions on immigration reform put themselves on the wrong side of history and an inevitable demographic trend that could cost them dearly in future elections. What is surprising, given their usually superb political instincts in the Karl Rove era, is that the mistake was avoidable, because the statistics quoted above represent a sea change in the Hispanic community, which had been going the Republicans' way.

In 2004, Republicans, with 9 million registered Hispanic voters, had a reasonable chance of becoming the permanent majority party in this country partly because of the strength of the president's support among Latinos. George W. Bush was reelected that year despite growing opposition to the war in Iraq and concerns about overreaching domestic surveillance and even allegations of corruption. And Hispanics helped save his presidency even more than Republicans had hoped. A *Los Angeles Times* exit poll showed that nationally, Bush got 45 percent of the total Hispanic vote, a gain of 7 percent over his take in 2000 and more than double the GOP Hispanic vote in 1996. As hard, cruel, clear political analyst Dick Morris said the week after Bush's 2004 triumph over John Kerry:

> Bush has worked incredibly hard for his Hispanic vote share. He reversed historic Republican Party positions on issues of importance to Hispanics and showed a willingness to listen to the needs of the Latino community.

That respectful romance with Latinos ended abruptly in the lead-up to the November 2006 elections when extremists on immigration hijacked the GOP.

One of them, Senator John Cornyn of Texas, may ultimately wish he had taken a more moderate stance instead of essentially adopting the position of the Minutemen and similar radical anti-immigration groups. These groups promulgate their wildly exaggerated portrayal of a cascade of brown people overwhelming our southern borders, running loose to rape, steal, and murder on the streets of our cities.

In August 2007, one of the top Hispanic Republicans in Texas announced he would back a Democrat instead of Senator Cornyn in the 2008 elections. Businessman Massey Villarreal told the *Rio Grande Guardian* and the Associated Press that he would throw his support to State Representative Rick Noriega, a Democrat. "I have decided to support Rick Noriega for U.S. Senate as a Democrat. I just don't think John Cornyn hears my community," Villarreal said. "Immigration reform is one of the defining positions in my community. I have got to support what is good for my community. At the end of the day, regardless of party, we have to come home to our community, where we grew up in the grass roots."

What makes the defection so important is Villarreal's status in the GOP establishment. A prominent Houston-area businessman, he served as Hispanic vice chairman of the Bush-Cheney for President campaign and deputy vice chairman of the Republican National Convention.

"Every time I saw a picture of John Cornyn speaking with Lou Dobbs or any of those talking heads, they show a picture of Mexicans jumping over the fence," Villarreal told the *Rio Grande Guardian*, adding, "The only reason they have to jump the fence is because he [Cornyn] does not have the gall to have a program, or a process, or a legal system to have legal immigration."

If the GOP is losing guys like Villarreal, the implications are grim for the party. As he departed the White House in August 2007, Karl Rove, for years the president's closest political adviser, warned against alienating Hispanics on the issue of immigration, saying that the party should not put itself out of line with "a vital part of the electorate that fundamentally shares our values and concerns."

How vital a part of the electorate? A record 8.6 percent of all eligible voters in 2006 were Hispanic, compared to 7.4 percent in 2004 and just 5.5 percent in 2000, and that number is expected to rise in November 2008. Census data shows that the number of Hispanic voters could reach 10 percent or more by then, according to the Pew Hispanic Center.

By adopting a position at odds with the president's moderation and with Republican Senate centrists like Arlen Specter or Lindsey Graham, the GOP insulted Hispanic Americans, helped fuel the rise of radicals like Venezuela's Hugo Chávez by appearing anti-Latino, and led the way to its own resounding November 2006 defeat.

While the war in Iraq was in 2006 the single most galvanizing issue for most Americans, for Hispanics it was immigration, and they made Republicans pay for their insults. In the elections of 2004, 40 percent of Hispanics voted for GOP congressional candidates. In 2006, that number was down to 26 percent. The effect of that seismic shift among the nation's fastest-growing ethnic group of perhaps 2 million votes was the utter defeat of radical candidates like Arizona congressmen Randy Graf and J. D. Hayworth. Graf ran a scummy ad showing a little blond-haired child walking by a slowly opening door as a doom-laden voice-over talked ominously about how the nation's open-door policy was leading to crime and decay (and presumably Mexicans raping little blond girls). In his noxious ads, six-term Indiana congressman John Hostettler appeared with representatives of the Minutemen and campaigned against the "nightmare of immigrant amnesty." None of it worked. "If running against illegal immigration were a winner, Arizona's J. D. Hayworth would still be in Congress," said the *Wall Street Journal* at the time.

The vote proved that most Hispanic Americans, although personally unaffected by immigration policy, would not ignore the insult to others who are here illegally. As for me, a professed live-and-let-live libertarian who has often voted for Republicans, I say here and now that I will never vote for any Republican (or Democrat) who opposes rational immigration reform and seeks to score votes on the backs of illegal aliens. Never. I don't care if I know the candidate personally or even if I have voted for him or her before.

Which brings me back to Carlos Santana and that night at the Congressional Hispanic Caucus dinner in Washington, D.C., when he was awarded the CHC's 1999 Medallion of Excellence. Carlos performed, thrilling the crowd of elected officials, bureaucrats, and luminaries playing his magical guitar alongside the legendary salsa artist Tito Puente.

Tito was a dear man, who with Cuba's Queen of Salsa, Celia Cruz, Willie Colon, and other Fania All-Stars helped popularize salsa, the driving, rhythmically seductive Spanish Caribbean music. He was a pillar of the Puerto Rican community and an old hang-out buddy of mine. In 1999, as the saying goes, we went way back. In the mid-1970s, I narrated a feature-length documentary film that is still in circulation that chronicled the rise of salsa music for Tito's pioneering producer Jerry Masucci. That night in D.C., Tito introduced me to Carlos and I suggested we get together for a drink. I was in the midst of reporting the *Nueva America* documentary for NBC and I wanted to interview the world's greatest rock guitarist (with kudos also to Eric Clapton). Carlos agreed and we went to a joint in downtown Washington, where after a couple (at least I had a couple; I don't remember if this deeply spiritual, Mexican-born mystic drank), we started talking politics.

I asked Carlos Santana what he thought of the pending Bush versus Gore election. That's when he told me, "Any Latino who votes for a Republican is an Uncle Tom." I have modified his Shermanesque statement to read, "Any Latino who votes for a Republican or a Democrat who opposes rational immigration reform is an Uncle Tom." The big political mystery going into the 2008 election cycle is whether the Hispanic votes like mine, lost to Republicans because of their rabid stance on immigration, will be made up for by an energized base among Anglo voters who have embraced anti-immigrationism as they once embraced opposition to gay marriage or abortion.

As the nationally recognized pollster Sergio Bendixen, who has worked for Senator Hillary Clinton and the Democratic Senatorial Campaign Committee, said in a New America Media piece following the 2006 election, titled "GOP Blew It: Latinos Are Moving Toward the Democratic Party":

> The immigration issue had a lot to do with energizing the Hispanic electorate, making them a lot more interested in politics and a lot more willing to come out to the polls and participate in the electoral process . . . many Hispanics have been offended by the tone of the debate in the Congress, by reactionary solutions that have been proposed by many members of Congress. . . . I think they blame the Republican Party for the unfair way that the issue has been handled and the way it has hurt the image of the Hispanic community nationally.

Mel Martinez, the Florida GOP senator, chairman of the Republican National Committee, and the only Hispanic Republican in the Senate, told his colleagues in what the *New York Times* characterized as a "stern warning," that "this is the first issue that, in my mind, has absolutely galvanized the Latino community in America like no other." When all the GOP presidential candidates except brave John McCain decided to skip an offered historic debate in Spanish sponsored by Univision, Martinez tried to be a good soldier, telling reporters, "I was hoping that there would be a good participation in the Univision forum. It's a very busy primary calendar, and their schedules are such that this forum didn't fit in. Now is this a rejection of Hispanic voters? Of course not. And I hope it's not seen that way."

Simon Rosenberg, who has studied the Latino electorate and runs the New Democrat Network, which helped set up the successful Democratic forum on Univision, commented in the *Washington Post*, "To be frank, every day Martinez's job is to put lipstick on a pig. It's not a pretty job, but he took it, and now he's got to live with it." Tellingly, the same week the GOP opted not to participate in the fall 2007 Univision network Voter Forum, the Spanish-language network captured the number-one ranking nationally among all adults eighteen to thirty-four, not just Hispanics. In doing so it outdelivered ABC, CBS, NBC, FOX, and the CW network. It was the first week that the Nielsen rating service calculated the ratings for all the networks with a single national panel (NPM). "Now with a single ratings source, advertisers [and politicians!] can see, more easily than ever, just how important Univision can be as part of their overall media plans," said Alina Falcon, executive vice president and operating manager of the Univision Network.

This is a good time to quote the born-in-Spain philosopher who curiously always wrote in English:

> **"Those who cannot learn from history are doomed to repeat it."**
>
> —George Santayana

In 1994, the California governor Pete Wilson, worried about a close election race, played the immigrant-bashing card, which among other odious aspects sought a referendum kicking the children of illegal immigrants out of schools and stripping their access to other public services. Outraged, I moved my daytime talk show to Los Angeles and did a series of shows demonstrating the unfairness and, more important, the obvious unconstitutionality of the proposals. We packed the audience with sympathetic students who would be adversely affected. The infamous Proposition 187 passed anyway and overwhelmingly, and Wilson managed to win reelection. The federal courts later tossed the measure, declaring the proposition unconstitutional, as every sober legal mind in the profession knew they would, but the Republican Party in the Golden State has never recovered from the perceived insult. Governor Schwarzenegger is a uniquely appealing anomaly. In terms of presidential politics, California is now solidly a blue state.

How bad is the erosion of Hispanic voter support for the GOP? Even Miami-Dade's famously Republican Hispanic voters are increasingly becoming independents. A *Miami Herald* survey found that less than half of the county's Hispanic voters are registered Republicans, down from 59 percent less than a decade ago. "It's a trend that I've seen happening, and obviously it concerns me," Jose "Pepe" Riesco, vice chairman of the Miami-Dade Republican Party, told the paper. "It's a problem we can't run away from."

The *Herald*'s survey found that statewide, where non-Cuban Hispanics constitute a much larger segment of the Latino community than they do in South Florida, about 37 percent of Hispanics are registered Republicans, compared with 33 percent registered as Democrats. "This is huge, because this is the state Republicans point to as a model of their Hispanic outreach," Florida Democratic Party spokesman Mark Bubriski told the *Herald*. "Clearly, the Bush era is dead."

The Reverend Luis Cortes, a Philadelphia pastor who is said to be close to President Bush and is the leader of a national organization of Hispanic Protestant clergy members, told the *New York Times* he had delivered a message at a pre–2006 election White House meeting: "I believe the Republican Party has hurt itself already," with its stance on immigration. The Reverend Samuel Rodriquez, who heads up the National Hispanic Christian Leadership Conference and is politically connected enough to participate in weekly White House conference calls, told William McKenzie of the *Dallas Morning News* that his congregants are natural Republicans, but are wondering now whether "the GOP is the party of [Alabama senator] Jeff Sessions, Tom Tancredo and James Sensenbrenner or the party of George W. Bush and John McCain? Xenophobia has triumphed over an appreciation for diversity. They completely abandoned us," he told reporter McKenzie, adding that he thinks Latino evangelicals will either vote Democratic in November 2008 or stay home.

I have always seen the *Wall Street Journal*'s editorial page as the place far right-wingers can go for extremist political rhetoric and silently move their lips as they read along. One of the personal ironies in the current immigration debate is how the page could be writing my material. Check out this editorial from June 2007:

> [Hispanics] know that when Tom Tancredo calls for an immigration "time out," he's not talking about the Irish. He means no more Mexicans, Hondurans or other Hispanics. . . . If the GOP wants to be deserted by Hispanics for the next few election cycles, that sort of talk should do the trick.

I agree with the *Wall Street Journal* editorial page 100 percent on this issue; the current anti-immigration hysteria willfully ignores our immigrant tradition, is bad business and bad politics. The page is trying to reach tax-cutting, business-oriented Republicans with dozens of opinion items like this one:

> Some conservatives insist that it's only the illegal aliens who have earned their wrath, but when the target of scorn is the mother or brother or cousin of someone here lawfully, that becomes a difference without much of a distinction politically. Moreover, Tom Tancredo, the pied piper of restrictionists in Congress, wants a "time out" on all legal immigration, and Hispanic voters are wise to the fact that it's not because he

thinks there are too many Italians in the U.S. Republican pols may decide to follow Mr. Tancredo, Lou Dobbs, Fox News populists and obsessive bloggers down this path, but it's likely to lead to political defeat.

—(*Wall Street Journal* editorial page, September 15, 2007)

"The GOP is being torn apart by the immigration debate," says the Southern Poverty Law Center's Mark Potok. "The weird thing is that the most right-wing administration in history is actually decent on immigration, but an increasing number of Republicans are pandering to the worst of their base, making a cynical calculation that trades short-term gain over the long-term interests of their party."

According to the *Wall Street Journal*, Massey Villarreal, who is also vice chairman of the U.S. Hispanic Chamber of Commerce, said recently: "I've been trying to put my finger in the dam of Hispanics leaving the Republican Party. I can't anymore. I've run out of fingers." By late summer 2007, the mainstream GOP began slowly panicking as polls indicated a wholesale desertion of the party by Latino voters. A coalition of Hispanic Republican organizations released the following statement on September 17, 2007:

> The Republican Party is and has been the Party of personal responsibility, free enterprise, and individual initiative; it's the Party of small business. . . . The Republican Party is not the Party of white people. The harsh and nativist-sounding rhetoric coming from some Party members on the issue of immigration reform is inflicting long-term damage to what should be a natural affinity between Hispanics and the core values of the Republican Party.

"There may be some short-term gain from this," Linda Chavez, formerly the director of the U.S. Commission on Civil Rights under Reagan and now chairwoman of a conservative public policy group called the Center for Equal Opportunity, told the *New York Times*. She was referring to the reenergized Republican social conservatives like Limbaugh and Dobbs, furious about illegal immigration. "But in the long term, it is disastrous for the Republican Party," said the no-nonsense columnist, adding, "The tone of the debate, and the way it was framed in sort of an 'us against them' way, has done great harm in wooing Hispanics to the party."

Perhaps surprisingly from a commentator who consistently railed against bilingual education and criticized my Puerto Rican community for welfare dependency and illegitimacy (and was punched in the nose when she showed up to speak at a community college in the Bronx), Ms. Chavez went further in a May 2007 column called "Latino Fear and Loathing." It had me cheering.

> They think Latinos are freeloaders and welfare cheats who are too lazy to learn English. They think Latinos have too many babies, and that Latino kids will dumb down our schools. They think Latinos are dirty, diseased, indolent, and more prone to criminal behavior. They think Latinos are just too different from us to become real Americans.

Then she really pissed off her party's conservatives by alleging that among the worst of the worst distorting the immigration debate were

> a fair number of Republican members of Congress, almost all influential conservative talk radio hosts, some cable news anchors—most prominently, Lou Dobbs—and a handful of public policy "experts" at organizations such as the Center for Immigration Studies, the Federation for American Immigration Reform, NumbersUSA, in addition to fringe groups like the Minutemen.

You go, girl! Ms. Chavez later apologized for perhaps overstating her case against her fellow conservatives and hurting some "erstwhile allies" in the GOP, but I think she got it exactly right. All that most of the undocumented want is a fair shake and a chance to work hard and realize what we proudly call the American Dream. Give them the chance to regularize and legitimatize their status, and watch as they become another unique component of the national mosaic. Maybe they will even become Republicans. But the chances of that happening in the current toxic environment are almost zero.

In criticizing his party's aggressively anti-immigrant tilt, particularly one delegate, who called illegal immigration "a stealth weapon by which Satan plans to destroy the free world," Gil Cisneros, the chairman of the Colorado state chapter of the Republican National Hispanic Assembly, quoted in the *Rocky Mountain News*, put it more colorfully: "Don't come to us on Election Day and eat our tamales and want us to vote for you." More likely, Hispanics will gravitate increasingly to the Democratic side of the aisle. And if that tilt can affect even Florida's Cuban-American community, as the Miami-Dade Democratic Party chairman Joe Garcia told the *Herald*, "There's no math in the world that will give Republicans the White House in 2008."

Conclusion

An Emancipation Proclamation for the New Century

"Can't we all just get along?"
—Rodney King

When Colonel Oliver North twice emphasized that the person he was about to introduce was a "friend," I should have known what was coming. The event was the fifth annual 9/11 commemorative Freedom Concert, with a portion of the proceeds benefiting Ollie's Freedom Alliance, the nonprofit he established in the wake of the Iran-Contra scandal in the waning days of the 1980s Reagan administration to promote patriotic causes, in this case scholarships to the children of military service members killed or injured in the line of duty. Cosponsoring the event was WABC radio, the big AM talk station in New York that carries Rush Limbaugh. The station's afternoon star, Sean Hannity, was cohosting the event, an all-day affair in which more than forty thousand people participated.

I had volunteered to attend, thinking the evening concert was a benefit for GIs, who I expected to fill the audience that misty, humid night in the ten-thousand-seat open-air arena at the Six Flags Amusement Park in Jackson, New Jersey, about sixty-five miles south of New York City. After six years as one of the Fox News Channel's main war correspondents, I have gotten very close to many men and women serving in the armed forces. My other reason

254

for attending was to extend an olive branch to Sean after the two of us had a particularly bitter on-air exchange on his evening cable news show concerning the alleged link between illegal immigration and crime.

The evening was starring Lee Greenwood, who sings that song about wanting to be an American, and LeAnn Rimes, who was onstage performing when I arrived. Sean gave a double take when he saw me, apparently surprised to see me despite my repeated assurances that I would show up.

Aside from one black radio technician, the crowd was all white, not mostly or almost all, but entirely white thirty- and forty-somethings, many wearing cowboy hats. I had no idea there were that many cowboy hats in New Jersey. When LeAnn finished her last song, which acknowledged all the painful things she had been through as a troubled teenaged star, but also that she was a grown-up woman now, the crowd roared. Then Ollie began my introduction. Without naming me, he stressed my support of the troops. As with Hannity, Colonel North and I have enjoyed a cordial personal off-air friendship that always trumps our political differences, and since we usually only interact on air in Iraqi or Afghani war zones, we tend to agree about most things. Despite the role he admitted playing in secretly funding the anti-Communist crusades in Central America twenty years ago, I admire him because he is a bona fide Marine Corps hero, twice decorated with the Purple Heart after being wounded in combat in service to his nation.

Colonel North finished my introduction and said, "Here's Geraldo Rivera." I strode confidently onto the stage, expecting the usual warm response, and was instead met by a wall of boos from the crowd. Not the whole crowd, as my lawyer and best friend Leo Kayser III later reported on our long, gloomy drive back to the city, saying in his resilient Alabama drawl, which has survived forty years in the Big Apple, "A third applauded yah, a third booed yah, and the other third was so stunned to see yah thar, they just sat and stared."

After my unequivocal support, sometimes at substantial risk and sacrifice, for the cause being commemorated that night, battling back after 9/11, being booed was a humiliation and an embarrassment. But my first reaction was anger; I wanted to flip everybody the bird and stomp off. Instead, I reminded the crowd that like Oliver North I had also been to Iraq eight times; that took the raw edge off their disdain. I made a lame statement about all of us having to be united if we were to succeed in the war. Still flustered, I introduced another Fox News colleague, the reporter Uma Pemmaraju, also the child of immigrants, in her case from India, who had driven down to Six Flags with Leo and me. Then we both walked off to thin, scattered applause mixed with a few muted jeers.

Those faux cowboys had booed me, but their real target was illegal immigration and all the toxic baggage the issue is generating. Like the on-air beat-down President Bush got from Rush Limbaugh and friends when he demanded their cooperation on immigration reform, and that they do the right thing for the country, the crowd was getting back at me for every word I had ever spoken for the cause of reform.

When I next appeared on Sean Hannity's TV show in September 2007, the topic, mercifully, was one of the few we could agree on, the bizarre Las Vegas arrest of O. J. Simpson for allegedly committing an armed robbery to retrieve items the acquitted double murderer said were stolen from him. The suddenness with which the Simpson story broke was like a breeze blowing away months of simmering tensions between Sean and me. Finally, we had a common cause. "I want to thank you for coming to the concert," he told me during a commercial break between segments.

"Yeah, sure," I answered sarcastically.

"What'd'ya mean?" He did his best to sound shocked.

"Well, it wasn't the warmest reception," I replied, giving him that line about not knowing there were that many cowboy hats in New Jersey.

"Well, you know they love you over Iraq, it's this immigration thing," Sean said honestly, his voice trailing off, leaving all the rest unsaid because we didn't want to start the fight again.

It was only the second time I had been booed in thirty-seven years of public life, and it was for the same essential reason: a disconnect between the audience and the once-trusted public figure they thought had turned on them and let them down.

The other time it happened was at a Puerto Rican Socialist Party rally held in a packed Madison Square Garden in 1975 or 1976. Attended by such antiestablishment luminaries as Jane Fonda, the purpose of that event was to advocate the independence of Puerto Rico. It was a cause I had supported as a younger man, particularly when I represented the Young Lords, but on which I had recently begun waffling. Still, I was sympathetic enough to agree to make a brief speech in Spanish about the dignity of self-determination, although I was already favoring statehood as a solution to the island's stagnation. The crowd that night was all island-born, hard-core, left-wing *independentistas*, and they let me have it with a cascade of boos and derisive catcalls that accused me of being a sellout to the Yankee imperialists. *"Geraldo abajo, Los Yankis son carajo!"* or, basically, "Down with Geraldo, the Yankees suck!" I was no longer left-wing enough for them, in the same way I wasn't right-wing enough for this crowd thirty-one years later at Six Flags.

Jane Fonda hugged me when I finally got offstage that long-ago night at the Garden, shaken after the longest few minutes of my life. She praised me for having the courage to go on—as if I would have done it had I known the reaction I would get. It wasn't courage either that time or at the Freedom Concert; it was naiveté, a willful arrogant ignorance with both those crowds that a middle road was possible and that the macho goodwill I had built up over the years could sustain a little disagreement. I had also woefully underestimated the depth of feeling, both for Puerto Rican independence by the socialists and for an end to illegal immigration by today's U.S. nativists.

After my Garden party, I never spoke again even in general terms about wanting Puerto Rican independence. I theorized then and now that any movement not big enough to include a moderate voice was too radical ever to garner widespread public support. Indeed, the independence movement was soon marginalized in Puerto Rico, withering to less than 5 percent of the popular vote in recent island elections as the inherently socially conservative people abandoned the wild-eyed romantics who would take them away from the safe harbor of commonwealth association with the United States and toss us off the cliff into the uncertain sea of independence. Their run is over.

I wish I could say the same fate awaits the opponents of immigration reform, but they are just now feeling their muscle. If you want a quick ratings fix on talk radio or cable news, bash an illegal immigrant. And when you do, show a picture of Latino wetbacks sneaking across the Rio Grande. For good measure Photoshop in a headshot of Osama. Indulge in some His-panic.

The worst is yet to come. Ignoring the nation's immigrant tradition and driven by fear of a country changing in a way they are powerless to prevent, the nativist crowd is becoming increasingly frustrated and militant. They are becoming more willing to do whatever it takes to foster harsh policies regardless of the economic, social, or political consequences, even if it means—since most immigration opponents vote Republican—sacrificing the GOP's chances in the 2008 election.

Here is one final e-mail I received on the day I completed this manuscript. It addresses a surge of stories regarding the self-inflicted economic hardships that increasingly befall communities that are getting tough on illegal migrants and driving them out of Dodge. It is leading to shop and restaurant closures, boarded-up storefronts, empty churches, and vacant buildings. As always this message is reproduced exactly as I received it, only the sender's name has been altered.

> From: Maria S.
> Sent: Sat Sep 29 2007
> Subject: GERALDO STOP AIDING ILLEGALS!
> Geraldo
> Any town that arose because of illegals who came in, and the residents gave them jobs and accommodations—should fail, and go back to the normal size it should
> Have been before they broke our immigration laws. THERE IS A WAY TO ENTER OUR COUNTRY LEGALLY, AND IT ISN'T BY COMING IN ILLEGALLY, AND SETTING UP LANDGRABBING TOWNS! GERALDO, if you don't like the regular mix of nationalities— including the Normandic and Germanic nationalities, then please shut up your treasonous mouth and go back to Puerto Rico. WE DON'T WANT ILLEGALS IN THIS NATION. Period! Your compadres are no better than those you accuse OJ of socializing with. You have had a fascination with the mob for years! That is my opinion based on your behavior.
> Maria,
> Washington

Now I am a traitor who must shut up and leave.

Sadly, this bad vibe is inevitably going to have a negative impact on other, quieter Hispanic-American citizens and legal immigrants, regardless of their station in life or how they feel about the issue. Social integration and assimilation will be slowed; segregation, or more precisely, separation, suspicion, and tension will increase, because the center, where immigration reform resides, has fallen. As neighbor turns against neighbor, for a time that will be measured by at least one presidential election cycle, no one backing a reasoned, measured, fair-minded approach to addressing this situation is going to be heard, much less heeded; not George W. Bush, the *New York Times*, Bono, John McCain, Madonna, Jimmy Carter, the late Mother Teresa, or the late illegal alien John Lennon, whose successful battle against deportation, the U.S. vs. John Lennon, I was proud to be part of, testifying as a character witness about how the legendary musician helped raise over $250,000 for my charity for the mentally retarded in 1972. We have seen it before with the Know-Nothings of the nineteenth century and the racist, restrictive immigration laws of the twentieth. This is a raw emotion that has to burn itself out, scorching domestic tranquility in the process. Hopefully, the flames won't be literal; but America is a resilient society, and in time, we'll figure this out.

I have an idea that would short-circuit this pending social collision, derail the coming catastrophe, save racial and ethnic amity, and rescue bipartisan politics. In doing what I am about to suggest, George W. Bush can forge a legacy that is worthy of himself, his long-serving family of patriots, and the live-and-let-live, pro-business, low-taxes political party to which they have long belonged.

President Bush can be a latter-day Lincoln or Tsar Alexander II and issue his own Emancipation Proclamation for this age. By threatening this suggested action, the president will force the Congress either to act rationally or be relegated to the scrap heap of history. What he would do is announce that if the legislative branch fails to pass meaningful immigration reform by a certain date, say within ninety days of his edict, as every president has done from the founding of the Republic, and as the Constitution specifically empowers him to do, Bush can pardon the illegal immigrants, grant a general amnesty, and say to the entire world that those immigrants who are here are absolved of any crime of status. They are free to stay here, so long as they are not convicted or indicted criminals, otherwise qualify, and if they register, are fingerprinted, and comply with other prerequisites, like background checks.

Since I consider those 12 million undocumented aliens my immediate and specific constituents in this fight, this act of amnesty would resolve the crisis for me. Immigrant freedom from fear of persecution and deportation is my minimum request. Those who are here for the various historic, political, and economic reasons stated in this book, after registration, must be allowed legally to remain. Not as citizens necessarily, but as holders of a valid, renewable visa, the specifics of which can be defined over time by federal authorities. They would live free from fear of congressional interference, or worse, the agitated talk-radio mob. Let them have driver's licenses, sign leases, work and pay taxes without fear of reprisal.

The specific details can be worked out in the ordinary course of business. What makes this suggested bold stroke profound and unprecedented is that this good man can boost the economy and end this crisis with a stroke of the presidential pen, doing something his original defeated bill was criticized for doing but never did: pardon all undocumented aliens.

With their status resolved, along with stricter border enforcement, which will curtail, but realistically speaking will not end, further illegal immigration until a new guest worker program can be hammered out, a grace period would be created that will give the various factions time enough to negotiate a sane, comprehensive immigration policy. The marketplace can help set the level of immigration. The policy must fit the geopolitical realities of the twenty-first century, while specifically recognizing the exceptional nature and necessary priority of Mexican immigration. They deserve a head start. Our shared history requires it.

This approach can replace gloom with optimism; exchange a paranoid, racially obsessed, cloistered and walled America like the one championed by the neo–Know-Nothings for an expansive, inclusive New World behemoth that appreciates its varied roots, celebrates diversity, and gains strength from its hybrid vigor. If my various e-mail correspondents don't want to hang out with me or people who look like me, that is cool, too. We don't have to be friends.

Different strokes for different folks. There is room, if not for every-body, then for a whole lot more than we have now. But no force on earth can take on America if her panoply of sons and daughters are in the fight together. We are the "New Colossus" Emma Lazarus wrote about for the Statue of Liberty. "Send these, the homeless, tempest-tossed, to me"; well, send the ambitious, and able, and ass kicking to me too. "I lift my lamp beside the golden door."

At the risk of alienating faith-based, fundamentalist activists, immigration is Darwinian. The Black Legend reputation of His-panics is bullshit. Who but the most eager and hardy can walk across forty or fifty miles of parched desert, dodge dopers, coyotes, and the feds, endure hardship and risk life and limb just to get a job at the other end of a gauntlet of discomfort and anxiety? Don't you want these tough sons of guns on our team?

This vision of a grand and inclusive America will comfort espe-cially our hemispheric allies, and it will be a giant step toward out-flanking Latin American radicals currently being agitated by Hugo Chávez and Mahmoud Ahmadinejad, and bring anxiety to the hearts of totalitarian enemies everywhere, especially the Castro brothers. It would define us as the nation for the new century, in a grand display of American vigor, competence, courage, compassion, ingenuity, adaptability, inclusiveness, and openheartedness.

Mr. President, do this for your father and grandfather, for the Hispanics you know, have known, and know about, for yourself, your legacy, and your country. It is what we stand for. "We hold these truths to be self-evident, that all men are created equal . . . we mutually pledge to each other our Lives, our Fortunes and our sacred Honor."

We can do this. *Sí, se puede.*